HOW AMERICA LOST IRAQ

Aaron Glantz

JEREMY P. TARCHER/PENGUIN
a member of Penguin Group (USA) Inc.
New York

JEREMY P. TARCHER/PENGUIN
Published by the Penguin Group
Penguin Group (USA) Inc., 375 Hudson Street, New York, New York 10014, USA •
Penguin Group (Canada), 10 Alcorn Avenue, Toronto, Ontario M4V 3B2, Canada
(a division of Pearson Penguin Canada Inc.) • Penguin Books Ltd, 80 Strand,
London WC2R 0RL, England • Penguin Ireland, 25 St Stephen's Green, Dublin 2, Ireland
(a division of Penguin Books Ltd) • Penguin Group (Australia), 250 Camberwell Road,
Camberwell, Victoria 3124, Australia (a division of Pearson Australia Group Pty Ltd) •
Penguin Books India Pvt Ltd, 11 Community Centre, Panchsheel Park,
New Delhi–110 017, India • Penguin Group (NZ), Cnr Airborne and
Rosedale Roads, Albany, Auckland 1310, New Zealand (a division of Pearson
New Zealand Ltd.) • Penguin Books (South Africa) (Pty) Ltd, 24 Sturdee Avenue,
Rosebank, Johannesburg 2196, South Africa

Penguin Books Ltd, Registered Offices:
80 Strand, London WC2R 0RL, England

Most Tarcher/Penguin books are available at special quantity discounts for bulk
purchase for sales promotions, premiums, fund-raising, and educational needs.
Special books or book excerpts also can be created to fit specific needs.
For details, write Penguin Group (USA) Inc. Special Markets,
375 Hudson Street, New York, NY 10014

An application to register this book for cataloging has been
submitted to the Library of Congress
ISBN 1-58542-426-9

Printed in the United States of America
1   3   5   7   9   10   8   6   4   2

This book is printed on acid-free paper. ∞

BOOK DESIGN BY AMANDA DEWEY

For my loving grandparents Jack and Evelyn Kramar
and the Nguyen family

ACKNOWLEDGMENTS

This book would not have been possible without the help of my courageous colleagues in the field with whom I reported many of these stories: James Longley, Raphaël Krafft, and Eunji Kang. Thanks especially to James Longley, who first encouraged me to write this book and then helped review the entire manuscript. Thanks also to journalists Andrew Berends, Julia Guest, Shannon Service, and Pratap Chatterjee for their help in Iraq.

Thanks also to Nadeem and Waseem Hamid, Salam Talib, and Istifan Braymook, without whose help as translators and friends in Iraq and Kurdistan I would have been lost. Thanks also to Ozlem Sariyildiz, Ezgi Saritas, Abdullah Anar in Ankara, and Oula Farawati in Jordan for their help with my earlier work in the Middle East.

Thanks to all my editors and colleagues at Pacifica Radio who have supported my work in the Middle East, especially Deepa Fernandes, whose vision has always been an inspiration to me. Thanks also to Tony Cross and Miranda Kennedy.

Thanks to my agent, Michael Bourret; my editor, Mitch Horowitz; and authors John Stauber and Sheldon Rampton for helping me to shape the story of postwar Iraq into a book-length narrative. Thanks to my friend Jennifer Schneider, my parents, Stan and Marsha Glantz, and my sister, Frieda Glantz, for reading the book as I churned it out. Without their encouragement I surely would have run out of steam.

Thanks to my fiancée, Ngoc Nguyen. Knowing you has changed the way I look at the world, in so many ways. This book would have turned out differently if we hadn't fallen in love. Or it might never have happened at all. I look forward to traveling the world with you. I love you.

CONTENTS

PART ONE

AFTER THE FALL

.1.

ENTERING AFTER THE FALL

I never went to Iraq when Saddam Hussein was the president. I didn't see much point in that. His government was a brutal dictatorship and the control it exerted over the foreign and domestic press was almost complete. Other reporters I respected who made the trip couldn't explain the situation on the ground better than I could from neighboring Turkey or Jordan. Almost always confined to Baghdad, always assigned a government escort or "minder," these reporters confined themselves to covering approved, staged events—among them a presidential election in which 100 percent of the Iraqi people turned out to vote, with 100 percent selecting Saddam Hussein for another five-year term.

Foreign correspondents in Baghdad were also welcome to attend press briefings from Ba'ath Party officials like Information Minister Mohammed Saeed el-Sahaf, whose statements included: "Lying is forbidden in Iraq. President Saddam Hussein will tolerate nothing but truthfulness, as he is a man of great honor and integrity. Everyone is encouraged to speak freely of the truths evidenced in their eyes and hearts."

But try to have an honest interview with a person outside the government leadership—impossible.

All this was driven home to me when my friend the American filmmaker James Longley left the country disgusted just a few weeks after scoring a rare visa.

In February 2003, I was in Jordan, working on a multi-part investigation into sweatshops that resulted from the kingdom's new trade agreement with the U.S., when a colleague of mine from New York, Barbara Nimri Aziz, arrived in Jordan on her way to Baghdad. A producer of my radio network's weekly program on issues in the Arab world, she had gotten her visa though the Iraqi department of education. She was a journalist of long standing, and she had used her connections in Saddam's government to get permission to attend something called the NASYO conference—the National Association of Students and Youth. NASYO was actually a non-profit based in Mauritius that had operated an office in Baghdad for years, and it was organizing a kind of formal antiwar protest in Iraq under the arm of the state.

Barbara offered to help me with my visa, but instead I asked her to help James, who had just released an acclaimed documentary about daily life among Palestinians in the Gaza Strip and hoped to be on the ground in Iraq as U.S. warplanes bombed the country. A quiet leftist from Seattle, he had studied in Moscow when the Soviet Union still existed, and then lived in Siberia with his girlfriend to make a movie about factory workers when Communism fell. He, like me, was committed to social change.

James had been to Iraq once before, in 2002, with a crew from the *Seattle Post-Intelligencer* to cover antiwar Congressman Jim McDermott's (D-WA) visit to Baghdad. On that trip, he had been assigned a minder and an official program of places to go and people to see. Ba'ath Party officials took him to Basra through the southern "No-Fly Zone" to film material on the effects of the 1991 Gulf War and the sanctions. He took a Geiger counter out to a tank grave-yard in the desert near the Saudi border, and took high-radiation readings caused by America's use of depleted uranium bombs. They also visited a diarrhea clinic, where children were being treated for the effects of drinking contaminated water. They made the rounds of hospitals in Basra and Baghdad that visiting journalists usually made, including the Saddam Children's Hospital and the Amariyah Bomb Shelter.

"By the end," James told me, "I hated the Saddam regime be-cause I had seen it and tasted a small measure of it myself. I hated being lied to constantly, hated being treated like a child by thuggish autocrats, hated being manipulated and used, I hated the oppres-sion and the shame of it, and the fact that whatever good inten-tions might have been there in the 1970s had been warped and twisted into something very ugly and foolish by the end of the twentieth century. But I was also very much against the Bush ad-ministration's plans for invasion and occupation of Iraq for pre-cisely the same reasons."

In short, James and I had very similar outlooks on the impend-ing war in Iraq. My employer, Pacifica Radio, was founded by con-scientious objectors who had refused to fight in World War II, and I largely believed in the line we pushed on the radio: that the U.S. military would kill thousands of innocent women and children in a war meant to benefit the big oil companies.

But I still saw no point in going to Iraq. As a radio reporter, my main job was to interview people and get their thoughts and ideas down on tape. If I couldn't interview anyone who wasn't hand-picked by the government—if it was impossible to honestly tell the stories of the Iraqi people—then I wouldn't go.

For James, images would suffice, and the images he wanted weren't necessarily political. He wanted to return to Iraq immediately before the war to film images of daily life to contrast with whatever happened after an American-led onslaught, and he thought that was doable.

Once he arrived with his visa, though, James found himself unable to do much of anything. Security was much tighter than before, he told me. It was much more difficult, he said, than working in Soviet Russia.

The NASYO conference, for example, was rapidly hijacked by Huda Amash, a member of Saddam's inner circle and the most politically powerful woman in Iraq at the time. "Under her guidance," James explained, "the conference was turned into a series of Stalinist rallies for the Great Leader. Attendance was mandatory. In the great hall of the convention palace children's choirs competed with dancing Japanese peace activists while odes to Saddam were screamed out in fake spontaneous outbursts from the crowd. A large number of doves were released in the hall and flew madly around the edges of the room, searching frantically for a way out. I sympathized with them entirely."

This would not work for James. A *vérité* filmmaker, he preferred to present his movies with no narrator, letting the images speak for themselves. But this time it was impossible to acquire permission even to film regular scenes on the street. "All channels were cut," he told me. One time, he slipped into the offices of Huda Amash under someone's mistaken impression that he belonged to another film crew and proceeded to beg for filming permissions. Huda brushed past him airily, advising that if he wanted to set up an interview with her, then fine: in anything else she had no interest.

James said she sped off under heavy guard in a nice, white Mercedes. Amash was later arrested in Baghdad by United States forces on May 5, 2003.

The dictatorship of Saddam Hussein even crept into James's hotel room. Surveillance was total. When James complained to his roommate that their air conditioner wasn't working, a helpful repairman immediately showed up at the door. They took to whispering their political conversations on the balcony, where there were fewer bugging devices, but even then Saddam's name couldn't be mentioned. They took to calling the Iraqi president "Bert and Ernie" to avoid waking the Ba'ath official who listened to their every word.

After being refused access to most of the places and people he wanted to film, James took to paying small bribes to Iraqi police officers to allow him to shoot material in the streets of Baghdad. The tactic worked out quite well. No formal permissions, he explained, just a little cold cash to grease the path. The material filmed was in no way controversial—just shots of markets and people in the main streets of the Iraqi capital—but it had been otherwise impossible to record.

But then James hit a snag, when he started to film a shoeshine boy in front of his hotel near the Tigris River. He explained:

One evening we tried to record an interview with a ten-year-old shoeshine boy who worked in front of al-Fanar Hotel. We were very cautious about it. We spent days getting to know him. We asked the hotel manager, explaining that we just wanted to have some narration material about life in Baghdad before the invasion—and that maybe we would continue to film him afterwards. The manager agreed. The shoeshine boy agreed. So that evening I set up my camera in my lap on the hotel steps and proceeded to film preliminary material of the kid shining shoes. In less than fifteen seconds three Iraqi policemen sporting AK-47 assault rifles appeared and started to haul the boy off toward their car, dragging him by the arm.

We ran after them and managed, with some difficulty, to convince them to let the boy go. He scampered off and hid behind a fence halfway down the block, watching us furtively. This was the breaking point for me. It was a small incident, really, but there was something about watching armed men haul off a ten-year-old boy that I found extremely repulsive. After that I decided to call it quits on Iraq until such time as the Saddam Hussein regime had been forced from power. It was quite obvious already that this was going to happen, and I was simply too tired of having to jump through their hoops to do even the smallest things. It was unacceptable to me that people I filmed would be put in danger by my filming. I was ready to see the regime fall.

Almost as soon as James left the invasion came. Less than a month later, U.S. troops toppled the statue of Saddam Hussein in central Baghdad and took over as the new rulers of the Tigris and Euphrates. Whatever its consequences for the Iraqi people, American control in Iraq meant free rein for foreign journalists, and James and I both thought this might be a rare chance to capture the true sense of the Iraqi street. We knew there would be a gap between Saddam's oppressive government and whatever system would be put in place when the Americans left.

At the very least, it was clear there was no authority on the ground to keep people quiet. There were over 100,000 American troops in Iraq, but they hadn't stopped looters from burning the National Museum and National Library, making off with some of the most important antiquities from ancient Mesopotamia. There were reports that armed gangs roamed the streets—some of them criminals, some vigilantes.

At the very least, there would be no censorship in the "New Iraq." I would be able to do the stories I wanted to do—stories about the human cost of war.

After a brief vacation on a beach in the Sinai Peninsula, I met James and a French colleague, Raphaël Krafft, in Amman, Jordan. It was Raphaël who had first introduced me to James. The two of them had lived together in Gaza. While James was working on his documentary, Raphaël had been reporting for Pacifica, where I had been his editor. But I had known Raphaël longer than that, albeit only over the telephone. We first spoke when I was editing a newscast he'd pitched about overdevelopment from Trinidad. The strapping Frenchman, I learned, had bicycled there from southern Argentina over a period of years, filing reports all along the way. Even over the phone I could feel his quick wit and warm smile. Though I had never been to a war zone before, I felt secure heading to Baghdad with experienced friends like Raphaël and James.

The next day, April 29, 2003, we headed across Iraq's western desert from Amman toward Baghdad.

James secured a seat in a white, air-conditioned General Motors sport-utility vehicle, the car of choice for the many journalists and contractors heading to Baghdad after the war began. These SUVs were often bulletproof and always outfitted with extra-large gas tanks, which allow them to cross the desert without a fill-up—a necessary feature since the U.S. military had bombed all the gas stations on the highway during the war. Normally, these seats went for upwards of $250, but James found an empty chair and made the trip for free.

Raphaël and I couldn't find free seats, though. So instead of buying seats in an SUV, we went to al-Mahata bus station outside Amman and rented the services of a driver named Majid, who drove a mid-1970s Chevrolet station wagon—an orange-and-white check-ered taxi. It was a typical Iraqi vehicle. Because the country had been battered by 25 years of war and economic sanctions, most Iraqis were driving older, reconditioned cars.

One problem Majid had, though, was that his car was not out-fitted with the special large gas tank the SUVs had. But he urged us not to worry. When we came back to the bus station at two in the morning (leaving in the middle of the night allowed us to cross Iraq's desert during the day, when it was safer), he had strapped a full tank of gas to the top of his station wagon. When we arrived at the no-man's-land at the Jordan-Iraq border the next morning, he revealed that he had hidden a third tank of gas under a desert bush.

Inventive to the fullest, Majid had given us a further discount because we didn't carry much luggage. That meant he was able to bring more than 1,000 cans of Pepsi from Jordan into Iraq, where canned Pepsi had been impossible to acquire during Saddam's rule.

The ride through the desert was much easier than I thought it would be. I imagined a series of U.S. military checkpoints where soldiers would sift through all our belongings. But there were no such stops or searches. There were no American tanks or humvees on the highway. After four hours, we drove past Ramadi and Fallu-jah and into Baghdad. Still no American checkpoints.

It wasn't until we arrived at our final destination that we met the American military. Upon reaching Baghdad, Raphaël and I had planned to meet James at the Fanar Hotel, a comfortable place with a backup generator that continued to power the air conditioner even after the war destroyed the electric grid. James had stayed there before the war, as had most of the peace activists who came to Iraq when Saddam was the president. The Fanar was conveniently located in central Baghdad on the banks of the Tigris River—and it was less than a block away from the Palestine Hotel, where most foreign contractors and international media had their offices.

Now that Iraq was under new management, a U.S. military checkpoint protected the Palestine and its surroundings, including the Fanar.

There, I met my first American soldier.

"Turn the car around!" the soldier yelled in English with a voice that seemed to indicate the Deep South. He was a young man, not more than 20. His helmet came down almost as far as his eyes. It seemed too big for his head.

"Turn the car around!" he yelled again, this time lifting his right hand into the international signal for STOP. The driver stopped the car and killed the engine. He and I got out of the station wagon to talk to the soldier.

"Hello, soldier, I'm American," I said, but he wasn't listening. All he saw was my dark hair, my mustache, and my three-day stubble. All he heard was the Arabic accent in my English that had developed during my months in the Middle East. I had grown my mustache in the Arabic style to blend in with regular Iraqis, and now I was being threatened by an American soldier for looking like a local. I wasn't sure what to do. I reached for my pocket to get out my passport.

"Turn the car around!" he screamed a third time, this time lifting his machine gun and pointing it in our direction. I tried to talk, but each time I opened my mouth he pointed the gun at me in a more hostile manner. I began to worry that I would die on my first day in the country, but then the soldier saw something that saved the situation.

He saw my French friend in the back seat of the Chevrolet station wagon. And Raphaël Krafft is blond.

"Now that's the man I want to talk to!" the soldier declared, throwing his machine gun over his shoulder and walking briskly to the car's rear window to speak with my friend. "You a journalist?" the soldier asked Raphaël in his thick Southern drawl.

"I am!" Raphaël declared, smiling an ear-to-ear grin.

"You got to tell your translator to show your documents for you," the soldier advised. "You can't just have him walk out like that."

"But of course," replied the Frenchman. I got back in the car and we drove through the checkpoint to the Fanar Hotel across the street.

We paid our driver and met James in the hotel lobby. We relaxed and drank dark Iraqi tea. "I'm really surprised," I said, "that these American soldiers weren't given any Arabic instruction before coming to occupy this country. They don't have to speak fluently, you know, but they ought to know how to say 'Stop' and 'Turn around.'"

Though we hadn't seen any American troops on the road on the way in, the area around the Palestine Hotel was highly fortified with them. In addition to the troop detachments, two tanks were parked out front to provide security for the contractors and news organizations located inside.

But I didn't have much interest in remaining in an area with so many American troops. I wanted to catalogue the lives of regular Iraqis, and that meant putting myself someplace where I would experience the American troop presence the same way that the Iraqi people did. James and Raphaël agreed, and we decided to find a new place to stay.

.2.

THE UNPOPULAR
RESISTANCE

Baghdad turned out to look quite different than I'd imagined it.
First of all, most of the buildings were still standing. Watching
television in Turkey during the war, I had imagined a lot more destruction. Smoke rising from the ashes of a devastated city. During
the war, I put little stock in statements coming from Washington
that only military targets and "symbols of regime power" were being targeted.

Every night, I turned on Turkish television and saw a sound-and-
light show of explosions over Baghdad. When Secretary of State
Colin Powell arrived in Ankara to mend fences with a Turkish government that opposed the war, a local journalist asked him to
comment about reports the U.S. military had attacked a hospital
maternity ward in Baghdad the night before. Powell didn't deny it.
Instead he said: "As you look at these scenes on your television sets,

I think you will realize that we will be as careful as possible, surgical as possible, as we can be in going after military targets and going after command and control targets that support the military forces of Iraq."

The hospital was just one example of U.S. bombs gone astray. In Northern Iraq, U.S. military bombers accidentally hit a convoy of America's Kurdish military allies—a high-profile party that included a brother of Kurdish leader Masoud Barzani and a BBC correspondent. U.S. Tomahawk cruise missiles missed Iraq entirely a number of times—and hit Syria, Iran, and Turkey.

When I visited the bombed Turkish village of Ozverin—more than 800 miles from Baghdad and 200 miles from the Iraqi border—the farmers I interviewed weren't surprised that their lentil field had been bombed. Elderly resident Burhan Yucal spoke on behalf of the village: "Bush is bombing all the civilians," he told me. "The hospitals, the mosques, the shops, and the bazaars. If a war begins in a country, this means destruction for all the people there. In a war only an army should be bombed, but war is destruction all the time."

No one was hurt in the accidental attack on Ozverin, but the fact that Turkey had been bombed three times by U.S. warplanes caused widespread discontent and fueled already overwhelming antiwar sentiment in Turkey. When U.S. soldiers came to Ozverin to inspect the mess and clean up the pieces of the Tomahawk, villagers surrounded their jeep and pelted it with eggs.

I was inclined to agree with the villagers. The few civilian bombings we knew about were probably only the tip of the iceberg. Because all reporters in Iraq at the time were either embedded with the U.S. military or confined primarily to their hotels under the rules of Saddam's government (whose official line was that the U.S. military was being slaughtered and Iraq was winning the war), I figured there was a lot more carnage that we weren't hearing about.

The civilian-casualty estimates coming from the Pentagon must, I thought, be hopelessly low.

So I was surprised when I arrived in Baghdad after the fall of Saddam's statue to find most of Baghdad's civilian infrastructure still standing. It occurred to me for the first time that the Pentagon might be telling the truth. Up and down Baghdad's main drags—Sa'adoun, Karada, and Palestine Streets—all the shops and apartments were standing, whereas military bases and government buildings had been destroyed.

This was not to say the city was fine. Anarchy reigned in the days following the fall of Saddam Hussein. With the streets unsafe after dark, I spent most evenings sitting on our small balcony, drinking dark, sweet tea or Iraq's native aniseed hard alcohol, *arak,* and listening to the gunfire. It went on all night long. James and Raphaël, who had lived in the battle-scarred Gaza Strip, began instructing me about different gunfire sounds and what each meant, and how to tell if the bullets were being fired toward us and when they were going away. Every so often there would be a loud *boom.* That was the Americans firing a tank's cannon. But the tanks could do very little to stop the violence. When the old Iraqi regime fell, the U.S. Army allowed mobs to loot Iraq's arms caches. Everything was taken. After the al-Qaqaa military site south of Baghdad was visited by invading U.S. troops, well-organized looters made off with 380 tons of powerful explosives. As a result, Kalashnikovs and RPGs were plentiful and thieves were numerous.

There was no telephone service, because the U.S. military had declared telephone switching stations "regime targets" and bombed all of them in an effort to destroy the country's wartime communications infrastructure. There was almost no electricity and lines for gasoline were blocks long—particularly frustrating in a country with the world's second-largest oil reserves. The tap water was dirty because there was no power to run the water-treatment plants.

All this meant that most of the shops on Sa'adoun were closed on my first Baghdad morning—bad news for Raphaël, who could not function without his coffee. *Leysh?* "Why?" he asked. "Why is there no coffee? Even in the middle of a battle in Palestine there is some kid with a coffee tray, you know, what is wrong with these people?" So we wandered for blocks along mostly deserted streets and shuttered storefronts before locating a solitary open cafe.

Still, the fact that the city was standing at all was pretty amazing given the defense strategy of Saddam's government. Determined to bring the war to the doorstep of every civilian, the Iraqi government had placed heavy weaponry into almost every school, library, and civil institution, effectively making most of its people involuntary human shields.

This was certainly the case at Baghdad College, an elite high school attended by Iraq's rich and politically connected youth. When I visited as school restarted after the war, I found a giant tank-mounted missile in the play yard. The students told me arms were stockpiled in their classrooms and troop detachments stationed at their school. Most of the students said they were happy about the possibility of getting new textbooks that weren't built around Saddam Hussein's status as a visionary thinker. Some were grateful, some merely surprised, that the U.S. Army had passed up the opportunity to bomb their school.

Elsewhere, civilian casualties seemed to follow guerrilla warfare by foreign Arab nationalists who had come to Iraq to fight the American onslaught. At Baghdad's al-Yarmuk Hospital, whose maternity ward was destroyed by the U.S. military, the director of the medical department, Walid el-Hitti, told me the story:

On April 7th, an American tank fired into the hospital's maternity ward and the medical staff fled. When they returned a week later, the doctors found 26 patients dead in the emergency room, apparent casualties of the advancing American military. The doctors first buried the dead patients in a mass grave in a lawn on hospital grounds before cremating them and sending their ashes away. But Dr. el-Hitti and his associates didn't focus their blame for the attack on the U.S. military. No, here, as in other cases, the Marines were only partially at fault. A Syrian fighter had taken up a position on the street and started firing his machine gun at an American tank. The American tank fired back with its cannon, destroying the hospital. This was not simple barbarity on the American side.

One of my first Iraqi friends was a man named Ahmed al-Rawi. Ahmed was a spokesperson for the International Committee for the Red Cross, and he knew James through a mutual friend in Egypt. A Ph.D. student, Ahmed had arranged for research materials to be smuggled into Iraq so he could complete his course of study. Now that the old regime had collapsed, he was excited by the expected arrival of the uncensored Internet. Under the Ba'ath regime, all e-mail correspondence was read by the government secret police and most websites from the outside world were blocked.

Unmarried and in his early 30s, Ahmed was a fit man who wore the thick mustache typical of middle-class Sunni Iraqis. (He told James he would have to grow one to be taken seriously in Iraq and taught me one of my favorite Iraqi Arabic phrases, *ana b'sharbek*—literally "I am in your mustache," but practically meaning "I trust you to take care of me.") Ahmed lived with his mother and his brother Zaid, a stocky fish-store owner with the same thick mustache, in the Sunni neighborhood of al-Khadra.

When I told Ahmed I was interested in hearing stories of civilian casualties for a report for Pacifica, he invited me to dinner at his house. "I can show you a place where the foreign fighters caused some civilian casualties," he explained. "Some of my neighbors' homes were destroyed." I accepted. I took his address and made an appointment for the next day.

Arriving in al-Khadra by taxi the afternoon of the next day, I found a neighborhood that looked a lot like suburban Los Angeles, complete with detached brown stucco houses with walled yards in the back for the children to play in. As in Los Angeles, date-palm trees lined the streets, although unlike those in L.A., Iraq's palm trees are native. Ahmed greeted me at the door and invited me in.

His house was dark, because the electric grid was down, and hot, too, since in late April the temperature was already starting to creep above 100 degrees and the lack of electricity meant there was no air conditioning. The ceiling fan was on, though, because Ahmed was running his car battery through an inverter. He could keep the fan on all day if the electricity came on one or two hours to recharge the car battery.

I never met Ahmed's mother, who cooked our meal. Like most Iraqi homes, the gender roles were very strict. Ahmed went into the kitchen to retrieve a dinner of lamb stew and puffy Iraqi bread with a cucumber-and-tomato salad. I thanked him for inviting me over and asked him to thank his mother for cooking us the meal. "We didn't want to fight here because we care about our homes and our city," Ahmed explained, "but for the foreigners, for the other Arabs, the situation is different. They just fought wherever they wanted, however they wanted."

After eating, we went across the street to meet one of Ahmed's neighbors, 42-year-old Ahmed Jalal al-Samari. Dressed in a full-legnth Islamic *galabiya* and a bit tipsy from the highly alcoholic *arak*, he pointed at an old government building on the corner that had been reduced to rubble. Some of the other houses on the street had also been destroyed. He explained another reason Baghdad was still standing: Whatever they thought of the American invasion, most Iraqis surrendered rather than fought. They saw the writing on the wall and wanted to save their homes and families from a terrible war.

The incident occurred near the end of the war, Ahmed Jalal explained, as the American troops entered Baghdad. He said that his neighborhood, the al-Khadra district, was a very peaceful part of Baghdad and had greeted the U.S. Marines with white flags.

I saw American tanks and two armored vehicles coming beside my house along with twenty American soldiers walking beside the armored vehicles. The American tanks were advancing toward the end of the street, and most of the civilian residents were outside their houses with white flags watching the American armored vehicles and the American soldiers too.

Suddenly, a foreign Arab *fedayeen* came and he was carrying a RPG-7 gun, and he shot at the American tanks. After that there was heavy fighting on the side of the American soldiers. A lot of shooting occurred and the American armored vehicles actually bombed many residential places. People got scared. The American tank was not affected at all by the shots of the Arab *fedayeen*.

Ahmed Jalal was no friend of the American invasion. "The American forces have no right to enter an Arab-Muslim country," he said. "We, as Iraqis, know our destiny and know our needs. No foreign country has a right to interfere in our country."

But at the same time, he said, he was not ready for the U.S. military to leave. "The occupying powers should work to restore Iraq's infrastructure—the wealth of Iraq and the wealth of the people, which has been looted. The food supplies should reach the population and order should be restored in Iraq so life will go on."

None of these stories went over well with my editors back in the United States. In nightly satellite telephone conversations from the roof of my Baghdad apartment building I was asked to file dramatic stories of the resistance's attacks on American soldiers, about Iraq's missing weapons of mass destruction, and about atrocities committed by the U.S. Army. They were seeking stories of American brutality and economic exploitation. The idea was to debunk the images of "liberation" being shown on TV in the U.S. and replace them with those of "occupation."

There didn't seem to be any space for stories about resentment toward the tactics of Arab fighters causing civilian casualties. I told my editors that the most critical stories I could find were about the lack of essential services like electricity and clean running water. They accepted my ideas, but I could tell they were disappointed.

Then events changed. On April 29, 2003, U.S. troops opened fire in Fallujah and killed more than a dozen demonstrators who had gathered to celebrate Saddam's 66th birthday and protest against the fact that the U.S. Army had taken over one of their schools and turned it into a military base. American troops said the protesters shot first, but local community leaders denied this, and no American soldiers were hurt. I guessed that demonstrators were brandishing rifles, but that the rifles had been fired into the air. Then, I guessed, nervous American soldiers had fired into the crowd.

In any case, tensions were supposed to be running high in Fallujah—a Sunni city of 200,000 on the banks of the Euphrates River, which, unlike most of Iraq, had benefited under Saddam's regime. The city was part of the so-called Sunni Triangle, and its residents were more likely to have been given good government jobs under Saddam, been members of the Ba'ath Party, or been officers in the Army under the old regime. Sunni Muslims from the west of Iraq had formed the backbone of Saddam's regime and had ruled over both Shi'ites and the Kurds, who together made up over three-quarters of the population. If there was any place in Iraq where support for armed resistance might be found, it would be Fallujah.

Indeed, the violence continued. The next day, protesters took to Fallujah's streets again—this time more than 1,000 strong—carrying signs condemning the shooting the day before. Demonstrators started throwing bottles and rocks and shoes at the U.S. Army's 82nd Airborne Division, which had set up shop in a compound formerly occupied by the Ba'ath Party.

U.S. Apache helicopters circled overhead but held their fire.

Then, a passing Army convoy fired into the crowd. At least one man, a 30-year-old Iraqi, was killed, and 16 more people were wounded. Major Michael Marti, an intelligence officer for the division's 2nd Brigade, told the Associated Press that the convoy "was engaged by what they believed was an AK-47."

Watching those events unfold on television from Baghdad, I figured Fallujah was about to explode into full-blown rebellion against the U.S. occupation. So, on Friday, May 1, 2003, Raphaël and I left Baghdad early (and without coffee) and hailed a taxi to travel the 30 miles east to Fallujah. Since it was Friday, we could attend a sermon by one of the city's leading preachers, which we expected would be followed by a protest march.

It was the same day George Bush piloted a fighter jet onto the U.S.S. *Abraham Lincoln* off the coast of San Diego and declared Iraq "one victory in the war on terror" in front of a banner reading MISSION ACCOMPLISHED.

Our taxi to Fallujah cost $10. It was, surprisingly, a relatively new car. The driver was a middle-aged Caldenian Christian who had hung a rosary from his rearview mirror and tuned his radio to the U.S.-government-run station, Radio Sawa (meaning "together"), a recent innovation by the State Department that broadcast a mix of English- and Arabic-language popular music along with news bulletins decidedly slanted toward Washington. The station had caught on quickly throughout the Arab world because of its music: the effect of the news bulletins remained to be seen.

As we drove west, our driver ripped down the rosary and put it in his pocket. "Fallujah people are bad people," he told us. "They like Saddam and they don't like Christians."

We smiled and told him we were journalists, which meant we didn't take sides in such matters. After a half-hour drive, we arrived at the market in the center of town. We paid the driver and told him not to wait for us. We'd arrived at 10 A.M., and we had some time to kill. Friday prayers would not begin until noon, so we thought we would check out the main marketplace. Then we heard gunshots.

We pushed our way past dozens of fruit and vegetable vendors and hundreds of chickens for sale in coops, and found there was no fight at all—just an open-air machine-gun market where looted Kalashnikovs were selling for less than $20 a pop. No one asked where the guns had suddenly come from; they just appreciated the low price and tested the automatic rifles by firing them into the air. A jubilant atmosphere filled the area, which seemed perfectly safe despite the events of the preceding days.

Safe, except that in the aftermath of the war there were no police on the street, and you knew some of the people buying these automatic weapons would become looters and thieves come nightfall.

When we got tired of hanging out at the gun market, we went to find out which would be the best mosque at which to hear Friday prayers. I needed a new watch, so we stopped in a watch store, and while I was shopping we asked where we could find the most political imam in town. The shopkeeper sold me a Seiko with a fake-leather band for $10 and asked his 10-year-old son—who was selling machine-gun bullets for 10 cents each on the street—to take us to the city's al-Kabir Mosque to hear Imam Shakur.

We followed him through the windy streets of Fallujah's *suq,* or covered market, to al-Kabir Mosque. At the mosque, we heard a speech much milder than we expected. Despite his history as a close associate of Ba'ath Party leaders, Imam Shakur denounced both protest and violence. "America has perpetrated an aggression against the people of Iraq and especially the people of Fallujah," he began his sermon. "The United States has killed innocent women and children and is guilty of crimes against humanity." In the culmination of his speech, Imam Shakur called on the U.S. Army to leave Fallujah, but he also told the congregation that he had been in meetings all week with the local commanders and advised the people of Fallujah to be reasonable. "Islam is a religion of peace," he preached. "Do not confront the Americans and do not turn out to protest."

After the sermon, congregants approached me to talk. "Please tell the American people an Iraqi farmer loves President Bush," one man in traditional long white robes told me.

Others wanted to complain. "There's no electricity, no food, no water, nothing!" a convenience-store owner screamed, slapping his hands together to emphasize each missing essential service. There was diversity of opinion in the city, which seemed still to be making up its mind about the Americans.

Before catching a ride out of Fallujah that day, Raphaël and I stopped for lunch at a kebab restaurant. As we stepped inside, we noticed another open-air gun market in the restaurant's entrance-way. As we ate, we reflected on the imam's sermon. Outside the restaurant window, another 10-year-old boy tested British and Russian rocket launchers that looked like they could have dated back to World War II.

"The Iraqi people are very pragmatic," Raphaël said, smiling. "They know there's no point in confronting the Americans." I had to agree with him, but I said, "I don't think the Americans are very pragmatic letting these gun markets run out in the open. These are the same guns that are being fired at them at night."

After lunch, we loitered for a while outside the school that had caused all the upheaval that week. Fallujah's Islamic School was now a U.S. Army base—guarded by tanks and snipers and surrounded with barbed wire. Every so often, a tank rolled through the middle of town. There was no protest that Friday, but there was anxiety in the air, because the locals had no idea when the U.S. military would depart from the school and leave the city.

.3.

NIGHTLY ARGUMENTS

After my experience in Fallujah I realized that covering the insurgency would be a no-win situation for me. If I gave the fighters a lot of airtime, I would have to report as well that the vast majority of the people I spoke to did not approve of their actions. When I told my editors back home about this phenomenon, they opted to pass on future reports. "That's just not what we do," I was told. "That's not what we're about."

What the Left was "about" was stopping George Bush and U.S. aggression in the war on terror, and stories broadcast on its airwaves focused on that goal. In the month and a half that had passed since the fall of Saddam, listeners were told of a succession of disasters that had befallen Iraq since the arrival of the Americans—the looting and pillaging of the country's museums and universities, the danger of unexploded ordnance and depleted uranium, the risk of civil war, the possibility of a fundamentalist takeover. All of these stories were important. But a very important one was left out: that despite everything that had happened, most Iraqis were overjoyed that Saddam was gone.

Since the key issue for me was to focus on issues of human rights and human dignity, I decided to investigate the general humanitarian situation. My first stop was the country's broken healthcare system.

I visited a number of hospitals and got the same story at each one. While there was a lack of medicine dating back to the sanctions imposed after the 1991 Gulf War and exacerbated by America's most recent invasion, the two biggest problems for Iraq's health system—the lack of electricity and security—were not directly related to doctors or medicine.

No electricity meant Baghdad's water-treatment plants didn't work and tap water was dirty. No electricity also meant no refrigeration, which meant food quickly went rancid in Iraq's already-blistering May heat. No electricity also meant Iraqis lacked fans and air conditioners, which meant they sweat more and drank more dirty water. So every day, hundreds of people, most of them children, came to Baghdad's hospitals seeking treatment for severe diarrhea and dehydration. Most of the ones who made it to the hospital survived, but many never came because of the lack of security.

For example, at al-Yarmuk Hospital, the one whose maternity ward had been destroyed during the war, there had been extensive looting. Everything had been taken, it seemed. Patient records had disappeared, all the drugs from the pharmacy had been stolen, even the air conditioners were gone (not that they would have worked, given the lack of electricity).

But the biggest consequence from the lack of security was that al-Yarmuk Hospital was empty. Only 150 of 1,000 hospital beds were occupied. With no telephone service to call an ambulance and no police on the streets of Baghdad, most Iraqis were staying home rather than risking a trip to the hospital.

"I understand their frustration, hell, I'd be the same way if I was them," U.S. Staff Sergeant Jaime Phillips told me. The 30-something Atlanta native was in command of two tanks and an undisclosed number of troops in charge of guarding the hospital. This battle-tested veteran had served tours in both Bosnia and Kosovo. He obviously commanded tremendous respect from the soldiers around him, most of whom seemed to be straight out of high school.

Every day, Baghdad's morgue received the bodies of more than a dozen Iraqis who'd died from gunfire on the streets of the city. The day before, as Sgt. Phillips' forces stood guard, a patient had been stabbed to death inside al-Yarmuk's emergency room. Phillips explained that three people had followed an injured man into the emergency room and stabbed him when it appeared the doctor might save his life. "When they bring people in, it's impossible to control them," the sergeant said.

He explained that his forces did their best to catch criminals but didn't get much support from local residents. "People are really scared, which I understand. I mean, everybody likes to stay alive." But, Phillips complained, "They don't give us identification, they don't tell us nothing. Every time anything happens, nobody knows nothing. We can't help them if they don't help us."

I asked Sergeant Phillips what his forces did when they caught someone. "Can't tell you that," he said.

"But you take them to prison somewhere," I pushed. "That's what you do when you arrest someone no matter where you are."

"Yeah."

"And then where are they held?" I asked.

"I can't tell you that," he said. "I don't even know that. They don't even tell us that."

"But where do you drop them?"

"I ain't gonna tell you that either." He went on, "You understand there are security reasons why we can't tell you that."

"Well, I mean if we were in Atlanta and I asked you 'Where is the jail?' You would say 'It's over here.'"

"Yeah, but in Atlanta if I tell you 'there' because you just killed somebody, that family that you just killed is not gonna come over looking for you to kill you. They would do that here. They're gonna come over looking to kill them."

This secrecy also meant, of course, that the families of those arrested had no idea what the charges were, where the U.S. military had taken their loved ones, or when they might see them again.

I thanked Sergeant Phillips for his time, but he wanted to add something. "Just speaking for myself and not for the Army," he said. "What they're doing to each other, I just don't understand it at all. I have so many mixed feelings about that. You're killing your own people. The way it seems to us—then again I'm a foreigner— these people don't even kill each other for a cause. They kill each other for a hobby. That's the way it seems to me. I don't know their traditions, but if killing each other is a tradition, it's pretty weird."

The security situation was slightly better across town at al-Ubaidi Hospital in Sadr City, a poor, predominantly Shi'ite section of Baghdad. This sprawling slum of at least two million inhabitants had been named Saddam City during the time of the old regime, but the residents had quickly renamed it for Grand Ayatollah Mohammed Sadiq al-Sadr after the fall of the dictator. The revered cleric had been gunned down by Saddam's forces in 1999 along with most of his family, after he called for revolt against the Ba'ath regime during Friday prayers. With the fall of Saddam's dictatorship, the late ayatollah's followers were rebuilding his organization under the leadership of cleric Muqtada al-Sadr, his sole surviving son.

So, in a kind of tacit agreement, there were no American tanks in front of the area's al-Ubaidi Hospital, which was guarded instead by armed youngsters under the auspices of Muqtada al-Sadr's *hawza,* or religious authority. While the streets of Sadr City were far from safe, no one had been hurt in or around the hospital itself, and doctors there reported that the hospital was full and that patients weren't afraid to come.

By and large, U.S. troops stayed clear of Sadr City entirely, leaving security to *al-hawza.* "We thank the Almighty God that Saddam Hussein is gone," Sadr's young, white-turbaned representative Sheik Mohammed al-Fartosi told me. "Now we will find out whether America has come to be liberators or occupiers. We are capable of running our own affairs."

Security wasn't the only function being performed by al-Sadr's movement. In the absence of electricity to run area streetlights, members of *al-hawza* had stepped in to serve as traffic police. When the UN oil-for-food program collapsed after the war, Sadr's mosques stepped forward with massive giveaways of staples like rice and tea. Followers of Sadr's *hawza* even took up garbage duty, making trash-pickup rounds throughout the slum. They started to guard nearby Mustansuriye University after U.S. forces allowed its library of ancient texts to be looted and burned after the fall of Saddam, and they donated large numbers of desks, chairs, and teaching supplies to replace those that had been destroyed.

The source of such aid was always clear, with posters of slain Ayatollah Mohammed Sadiq al-Sadr plastered throughout the neighborhood that now bore his name. In the posters, the ayatollah's face basked in soft light, with his white beard spreading out below his kind smile and gentle eyes. There were also posters of Muqtada al-Sadr's uncle Grand Ayatollah Mohammed Baqir al-Sadr, a well-respected scholar who was murdered by Saddam's regime in 1980 after he refused to declare the Ba'ath Party in accordance with Islam. In the streets and main squares of Shi'ite Baghdad, new murals were being painted highlighting the Sadr lineage—with young Muqtada al-Sadr painted behind his dead father and uncle.

I was quite impressed by the whole operation, I told Raphaël, who had traveled with me that day. The situation in Sadr City suggested that Iraqis were capable of taking care of themselves and that, indeed, they were doing a better job of keeping the peace and providing essential services than the American army.

But Raphaël had a different view. "I just hate this cult of personality they've built around al-Sadr. Look at all these posters with his face—so wise, so kind. It reminds me of Saddam Hussein. You know, before, Saddam's face was everywhere, and now it is al-Sadr. There is a totalitarian streak here."

Raphaël was also concerned about the religious aspect of the Sadr movement. "It's like in Gaza," he explained. "Hamas started with social services, and that's how they took over. People become dependant on the fundamentalists for food and schooling, and gradually no one is able to contradict them."

Perhaps proving Raphaël's point was the new "justice system" the Sadr movement had set up after the war. When I asked Sheik al-Fartosi what his security guards did with the people they caught, Muqtada al-Sadr's representative told me his followers don't arrest people and bring them to prison.

"Mercy is a humanitarian principle as it is conveyed by the almighty God, peace be upon him: 'My mercy came before my anger,'" the sheik explained, quoting the Qu'ran. "So what we are doing with these people—we are not going to do with them what the old regime was doing. We are going to treat them as sick people, as ill people."

Instead, al-Fartosi said, criminals were taken home to their families for a conversation with a cleric. "We go to their families, telling them 'your son has done so and so,' and we advise them that this act is not correct, and we will release them." Al-Fartosi explained that no trials are "necessary" under this justice system. "As soon as the cleric visits the man's family, the clerics are accepted by that man's family and the problem will be finished."

But despite its efforts to keep the peace in Baghdad's Shia slums, there was little that Muqtada al-Sadr's movement could do to restore the massive infrastructure systems destroyed by the war. And this had the temporary manager of al-Ubaidi Hospital, Elhan al-Rashed, praying for a phone. "It's very difficult to contact patients," she complained, stating the obvious. "The people come by themselves to the hospital, and if they need an ambulance, they send somebody to take the ambulance to their homes. Sometimes, by the time we get the ambulance there, the patient is dead."

The phone was all the more important, she said, because of a nighttime curfew the Americans had imposed. Only ambulances and other emergency vehicles were allowed out at night. "From eleven o'clock until six in the morning no one is allowed on the street," she said. "It is very difficult. They let the patient die and they don't come to the hospital. They are frightened to come, not only to this hospital but to anywhere—to any other hospital."

The destruction of the telephone grid had really hit home for Dr. al-Rashed. Her house across town in Baghdad's middle-class Adamiya district was next-door to a block-sized neighborhood telephone switching station that the U.S. military had bombed. A month after the war, the rubble of the switching station was 20 feet high in places, with iron rods sticking every which way out of stray cinderblocks. The telephone switching center had been bombed three times by a total of six American cruise missiles. The explosions were so big, six neighboring houses were destroyed.

"I have cried so much," Dr. al-Rashed told me, tears welling up again. "I have cried so much. And all the glass in our house was broken because of the bombing of this station. Just because my house is near the station."

Since they had taken over as the new rulers of Iraq, the U.S. military had done nothing to repair the telephone station or even clear the rubble. When I visited the station a few days later, I found a group of children from the neighborhood wrestling club climbing amid the wreckage.

Dr. Elhan al-Rashed told me she had been desperately hoping for the phone service to come back. "My daughter lives in the [United Arab] Emirates in Shariqa. My daughter Sura Kalemshi. She is just married now. Her wedding was in January [five months before], but I couldn't go and I haven't heard her voice for three months. If I could talk to her," the doctor said, "I would tell her 'Congratulations on your pregnancy and I hope I will be a grandmother very soon.'"

While I reported the sad state of Iraq's civil infrastructure, James spent his days in Sheik Omar Street, Baghdad's Auto Row. James was convinced he would find a person there whose situation typified that of Iraq. Then he would follow the person for at least a hundred days in an effort to communicate the experience of regular Iraqis after the fall of Saddam. Raphaël followed my lead and focused his reporting on the human costs of war, hanging out with residents as they waited in day-long lines for gasoline, and visiting Baghdad's oil refinery (which was not harmed during the war). Staffers at the refinery told him there wasn't enough electricity to refine crude oil into gasoline for cars. Raphaël also did his best to figure out why there was almost no electricity in Baghdad, though that effort led him nowhere.

But even as he looked into these problems, Raf was becoming increasingly irritated at our left-wing editors at Pacifica back in the States, and this became the subject of late-night arguments between James and Raphaël.

"I am so sick of these Berkeley salad-eaters," Raphaël would say—using the phrase to describe our editors as well as the peace activists who had descended on Baghdad before the war. "They really could give a shit about the Iraqi people. You know, it is always America that is the bad guy, but here you have one of the worst dictators in the history of the world killing millions of people. And what do they say? They defend him. They want to hear stories about the lack of electricity and clean water. What about the mass graves of Saddam Hussein?"

Ironically, we had moved into a building whose owner had no problem with the Saddam years. Our new home was a two-bedroom apartment in a building owned by the Dulaimi family. They had supported Saddam during his reign and had been rewarded handsomely. Our complex was but one of the Baghdad buildings owned by the clan.

Our building was situated along a row of hotels that catered to newlyweds, and every night a parade of wedding parties would enter the hotel to send honeymooning relatives upstairs to consummate their marriages. We were the only Westerners when we moved in, although over time other foreign journalists would become our neighbors.

The flat itself looked like it was right out of a 1970s blaxploitation movie, with mood-blue carpets, fake ivy wrapping around the ceiling fans, and a lounge off to the side with low couches. An odd look, but not completely strange given the circumstances. "The 1970s were the last happy time in Iraq," James reflected, surveying the black tile and light-blue backlighting of our new living room. "Before the war with Iran, before the 1991 war and the sanctions. Why wouldn't you want to preserve the memories?"

James got the master bedroom with a big bed and a walk-in closet, and Raf and I shared the kids' room with two beds squished against each other. The apartment had generator power that kept the fans and refrigerator running when there was a power cut. We went to a corner store and bought staples—clean water, rice, beans, tea, sugar, and coffee. Raphaël was happy. We would no longer have to wander Baghdad's empty streets looking for an open cafe.

For the rest of our stay in Baghdad, the first one awake would go to the kitchen, light the stove, and make strong, Turkish coffee for himself and the other two. The combination of a comfortable home and unsafe streets made for very long arguments every night.

"You can't just look at the mass graves in a vacuum," James would tell Raphaël, cooking up a simple dinner in the kitchen. "Look at how Saddam came to power. In a coup backed by the CIA. Then who sold him chemical weapons? The United States government. Do you really think the Bush Administration had the benefit of the Iraqi people in mind when it invaded? Maybe it's oil or Israel or whatever, but it's not the Iraqi people that brought the U.S. military here."

"I agree with you!" Raf would exclaim. "The United States has sold Saddam Hussein a lot of arms and chemical weapons during the Iran-Iraq war, and now the U.S. has changed its mind for reasons that may not be entirely humanitarian. But that doesn't matter so much to the Iraqi people who have been suffering under Saddam Hussein. I don't give a shit about WMDs. . . . I must tell you I am really ashamed of my country. France has also sold Saddam a lot of chemical weapons. Jacques Chirac was a very good friend of Saddam. He has even sold Saddam Hussein nuclear reactors in the 1970s. And you know what? I am really happy Israel bombed them in 1982 or else we might be in very big trouble today."

Listening to these arguments every night, I found it difficult to take a side. On one hand, the reality that I saw was similar to Raphaël's. Almost everyone I met seemed happy that Saddam was gone. Taxi drivers smiled approvingly when they learned I was American. Artists were beginning to organize exhibitions that would have been illegal under the old regime. Children *did* come up to the American soldiers to give them flowers and, overall, the occupation seemed quite friendly. At the ice-cream parlor near our apartment, American soldiers regularly lined up among the locals seeking a respite from the summer heat. People felt free, even if they didn't have electricity or enough security to send their kids to school. They said they were happier than they'd been before the war, since they assumed the current situation would be temporary.

But despite these observations, I harbored doubts. I agreed with James that the Bush Administration's motives were hardly pure in invading Iraq, and I wondered what might happen down the line if the situation didn't improve. "I guess we'll just have to wait and see," I said. "It's still early. If I were George Bush, I would be putting every cent into fixing the electric grid and the telephone grid. If America could get this country to function again, people might love them enough that they would elect a pro-American government."

It was an argument that did not end, but instead rotated around a circle every night. Raphaël would mention that Baghdad was not nearly as bombed-out as Sarajevo in Bosnia, for example, to which James would respond that the streets of Baghdad were silent except for the gunfire of looters and thieves. Nearly every statement registered as true in my head. Sometimes I found the nightly arguments annoying in their repetition, but mostly the exchanges gave me a new way to process my experiences. After each new observation of my surroundings, I'd think: What would Raphaël say? What about James?

Raphaël's opinion was shared in the home of Manu Nur, an educated Iraqi Christian who lived with his family in a housing-project-type complex called al-Zeuna, across the street from the Army Canal and the United Nations complex. Manu's apartment was one of our first stops in Baghdad because he was the brother-in-law of a friend of ours, Salem Nur, a heavyset Iraqi refugee living in Jordan.

Raf and I had met Salem in Amman's al-Monzer Hotel a few months before. Although it was a bit dirty, the hotel was a nice place with a familial atmosphere, a central kitchen, and a large TV with a satellite dish alternately turned to the BBC or al-Jazeera. Most Western peace activists traveling to Iraq before the war stopped at al-Monzer because it had the advantages of being cheap and across the street from Jordan's central bus station. Most of the activists came and went so quickly that they didn't have time to meet the Arab guests, but since Raphaël and I had made al-Monzer our home for months, we got to know most of the regulars, chief among them Salem; drinking a morning tea with him in the kitchen, watching the news, drinking a late-night beer.

At 62, Salem looked much older than his age. He was missing most of his teeth, and he drank *arak* and chain-smoked all day long despite an obviously severe lung condition. A large teddy-bear of a man with gray hair and a big Arab mustache, Salem was an air-conditioning repairman who had been fixing the cooling systems of the American Embassy in Baghdad in 1963 when Saddam's Ba'ath Party came to power in a Washington-backed coup. In the years since, he had been thrown in prison twice by Saddam's regime, once for two years. He rarely spoke about these experiences and never told us why he was arrested.

Salem was alone in Jordan trying to get a visa to join his wife in Europe. His wife had been able to flee to Sweden years ago with his children, who had grown up without him and now lived in Germany. Salem carried the pictures of his wife and kids wherever he went. He came to Amman seeking a visa to Sweden so he could reunite with them, but for months the diplomats told him to wait.

Unable to work, running out of money, and afraid to go back to Iraq for fear he would never be able to make it back to Jordan to pick up a visa, he sat in front of al-Monzer's television most of the day during the war and its immediate aftermath. Like so many around him, he cheered when Saddam Hussein was toppled, but then cried when U.S. troops protected the oil ministry while allowing the National Library and Museum to be looted.

When Raphaël and I told him we would be going to Baghdad after the war, Salem asked us for a favor. Could we locate his relatives that still lived in Baghdad and use our satellite phone to call him so he could know everything was okay—that none of the members of his family had been killed in the war? We told him, yes, of course. He even offered us his apartment, which was below his brother-in-law's in the same building, but we knew security would be such that it would too difficult to live in a regular Iraqi residential building, so we politely declined.

As we approached Manu's complex in a taxi, we saw about a dozen men with AK-47s milling around the neighborhood. Whether they were vigilantes or criminals or resistance fighters, we couldn't be sure. Some of them walked up and down the street in what could have been a foot patrol. Others sat on the steps of the neighborhood mosque smoking cigarettes.

Unsure of the exact location of the building, the taxi driver pulled over and asked the armed men for directions. After a brief discussion and a few minutes of circling the neighborhood, we arrived safely at the correct location and walked up to Manu's second-floor apartment. The stairwell was dark with lack of electricity. We knocked on the thick wooden door, and a fit man in shorts and with a thick mustache answered the door.

We explained that we were friends of Salem from Jordan and asked if everyone was okay. "*Al-hamdu l'Allah*," Manu responded, the whole family was healthy and safe. Indeed, they were more concerned about Salem than their own predicament. "How is he?" Manu asked. "Is he okay? Does he have his visa?" We went to Manu's balcony and called Amman on the satellite phone. Everything was going fine, he told Salem, a big grin reaching across his face.

Manu asked us to sit, and his wife, a college professor who spoke fluent French, emerged from the kitchen with a tray of cookies and tea and set it down on a table in the center of the room. Raphaël tried to engage her in conversation, but she declined, slipping, after a brief period of time, back into the kitchen.

"Sure, things are difficult now, but it's only temporary," Manu explained to us over dark tea and cookies. "So there's no electricity. The Americans will fix it. They have come to Iraq to lift us into the Western world."

We asked Manu about the armed men near his house. He said they were vigilantes charged with keeping looters and thieves away from the neighborhood mosque. He said he was concerned about their presence, but not overly so.

"You know, people here have been oppressed so long," he said.

"For thirty-five years they have had the Ba'ath Party. They have not been able to say anything, so the first response will be to go to the gun. There are no police now because America has dismissed Saddam's forces. This will take time but everything will be okay. It will be much better than before."

Then Manu switched the topic to his passion, religion. "Do you love Jesus!?" he implored, leaning across the coffee table. "Do you accept Jesus Christ as your Lord and savior?"

James said he was an atheist and I had to admit (for the first time in Iraq) that I was Jewish, but Raphaël won Manu's approval by declaring himself a Catholic, albeit lapsed. "Jesus changed my life," Manu implored. "He can change yours."

This seemed a little strange coming from an Iraqi—even a Christian. Most Iraqi Christians, either descendants of the ancient Caldenians or Assyrians, had lived among Muslims for centuries without ever trying to proselytize. The silence had paid off and— for the most part—the Christian minority remained respected in Iraq. But Manu was different. Unlike the rest of his family (whose Christianity had gone back generations), Manu's Christianity was of the "born again" variety. In this, even his loved ones found him a bit strange. Attending church with him the next week, we found that Manu was one of the few Iraqis to attend Baghdad's only Protestant evangelical church. (Most of the parishioners were foreign diplomats or aid workers.)

But despite the strange looks and sighs from his family, Manu held fast to his faith. He told us he had "found Jesus" in the mountains of Kurdistan along the Iranian border in the late 1980s. After he finished school, Manu had been conscripted into the Iraqi army and served for all nine years of his country's long war with Iran. The war, which cost more than a million lives, became the longest conventional war of the twentieth century. More than the 1991 Gulf War or the recent American invasion, it was "the war" in Iraq.

Fifteen years after the end of the Iran-Iraq war, there were still Iraqi POWs in Iranian custody.

But the Iran-Iraq war wasn't just between two armies. With Europe and America backing Saddam Hussein during the war, Iran's leader, Ayatollah Ruhollah Khomeini, turned to Iraq's Kurdish minority for support, promising the Kurds autonomy in exchange for their opposition to Saddam. As a result, many Kurds fought in the Iraqi army during the day, but took to the hills as guerrillas at night and attacked Arab members of the same army. "I don't blame them," Manu explained. "They were being oppressed by the Ba'ath more than anyone. I just got depressed fighting in the same mountains year after year. I couldn't get married. I couldn't have a family. I'm sure I would have lost my life, too. But one night I was sitting in a trench, the Kalashnikovs of the *peshmerga* (Kurdish guerrillas) firing all night, and I saw Jesus Christ and he saved me. He saved my life in those northern mountains and he filled me with love for all my fellow human beings and I was born again when I found Jesus."

Sensing a favorable audience, Raphaël prepared to explain one of his forming ideas on George W. Bush's war.

"You know, during the Iran-Iraq war we French people have sold Saddam Hussein a lot of Mirage [fighter jets]," Raphaël told him. "I mean a *lot* of Mirage. And chemical weapons. And Jacques Chirac was a very good friend of Saddam Hussein. France has supported the Ba'ath very much during the war with Iran. And America has also sold Saddam a lot of chemical weapons, but now at least the American government has the dignity to realize its mistake in supporting such a terrible dictator, and they have gotten rid of Saddam Hussein, and it's a great service to the Iraqi people."

Manu turned to me. "Your friend's a sharp one," he said of Raphaël.

Raphaël smiled. "I am just so sick of the game France plays with the Arab masses. Jacques Chirac opposes the war, and wherever I go in Jordan, or Egypt, everybody says 'France! Jacques Chirac! Very good!' But France is not very good. Jacques Chirac is a very good friend of Rafik Hariri in Lebanon and Bouteflika in Algeria and ben Ali in Tunisia, and Jacques Chirac was a very good friend of Saddam Hussein. And all of these damned Arab leaders are dictators. But France supports them for strategic advantage."

Manu agreed completely and invited us to attend church with him on Sunday, and to have lunch with his extended family a few days later. As we left, Raphaël turned to James. "You see, Jamesy, the Iraqi people are very pragmatic and not so anti-American as you leftist Americans."

"Sure," retorted James. "The educated Christians."

But Christians weren't the only ones overjoyed at the fall of Saddam Hussein. In the north, the Kurds were taking to the streets in massive celebrations, and in the south, the country's Shia majority was beginning to pick up the pieces after 35 years of Ba'ath Party rule. Every day, it seemed, new mass graves were being uncovered in southern Iraq, including a huge one under a wheat field outside Hilla near ancient Babylon.

It had only been one day since the field had been identified, but already 16,000 bodies had been pulled from the land, which had been owned by a local Ba'ath Party boss. For almost a month after Saddam put down a Shi'ite rebellion in 1991, busloads of prisoners were taken to this field three times a day. With Saddam Hussein removed from power, Shi'ites were coming from all over Iraq, sifting through the dried bones, hoping to find their loved ones.

When I arrived, an American military Caterpillar was digging a fresh hole, turning up fresh bodies. "We found a car and a big bus in there filled with people underground," explained a local man, Sa'adin Amin, as he searched for his brother through the turned-up remains. "They were buried in the car in the ground. A lot of them. Many of the bodies don't have any name or any dog tag to tell who they are. So the Americans just gave him a number. They just have numbers and no names. We don't know anything about them."

But Sa'adin nonetheless continued to look at the excavated skeletons, hopeful that he could find his relative. "We're looking at the name tags trying to find some document that shows it's him. He was twenty-one years old. It's a young age to die. He was small. They took him without any reason."

A woman in a traditional all-black *chador* that covered her entire body wailed as she sat on the ground lifting different clusters of dried bones, screaming at them as if to ask each skeleton, "*Why aren't you my son!?*"

"Where are you, my son!?" she cried. "Where are you, Ali?! I've come here, where are you?! I want you! I love you! I am looking for you between the graves and there is nobody here with your name. The addresses and the hair don't match yours."

A factory worker from the holy city of Najaf sat nearby. "I just stay here hour after hour trying to find my sons," he told me. "I left my job. I left everything to come here. We must find them to make a grave for them and bury them properly.

"American forces did a very important thing for the Iraqi people," he continued. "They finished Saddam. The second step must be the whole Ba'ath Party. They didn't help the Iraqi people and they must be punished."

A man named Khadem told me he was looking for his son Laith and his wife's brother, Haider Ibrahim. He had nothing but kind words for George W. Bush. Like so many of the Iraqis around him, he directed his anger toward the current president's father, George H. W. Bush. At the end of the 1991 Gulf War, the elder Bush had called on the Iraqi people to rise up and promised American support for their revolution. But when the people of Iraq rebelled, the

American president withdrew his support and allowed Saddam to engage in a mass slaughter of Shi'ites in southern Iraq.

"The first Bush is the reason for this mass grave," he told me, "and what happened to all the Iraqi people from 1991 until now. Because if they finished Saddam in 1991, nothing would have happened and we would have been safe."

Sitting in the car on the way back to Baghdad, I started to wonder if Raphaël wasn't right after all. Perhaps the main problem with the war wasn't that George W. Bush had launched it, but that it had come too late.

.4.

CIVILIAN CASUALTIES

When I got back to Baghdad that afternoon, I felt physically sick. Added to the depression I felt at seeing thousands of rotting skeletons coming out of a single field was a physical reaction to the sick stench of death. I wanted to vomit before crawling into a corner of my apartment and curling up in a ball. I listened to the material I'd recorded again and again—the wailing of the women, the cold sound of bones rattling together as the men climbed into a pit and pulled them out. How could any human being do this? I wondered. What kind of monster could order it? And how could he get so many people to follow him in carrying out such a massacre?

Making things worse was the knowledge that the mass grave I had seen in Hilla was just one of many being found across Iraq. In addition to the dead exhumed in Hilla, mass graves had been unearthed in the northern city of Kirkuk, where Kurdish officials reported the discovery of 2,000 bodies. In Muhammed Sakran, outside Baghdad, 1,000 skeletons were exhumed. Smaller mass graves were discovered almost every day. 150 dead bodies in Basra, 72 unnamed skeletons in Najaf. In Babylon, children's bones were among the remains. Eventually, human-rights groups would identify 300,000 bodies buried in 263 mass graves during 35 years of Ba'ath Party rule.

After a few hours of sitting silently alone in the apartment, I gathered up some motivation, made some sweet tea, and sat down at my computer to write. I knew a story for a left-wing American radio network couldn't focus on Saddam's brutality alone. The editors wouldn't accept it. So instead, I built my story around former President George H. W. Bush's complicity in the 1991 massacre. There would have been no mass graves, I wrote, if George Bush Sr. had followed through on his promise to support the domestic uprising to overthrow Saddam Hussein.

When Raphaël and James came home, I showed them the script of my story. "You cannot blame America for everything," Raphaël said. "It is true that George Bush withdrew his support for the Shi'ite uprising in the south after the 1991 war, but you must also understand that he was under tremendous pressure from his allies—from Saudi Arabia, and Syria, and Egypt. These countries were members of his war coalition and they were terrified that a new Shia state in Iraq would ally with Iran and make them less powerful. If you want to point a finger at George Bush, fine. But you must also point a finger at the Saudi royal family.

"The most important thing," Raf continued, "is that Saddam Hussein was a bastard. He was one of the worst dictators the world has ever seen. Number three after Hitler and Stalin—"

"Oh, please," James interrupted. "Number three? What about Pol Pot?"

"*Okay,* number four," Raphaël responded. These debates were getting ridiculous. "But you must remember that he was a terrible dictator and now he is gone because of America and that is a good thing. Or do you disagree?"

"But the point is you can't just say 'He is a terrible dictator and so we should invade the country,'" James countered. "If we said that, we would be invading a lot of countries—including countries that are currently being supported by the United States. And you can't forget that the only way Saddam was able to get powerful enough to kill so many people is that the U.S. supported him all those years when he was fighting with Iran. You have to look at the motives for the invasion—the oil, the water, Israel—and decide if Iraq will get better under occupation. I don't think it will."

Again, I couldn't decide who I agreed with, James or Raphaël. It seemed they were both right. So I interrupted their argument to ask them both for suggestions on how to follow up the mass-graves story. Raf suggested that I visit the Free Prisoners' Committee that had just been set up. The Americans had given Saddam's political prisoners an old Ba'ath Party building and custody of many of the regime's prison records. A visit there would be an opportunity to delve deeper into Saddam Hussein's human-rights record, and I firmly believed that human-rights abuses needed to be broadcast, regardless of the culprit and who was to blame for the current bloody conflict.

The next day, Raphaël and I hired a translator. Asking people nearby to help translate between English and Arabic had worked well in less-stressful environments like Jordan, but it was proving difficult in postwar Iraq. So I asked other reporters if they could suggest anyone for us to work with. A freelance photographer suggested Nadeem Hamid, and said he would tell Nadeem we were interested so he could stop by our apartment. Since telephone service in Baghdad was completely down, any other arrangement was out of the question.

Nadeem arrived the next morning. He was a striking young man—age 20 and well over six feet tall. Well-built and a hit with the ladies, Nadeem had been studying biology at Mustansuriye University when the Americans invaded, but since his college had been looted and burned after the war, his classes had been cancelled, and Nadeem had started working as a translator.

Nadeem was also the front man for an English-language Iraqi boy band similar to America's N*SYNC. For him, the fall of Saddam Hussein meant his first chance to introduce his band to journalists and record producers from Britain and the United States. He said he had already gotten promising signs from a music promoter in London and was optimistic about a record contract. Under Saddam, he said, communication with foreigners was only legal with Ba'ath Party permission.

As we served Nadeem coffee in our kitchen and negotiated a rate of $25 a day plus lunch, Raphaël explained his current view on the situation in Iraq. Nadeem responded dryly: "Saddam Hussein was his own weapon of mass destruction," he said. "He didn't need any special weapons to destroy his people."

We all shook hands, and Raphaël explained that today he would be going out in the field with some French reporters he knew. So Nadeem and I walked down our building's three flights of stairs to the street and hailed a cab. For $2 we rode for a half-hour to the other side of the Tigris River and the offices of the Free Prisoners' Committee, which were housed in a jail Saddam's regime had used to hold political prisoners.

Exiting the taxi at the Free Prisoners' Committee, Nadeem and I faced dozens of pieces of paper taped to the building's exterior. Each paper listed the names of dozens of people killed by Saddam's regime. It was a kind of low-tech version of the Vietnam War

Memorial in Washington, D.C., with relatives of those who had gone "missing" in custody during Ba'ath Party rule standing around the posted lists, closely perusing them. If they were lucky, the family members would find an official notation of the death. Then, they would break down crying, finally knowing with certainty that their son or brother or father was dead. If not, they would leave, promising to come back later when more names were posted, still unsure if the missing were still alive.

We decided to start by talking to the security guard, a dark young man with scruffy cheeks and an AK-47. "My name is Mohammed Nuri Abu al-Hussein Jabari," he volunteered. The 24-year-old lived nearby, in the middle-class Shi'ite neighborhood of Kadamiya.

"I work in this committee as a guard," he explained. "A lot of people want to hurt people who work in this committee. There are some of Saddam's *fedayeen* still around and also members of the Ba'ath Party." Mohammed said members of the Ba'ath Party had attacked the Free Prisoners' Committee four times since its founding—about once a week since the fall of Saddam Hussein. "One time we found a car bomb across the street, and we called the Coalition forces, and they came and took care of the car."

I asked Mohammed how he came to be involved in the Free Prisoners' Committee. "I'm here to serve these people because I was put away in prison and I've seen the way these people used to be humiliated and tortured," he said. "People were thrown in prison for no reason. Just for walking in a place they weren't supposed to be walking. Even if they didn't have anything bad to say about the Ba'ath Party. I want the whole world to know what has happened to us—to the Iraqi people."

Mohammed said he knew about the torture firsthand. "I was in the army," he explained, "but I was scared, so I crossed the border into Iran. Then I got homesick and when I came back they captured me and threw me in prison. They tortured me. They charged me with electricity. They beat me very severely."

Mohammed said he served two years and six months in prison before being released in a general amnesty announced just before the war. Immediately after being released, though, he was redrafted into the Iraqi army to fight the American invasion. But when the war came, he deserted. Now, he said, he has to live with four bullets embedded in his chest and one in his leg.

"It was actually the Americans who shot me," he explained. "When I was running away from a battle, the American soldiers saw me and shot at me, and I got hit."

I asked Mohammed what he thought about George W. Bush. "Even though American soldiers shot me, I am very thankful to him. We are very thankful to him because he got rid of Saddam," he said. "He saved us from the former regime and we're now living in this house (the Free Prisoners' Committee) as a family. We're here to serve people and let them know what happened to their loved ones."

Like the relatives at the mass grave in Hilla, most of those searching at the Free Prisoners' Committee had lost their loved ones to Saddam's regime because of the uprising after the 1991 Gulf War— when George H. W. Bush had urged the Iraqi people to rise up, but then withheld promised support for their revolution.

Most of the people searching were Shi'ite women, clad in the traditional long, all-black *chador.* Most of them were still searching, unable to find their loved ones' names on the papers outside the Free Prisoners' Committee.

"My son was in the army during the 1991 war," one woman from the city of Babel told me, "and after the war, he joined the revolution when the first Bush told us to rise up. We haven't heard from him since that day in 1991." She started crying. "I can't even find his name on a list."

"What do you think happened to him?" I asked.

"He's dead," she replied behind tears. "I'm sure that he's dead. Saddam didn't leave any one of them. He killed so many people."

She began pointing at random to the names taped to the walls. "This one was killed in 1984, this one in 1985. My son was killed in 1991 for rising up against Saddam. He never stopped killing."

A few feet away, a heavyset, 35-year-old man named Ali Mohammed started weeping. All four of his brothers had disappeared more than 20 years ago, after Saddam Hussein destroyed the Da'wa (or Islamic Preaching) Party in the early 1980s.

"I just found two of them," he said, trying to keep his tears from flowing, his hand pointing at a paper on the wall. "My brother Karem Mohammed was executed March 12, 1983. My brother Adel Mohammed was killed January 2, 1982. The last time I saw them was in March of 1981, twenty-two years ago. I was thirteen and my brothers were older. They were studying for their exams."

His other two brothers were still missing, he said, but he was heartened to learn that at least two of them had been executed by Saddam's regime. "I'm very proud that they are martyrs," he said. "I know they are all dead, but they are heroes. The regime tried very hard to get them to join the Ba'ath Party, but they wouldn't. They stood on their principles and for that they got executed."

Founded as a movement to make Iraq an Islamic republic, the Da'wa Party became emboldened after Ayatollah Khomeini overthrew the Shah of Iran and imposed his version of Islamic law in 1979. After the revolution in Iran, the leader of the Da'wa Party, Ayatollah Mohammed Baqir al-Sadr (uncle of current U.S. enemy, cleric Muqtada al-Sadr) issued a religious order, or *fatwa,* prohibiting Muslims from joining the Ba'ath Party or its affiliated organizations. He then led a wave of massive demonstrations against Saddam's regime throughout the country.

In response, Saddam detained Mohammed Baqir al-Sadr and transported him to Baghdad, where he was put under house arrest. His sister, Amina al-Sadr, commonly known as Bint al-Huda, went to the holy shrine of Imam Ali and gave a fiery speech urging Iraqis to demonstrate against the government and to protect their leader. As the news of his arrest spread, riots broke out across Iraq—in Baghdad, Basra, Diyala, Samawa, Kuwt, Diwaniyya, Karbala, and other cities. The bazaar in Najaf shut down; angry crowds clashed with the police. The whole city seemed under siege as the government rapidly increased its security efforts. The spread of violence in the country forced the regime to free Sadr the next day.

But the victory for the Da'wa Party was short-lived. Tension between Saddam's secular Ba'ath regime and Sadr's Islamic Da'wa Party continued to build. Islamic activists threw a bomb at Ba'ath Party leader Tariq Aziz (now in American custody as one of Iraq's 52 most wanted) at Mustansuriye University, injuring him and killing his bodyguards. At the public funeral for the guards, another bomb was thrown at the funeral procession, killing several people.

Saddam responded by calling for revenge against the perpetrators. On March 31, 1980, the regime's Revolutionary Command Council passed a law sentencing all past and present members of the Da'wa Party, its affiliated organizations, and people working for its goals, to death.

To the end, Sadr refused to back down. In a message issued shortly before his execution, Sadr issued an ultimatum to his followers: topple the regime and establish an Islamic government in its place. "It is incumbent on every Muslim in Iraq and every Iraqi outside Iraq to do whatever he can, even if it costs him his life, to keep the jihad and struggle to remove this nightmare from the land of beloved Iraq, to liberate themselves from this inhuman gang, and to establish a righteous, unique, and honorable rule based on Islam."

The security forces came for Sadr and his sister on April 5, 1980, and detained them in the headquarters of the National Security Agency in Baghdad. Two weeks later, Iran's new ruler, Ayatollah Khomeini, announced their executions. When the expected revolt came, U.S. President Jimmy Carter stood by as Saddam's forces killed tens of thousands. The last thing Washington wanted was a second Khomeini in Iraq. Carter, it seemed, preferred Saddam.

But it was not through this geopolitical lens that visitors to the Free Prisoners' Committee viewed the deaths of their loved ones. "Terrible things were happening to all us Iraqi people under that psychopath Saddam Hussein," Ali Mohammed told me after finding two of his four brothers on the death list. "I don't want to thank America for that because God is the person who pushed America to liberate us from Saddam Hussein. We are thankful to God.

"God alone has liberated us," he concluded. "The Americans are invaders."

I asked Ali Mohammed if he was optimistic about the future.

"Only God knows," he responded. "If the Americans stay here, I don't think the future will be good."

"Why?" I asked.

"We are Muslims," came the answer. "We can't allow other people who are not Muslims to come here and rule us. No man could just let the invaders rule. We will fight against that. Invasion is not the right thing to do for any people. We don't hate the American people, but we don't like invasions and we will fight."

We don't like invasions and we will fight. This statement was similar to the ones that came from Saddam Hussein and his underlings in the months before the war. But it was said differently here, with different implications. Ali Mohammed and his family didn't fight the advancing U.S. Army because they were eager to see Saddam go. They, like Muqtada al-Sadr's representative, Sheik Mohammed al-Fartosi, were waiting to see if the American army had come as liberators or occupiers. I wondered what U.S. officials were doing in response to this sentiment.

I already knew what Raphaël would say if I asked him: "No matter what the Americans do, there is no way they could be as bad as Saddam Hussein." And what James would retort: "When the Iraqi people see what America has planned, that's when it will get messy here."

Regardless, I knew I could not broadcast a story about the Free Prisoners' Committee on Pacifica Radio. My network had already run my story on mass graves and I had been told that additional coverage of Saddam's brutality would not be welcome for a while. "We get so much of that here," a colleague in the States told me. "Even if it's true, we can't focus on it. There's so much more that we're not hearing about here in the mainstream media."

"But," I protested, "from here, these crimes seem like the most important thing. I believe in the big story, you know, and right now the full revelations of the true scope of the crimes of Saddam Hussein is the biggest, most important news."

"I don't know, Aaron," she said. "Find something else to focus on. You've already looked at those killed by Saddam Hussein. What about the civilian casualties caused by the American side?"

It was an obvious human-rights story and, despite my reservations that it was not the most important story to be reported, I agreed to pursue it. After a few days of research, an opportunity presented itself when I met an Egyptian-American journalist, Kareem Fahim. The Middle East correspondent for the *Village Voice,*

Kareem was living in a more modern building across the street from me. We met often for dinner, and one day he told me he was putting together a story on civilian casualties for the *Voice*. He said he was planning to travel to the south of Baghdad to some of the places where the fighting had been fiercest and asked me if I wanted to come along. I accepted, and we left with his translator and a rented car the next morning.

Our first stop was the main hospital in Kuwt, a mid-sized city two hours south of Baghdad. Unlike Nassariya farther south, where the U.S. Army had met stiff resistance and documented civilian casualties were high, Kuwt had fallen without a fight. The head of the hospital told us the Americans had surrounded the city, laying siege until the Iraqi army deserted and American tanks simply rolled in.

But, he told us, there were civilian casualties nonetheless, mostly outside the city, where U.S. airplanes and tanks had destroyed houses and killed innocent women and children. He recommended we go to a village called al-Mufwrakiyya, on the banks of the Tigris farther south. At least four women had been killed in that village, he told us—all of them while hiding in their homes.

We drove down a poorly paved road along the Tigris toward al-Mufwrakiyya and my body relaxed. It was easier to unwind without Baghdad's Los Angeles–style smog and sprawl. The air was clean and the countryside calm—reeds floating in the river to my right, date palms and wheat and vegetable farms to the left. There were fewer American tank patrols than in Baghdad, and the weather, already well over 100 degrees in the capital, felt like a cool 90 in this small town.

As we arrived in the village, we saw a row of a dozen destroyed apartment buildings on our left. On our right was a bridge across the Tigris—on it a tank and a handful of U.S. soldiers playing with Iraqi children. "It's journalists!" one of the kids screamed in Arabic.

The group of children migrated toward us. We were more of a novelty than the American soldiers.

"Are you Arabic?" one of the kids asked. "What's your name?" asked another. "You're Saudi?" asked a third. When I said no, the kids determined I was from Qatar. I made no effort to discourage the impression. As the locals surrounded me, Kareem quietly made his way to the U.S. soldiers. "We're fixing the bridge," one of them told him, though there didn't seem to be much work going on.

"How did it break?" Kareem asked.

"There was some kind of gunfight here," the soldier explained, "but I don't know how it happened, exactly. You know, some people fired and it broke." He apologized for not knowing more, explaining he was with an Army unit that had arrived that week, not with the Marines that had taken the city six weeks before.

Meantime, the chorus of children turned their excitement to their favorite topic—*maku*, Iraqi Arabic for "there isn't any."

"There isn't any water," one said.

"There's no electricity," added another.

Other children shouted about the lack of cooking fuel and of gasoline for cars. The chorus culminated in a chant: "*Kulshe maku!*" Of everything, there is nothing.

During a brief pause in their game, I was able to ask a question. "How can there be no water?" I asked, pointing at the Tigris below our feet.

"There is no water because there is no electricity to pump the water," explained an adult who had pushed his way through the children to represent the village. He was a dark man, with a short, scraggy beard typical of the area.

"And the plant doesn't have a backup generator?" I inquired.

"There's no generator," he responded. "In the entire area, there's no generator. But even if there was a generator, there's no diesel fuel in the whole town to run the generator."

Then, again, the *maku* chorus arose from the assembled children.

"Before, under Saddam, we used to swear when there was no electricity," joked the man, who introduced himself as Amar Khadem, 45 years old. "Now, who should we swear at? Now I don't know who to swear at. Who do I insult?

"The most important thing," he added, "is that the Americans promised everything but they didn't fulfill their promises. At the beginning we were happy that the Americans came here. We thought they would save us, but now we see it's just a lie. They were supposed to help us. I thank Bush and the Coalition forces for getting rid of Saddam. I thank Bush and Tony Blair because they got rid of the Ba'athists and Saddam, but we need them to help us a little bit."

"What do you want from America?" I asked, knowing the answer that would come.

"We want electricity, gas, oil, all the national services we had before. Before the war, I sold ice cream. Now there's no job, no work, no nothing."

"There's no ice cream," I noted.

"That's right," Amar responded, laughing. "There's no sugar or milk because the government rations have run out, and there's no electricity to make the ice cream.

"Say 'hi' to Bush," he added with a mocking grin.

We asked Amar about the destroyed houses we'd seen on our way into town. He then introduced us to a 23-year-old farmer named Tamar whose cousins had lived in one of the houses. He was supervising a crew of locals who had begun carrying away the debris.

"No one was hurt, thank God," he said. "There was no one in the houses at the time. The people got out of the houses before the Coalition forces came." Tamar said Ba'ath Party activists had come through town and urged residents to flee as the Americans advanced. Most had evacuated and escaped unharmed. Still, Tamar explained, his cousins had lost their homes. Tamar complained they had received no help from the U.S. Army to reconstruct the houses. The families would have to bear that cost themselves.

"So, who destroyed these houses?" I asked. "The Americans or the Ba'ath?"

"This is the result of the American army," Tamar said. "There was no resistance inside these houses. Most of the Iraqi army deserted this place, and only two people in the whole town were resisting. They were standing next to the bridge, and the Americans came with their airplanes and fired missiles from the sky. They bombed these peaceful houses because of Saddam's *fedayeen*? It's not right."

He said he was happy no one had died in the buildings near the bridge, but added that four women had been killed, cowering in their homes in another part of town. He said he would introduce us to those families, but first there was something important Tamar wanted to tell us. "We are Islamic," he said. "Take our voice to Mr. Bush. . . . In his speech, Bush said 'We came to Iraq as liberators.' So, we only want them to do what they said, not what they are hiding. . . . Sometimes a person will say something and do something else."

"What are they hiding?" I asked, as we walked through the deserted streets of al-Mufwrakiyya. All the storefronts in town were shuttered. On a Thursday afternoon, all the shops were closed. No sense in opening if there was no electricity and no goods to sell.

Tamar continued:

I listened to Bush's speech and Bush said that Iraq has all the necessities, but it's been a month and there are no services. We only want him to keep his promises. The American soldiers are now using sexy pinup pictures and showing them to our children, but we are an Islamic country and we refuse this thing. At last we got rid of Saddam.

He did whatever he could against the religion and now the Americans come and they have their sexy pinup pictures. These attitudes are not moral. We want an Islamic state in Iraq. We want the American leader to act against these things and to work with Islamic opposition parties to make a government.

Tamar knocked on the door of one of the small, square-built homes, and a young man answered. Our translator explained that we were interested in speaking to family members of those killed by the Americans. After we'd waited for a few moments outside, an older man came to the door and invited us into his living room.

We sat on the floor. He was a poor man, 63 years old, with no furniture and no art on the walls. The only color in the room was a faded Persian area rug. We were soon joined by his nephew. They offered us tea and we accepted.

"I've lived here for thirty years," the old man said. "I used to live in Baghdad, before the Ba'ath, but they were terrible to the Shia and they wouldn't give any jobs unless you joined the party, so I moved back here to my ancestral village."

Kareem asked him to describe what had happened during the war.

"It was on April first at eight in the evening. That's when my wife died," he explained, showing her death certificate.

"The planes came and hit this area. There were four airplanes and when they came they started to bomb the civilian houses. Most of the people had already left this area when there was heavy bombing, but we stayed in our homes. We were happy when we heard the Americans coming. We were just waiting for the Americans to come."

"But everyone else was leaving," Kareem said. "The Ba'ath officials told everyone to evacuate."

"Yes," the old man said, "and the Americans, too. They called on their microphones and loudspeakers: '*Evacuate this neighborhood, we are coming.*' . . . Most of the people ran away. If you saw it, you might cry at the sight of the people running away from their houses. I was asked to evacuate my house, but I refused. There were too many children in this house and it was hard for us to leave. We stayed in our home."

He explained that 13 people were crammed into the small house that day. All of his daughters, his daughters-in-law, his sister, his sister-in-law, and his mother. Some of them used to live in Kuwt, he said, but when they heard the war was coming, they fled the city for the comparative safety of small-town al-Mufwrakiyya.

"After that, the tanks began to shoot the area, targeting a few of Saddam's *fedayeen,* and then the airplanes bombed the town," he said. His wife and niece had died when a missile hit his home. Shrapnel hit his niece in the neck while her two-year-old baby was in her arms. "The baby was injured, too," he said, "but thanks to God, the next day we got her to the hospital."

"We had to stay here all night with the dead bodies," said the man's nephew, 42-year-old tailor Zhreher Shabuk Muassen, whose wife had also died in the air strike. "The next morning we took them to Kuwt to be buried."

They offered to give us a tour of the damage.

One bedroom had been completely destroyed by a Tomahawk cruise missile. The steel door separating it from the rest of the house was full of shrapnel. This door, the old man said, was all that saved his life. "I would have been killed, too," he said. "As it is, I have pieces of shrapnel in my stomach and the back of my head."

His nephew Zhreher pointed to huge cracks in the house's walls and foundation that would need to be repaired before the winter rains came, or the whole house would collapse. But since there had been almost no electricity in al-Mufwrakiyya since the war, he had been thrown out of work like most Iraqis. He didn't have the money to support his family, let alone repair the house.

The old man pointed around the room. "I will have to sell everything to pay for the repairs," he said. He didn't have much to sell. His furniture and television had been destroyed in the blast. "I will have to sell my stove, my cabinets, my silver. I will have to sell it all," he said.

I asked him a question. "You said earlier that you were very excited to hear that the Americans were coming. How do you feel now that the Americans have come and such terrible things have happened to your family?"

"There are mass graves everywhere," the man said as a way of answering my question. "Every day they find another one."

"So you feel like it was the price you had to pay for freedom?"

"Yes, of course."

"Do you think that Saddam could have been removed any other way but this way?" I asked.

"Only America could do this," he responded. "If it weren't for America, Saddam would stay. Then his sister would take over and rule the same way. It would go on for generations. Even his grandson would come and grow up and rule Iraq in the same way as Saddam. But, thank God, now he's gone. God brought America to get rid of Saddam and take him away. Now, when the tanks pass in the streets, the children greet them."

Zhreher spoke up. "There will always be sacrifices," he said of his dead wife. "We wanted Bush to win the war, so we encouraged the Iraqi military and *fedayeen* not to fight here."

He told me he had been jailed twice by Saddam Hussein. The first time was for a year, beginning in 2001, for making a banned pilgrimage to the Shi'ite holy city of Karbala. In February 2003, he told us, he was jailed for marrying in a traditional Shi'ite wedding.

"I was taken to Abu Ghraib prison in a special section for political prisoners. I was held upside down with my feet tied to a rope behind bars and then they shocked me with electricity," he told me. "It went on for two days. It would have continued forever, but one of my relatives bribed the jailer with 400,000 Iraqi dinar [about $250, a fortune in a country where the average factory wage was $20 a month] and I was released.

"Thanks to God they got rid of Saddam," Zhreher summed up. "We are thankful to the Americans. So it depends on them now if they will stay in Iraq or go back to America. They did their job. They took away this criminal, Saddam, they should go home. They saved all the Iraqi people from Saddam."

Zhreher invited us to lunch with his family, but we declined. We had to get back to Baghdad before nightfall, we explained. Heading back late, we said, would have been an invitation to robbery or worse.

As we pulled out of al-Mufwrakiyya, Kareem sulked next to me in the car. The townspeople's story wasn't the one he wanted to hear. "I can't write about this," he told me. "I'm not going to write a story about civilian casualities who want to thank George Bush."

"But it's the truth," I said, noting that it corresponded to stories I'd heard in Baghdad.

Kareem wouldn't budge. He argued that the story of these villagers was hardly representative of the overall story of civilian casualties in Iraq and asked if we could stop at the Marine base in Kuwt on the way home. The city's hospital director had told us that the ex-Ba'athist who had been tapped to run the new U.S. Army prison there had just been killed in a motorcycle drive-by shooting. Kareem said he was interested in doing a report on communal acts of revenge against the former regime. We parked the car a block away from the U.S. Marine base, which was located in a former Ba'ath party building in the center of Kuwt.

With the exception of the U.S. base, the entire area was plastered with posters of Grand Ayatollah Mohammed Baqir al-Hakim, a sad-eyed cleric who had gone into exile in Iran in 1983 after the assassination of Ayatollah Mohammed Baqir al-Sadr and the destruction of the Da'wa Party. There, he had used money from the Iranian government to build an organization called the Supreme Council for Islamic Revolution in Iraq, and raised his own army, called the Badr Brigades. Saddam responded by arresting 125 members of al-Hakim's family and executing 18 of them.

But al-Hakim kept fighting. A well-respected figure in Iraqi society, the ayatollah helped organize the Shi'ite revolt in 1991. When George W. Bush and the U.S. military toppled Saddam in 2003, he returned to Iraq and began leading Friday prayers at the holy shrine of Imam Ali in Najaf. In Baghdad, his picture was rarely seen, but Kuwt was apparently a stronghold of his support, and his visage was everywhere: on posters, on billboards, in shop windows, and on lampposts. In Kuwt at that time, it was hard to turn around without seeing a picture of Mohammed Baqir al-Hakim.

We asked Kareem's translator to wait in the car while we went to see the Americans, and then we climbed past the razor wire that surrounded the base to meet the U.S. guards.

"Hi there," Kareem said to two young Marines, neither of whom could have been older than 20. "We're Americans. I'm from New York and my colleague here is from California."

We showed them our press passes and, after a brief delay, were waved in.

Inside, the building was almost empty. A man who introduced himself as Major Todd Melby came up and greeted us. He was wearing a floppy, camouflage-print military sunhat and had the kind of small, thick moustache that had gone out of style years ago because of its similarity to the facial hair of Charlie Chaplin and Adolf Hitler.

"How are you guys doing?" the major asked with a kindly Minnesota accent. "Good to see you."

"I'm from the *Village Voice* in New York," Kareem stated blandly. He would be doing all the talking here. I introduced myself as well. "I'm doing a story on revenge killings," he explained. "You know, people who go after the Ba'athists and kill to make sure they never come back."

"Yeah, we had something like that," the major responded, walking us upstairs to a large, equally empty room. There were a few maps on the otherwise bare walls. "Our jailer was killed yesterday."

"*Our* jailer?" Kareem asked.

"Yeah, he was the jailer under the former regime, and when we took over, we still needed someone to run the jail so we kept him on. But then yesterday, two guys on a motorcycle drove by and pumped him full of bullets. It was a drive-by, except they were on a motorcycle."

"Do you know who did it?" asked Kareem.

"Not really," Major Melby answered. "It's under investigation. But I don't think we'll find out. You know, we Marines are leaving Kuwt in a few days. The Army is taking over, so we don't have much time to investigate. It could be a lot of different people. The guy [the jailer] was a member of the Ba'ath Party. Not a very big member, but a member still." Major Melby saw a look of surprise come across our faces. He could tell what our next question would be and cut it off before we asked it. "We needed someone to run the jail and he had experience."

We thanked the major and started on our way. "I know the *Village Voice*," the major told Kareem. "You guys are kind of left. Against the war. But there are a lot of good things happening here, too. I hope you write a fair story."

A pledge of fairness was made and we left the base. As we walked past the razor wire and back to the car, I was reminded again of the resurgent power of Ayatollah al-Hakim in this area. During the war, his Badr Brigades had joined the American-led coalition against Saddam Hussein, but after a month of occupation, the ayatollah had become more critical. He had just given an angry sermon in Nassariya. "Do the Americans accept it if the English govern their country?" he asked his congregation. "Even though they share a similar culture? How can we accept a foreign government whose language is different than ours, whose skin is different than ours? Our brothers, we will fight and fight, so that the government we have is independent, that it is Iraqi."

It's possible, I thought, that al-Hakim might have been responsible for the hit. In any case, it was al-Hakim's Badr Brigade that was patrolling the streets. The only thing the Americans controlled here was their base.

When we got back to Baghdad at dusk, no one was home. James was filming his subject—an 11-year-old kid nicknamed "The Screw." The kid was a mechanic on Sheik Omar Street, Baghdad's Auto Row. He came from a poor Shi'ite family, and James had decided that following this child's experiences for a year could provide an interesting insight into how Iraqi life would change after Saddam. Raphaël was staying in a pricey hotel courting a female journalist from a French wire service. The day before, he'd told me he was in love.

I wished there was someone at home to talk to. It was incredibly hot and I had yet another huge headache. I walked to the refrigerator and gulped down a liter of water and then hopped into the shower. Walking out of the bathroom dripping naked, I nearly cried as the water dried almost immediately. The electricity was down, and the building management was resting the generator, so there was no fan. I wouldn't be able to sleep.

I thought, "This is the only story in which I am confident. If there is no electricity next month when the temperature goes to 130 degrees, there will be a lot of angry, sleep-deprived Iraqis. And they will all have Kalashnikovs they bought for a few dollars at the corner market."

About anything else, I had no idea. I wondered what I was doing in Iraq. For the first time in months, I wanted to go home.

.5.

A DYSFUNCTIONAL
OCCUPATION

I don't know what to do," I complained to James as we walked toward an ice-cream shop four long blocks from our apartment. Raphaël had just announced that he would be leaving at the end of the week. His new love had recently journeyed back to Paris and he was determined to follow her. In any case, he said, he had been on the road for long enough. After four months in Egypt, Jordan, Syria, and Iraq, he was ready to go home. I was burnt out, too, and had been living out of a suitcase even longer, but I had only been in Iraq for one month and it didn't seem right to leave when there were so many stories to tell. James explained that he was staying for the long haul—more than a year if necessary—and urged me to stay, too.

"Go to Jordan with Raf if you need to," he said. "Go to the Dead Sea and float in it. Enjoy some good food and some air conditioning. Get some sleep and then come back."

But I wasn't sure a vacation would do the trick. "I just don't know how to be a reporter here," I said. "I don't know what stories are important. I'm thinking of leaving. I need to go back to the States and talk to some people about the situation here. Then maybe I'll come back."

I had been away for months and I didn't understand the reactions of my editors back home. I didn't know what the American people were thinking and what they were hearing in the media, so I couldn't analyze their motives on the left or the right. Maybe I just wanted to work somewhere where the issues were simpler. "What do you think you'll learn there that you can't learn here?" James asked. "Everything is happening here, *habibi,* here is where you can learn about here."

"It's true," I admitted, as we crossed a giant traffic circle. In the center, where a monument to the former regime once stood, were an American tank and U.S. soldiers, showing their machine guns, playfully, to Iraqi youth.

"You're stressed and tired," James responded without much sympathy. "Take a vacation and then come back to work."

Since my trip to al-Mufwrakiyya, I had done a number of stories, but none of them had helped me discover any greater truths about the Iraqi situation. Nadeem and I went to his university and made a report about difficulties in restarting school. (The U.S. military wasn't sure what to do about the fact that most professors were Ba'athists.) American authorities had also allowed the universities to be looted—which meant no libraries, no science labs, no desks, and no chairs. Electricity remained a persistent problem. One of Nadeem's friends at school joked, "If you gather something like sixty students in a classroom with the hot weather and no electricity to run a fan or air conditioner, most of them would get out of the room during the class. It happened yesterday. We held a class that did not last more than fifteen minutes. If the temperature is more than 120 degrees, the teacher can't pressure a student to stay in the room."

Nadeem and I also checked out one of Baghdad's biggest refugee camps—a tent city of 500 families, thousands of people, in a former soccer field called Haifa Sports Stadium in the center of the capital. The camp's occupants were all Palestinians, many of whom had come to Iraq under the rule of President Saddam Hussein. In an effort to portray himself as the leader of the Arab Nation, Saddam had invited tens of thousands of Palestinians to Iraq and forced private landlords to rent apartments to them at rates far below market—rents he did not allow to be raised for more than 20 years. When Saddam was overthrown, the landlords acted quickly to evict their unwanted tenants, rendering many of Iraq's Palestinians homeless.

The basic story seemed pretty straightforward, but what was curious was that the Palestinians were living in tents rather than in one of the plentiful government housing projects that stood vacant after the regime's collapse. The camp director, Dr. Salem Alawde of the Palestinian Red Crescent Society, was similarly perplexed. He told me he badgered American soldiers every day, demanding that an abandoned building be provided, so the refugees wouldn't have to spend July and August outdoors in Baghdad's brutal 130-degree heat.

"There is a building right across the street that's completely empty," he told me, pointing in its direction, "and I have some businessmen from Dubai who would be willing to pay for it. I keep asking the American soldiers if I can have one of them for the refugees and they never respond." I told him I would try to get a response.

Leaving the refugee camp, I walked with Nadeem along the main road toward the nearby abandoned government buildings. Eventually, I saw a group of U.S. soldiers in a second-floor sentry post who watched the traffic as it went by. I needed to ask them who their commanding officer was so I could get an answer for my story about the Palestinian tent city. Remembering my experience at the American checkpoint when I first arrived in Baghdad, I briefly composed myself and then screamed, in as American an accent I could muster, "Hi! My name is Aaron! I'm from California!"

A voice came back from the sentry point: "I'm from Ohio! We've been here for eight months." He was counting the prewar buildup in Kuwait. "Do you have any idea where I could find a woman?"

Nadeem shook his head and looked around us. Luckily, there were no other Iraqis close by. It was a busy street for cars, but there were no shops to draw pedestrians. I screamed up that I didn't know where to find a prostitute, but that I was interested in finding their commanding officer so I could ask him about the Army's plan for the buildings. The soldier told me where to go—to the area Civil Affairs headquarters on the Army Canal near Baghdad's United Nations headquarters, which since then has been bombed and then shuttered.

Nadeem and I hailed a taxi and went off to Civil Affairs headquarters. It was the first time I had gone to see any kind of military authorities since my arrival in Iraq, and what I saw there was much less intimidating than I thought it would be.

There was only one guard at the entrance, a thinly built, thinly mustached Iraqi who took my press pass back to his American boss inside before returning to wave me in. After being patted down by a rather large female soldier with a long blond ponytail, I was escorted into the headquarters of Alpha 411 Civil Affairs Battalion, which was responsible for half of Baghdad. The office's electricity was down, and as far as I could tell, the building held only two civilian administrators.

The head of the office, Major Scott Hill, seemed like a nice man. An Army reservist from Connecticut, he had worked as an engineer for the state's Department of Transportation before being shipped off to Iraq. The only other man in the office was a radio operator. He was adjusting the radio, which appeared to be broken.

When I entered their office, Major Hill and the radio operator were talking about a large fire that had occurred the day before. On May 12, 2003, Baghdad's main telephone switching station, a seven-story structure near the Tigris River, was gutted in a spectacular fire that sent smoke billowing into the air for hours. All the telephone circuits were destroyed.

"The Iraqi firefighters kept coming to me, asking to put the fire out," Major Hill explained. "But we don't have the resources to fight every fire that comes along. I kept telling them no. Most of the buildings here are built out of cement. They're not like American buildings constructed from wood or a more flammable material, so the best thing we can do is just let them burn themselves out."

No mention was made of the lost telephone-switching system. Maybe it didn't matter much to him, because most of the city's local switching stations had been targeted and destroyed during the war as part of the U.S. bombing campaign's effort to disable the enemy's ability to communicate. (As of this writing, almost two years after the war, it remains almost impossible to use a land-line telephone to call from one part of Baghdad to another. To make such a call, an Iraqi has to go to a special international call center, which dials the international operator, who connects to a satellite in Europe, which then uses a separate satellite grid to call a land-line phone that's just a few miles away in another part of Baghdad. The cost is about $1 a minute, a fortune in a country where the average working-class wage is less than $4 a day.)

Eventually, Major Hill and I started talking about the main reason for my visit—the Palestinian refugee camp. "I understand their desire to get into a hard building," he told me. "But I think that in the grand scheme of things right now in Baghdad, they're living pretty good." He then cited the water provided by the Red Crescent and food coming from the United Nations Children's Fund as examples of their good life. In any case, he told me, his office, a civil affairs battalion of the U.S. military, had no authority to give out Iraqi government land.

"Only the Iraqi government can do that," he said. "Once we have a functional Iraqi government up and running they will be able to decide what to do with these buildings." When I asked him what he would say to the refugee families in tents, he told me they should sit tight and wait for an Iraqi government.

"Patience," he told me, "that goes for all the Iraqi people. Patience is something that's hard to come by, but we're trying to take a dictatorial society that's been run into the ground over the last twenty-five years and we're trying to fix everything in one month. The problem that we're running into is they want everything fixed yesterday.

"We're trying our best to help these people," he hastened to add. "We're exhausted already and we've only been here a few weeks."

Nadeem and I bid Major Hill farewell, walked out of the sparsely populated offices of Alpha 411 Civil Affairs Battalion, and hailed a taxi. On the ride back to my apartment, Nadeem and I wondered why the United States military was putting so little money toward civil affairs. "Is it because the Bush Administration doesn't care about the reconstruction of Iraq, or is it because all the money is going to big companies like Bechtel or Halliburton?" I wondered. The two companies had been given giant "cost plus indefinite quantity" contracts to reconstruct Iraq. That meant all their costs of doing business would be paid by the American taxpayer plus a tidy profit for their shareholders. It also meant they would get taxpayers' money whether they fixed anything or not. Initially, San Francisco-based Bechtel was given $1 billion to repair and refurbish the country's electric, sewage, water, and school systems. Houston-based Halliburton, meantime, was given $2 billion to rebuild the oil industry and provide logistical support to the Army, including meal service, laundry, communications, and housing. Both numbers would climb as the occupation dragged on, but little would be fixed.

Despite the insights I gained from this reporting, it left me wanting. I longed for a "good guy" and a "bad guy" in my stories on the war, and while it was always clear Saddam was bad (so bad that nobody could ever be as bad), I had trouble labeling anyone else "bad" or "good." I talked to other journalists about ways to get the opinions of regular Iraqis, and an independent photojournalist, Kael Alford, suggested I go door to door asking for people's opinions. Because of the lack of electricity and security, most Iraqis could be counted on to be at home during the day. Almost no one was working, and almost no one was going to school. Going directly into people's homes seemed to be the best way to get to the root of public opinion in Baghdad.

Kael suggested I go to a dilapidated building in downtown Baghdad, where she had been shooting a photo essay. One of the "regime-approved" families lived there, and before the war it was a regular stop for peace activists and left-wing journalists interested in the effects of 13 years of economic sanctions on Iraq. It was one of the few families in Baghdad that was allowed to talk to journalists. Before the war, they could be counted on to speak about the hardship of not having access to necessities, such as books and pencils and medicine for their children. They would blame these problems on America, which maintained the sanctions through its veto power at the United Nations Security Council.

Kael arranged for me to go to the building the next day with her translator, an unemployed engineer named Hashem, who was already well-known to people in the area. The next day, we drove 15 minutes through the downtown neighborhood, Karada, where the boulevards are full of nice restaurants and department stores, but where the housing on side streets verges on deplorable. Hashem squeezed his economy car into a small space, and we got out and walked to a brown four-story apartment building. The front door was open and we walked in.

Inside, it was completely dark. There were no windows to let light in, and because of the lack of electricity, all the interior lighting was out. Hashem let the flame rise from his lighter and we walked past the building's bare walls. The paint had peeled off a long time ago.

"Let's knock on some doors and see who lets us in to talk," I said.

So we walked carefully through the darkness, up the concrete stairwell, until we reached the top floor. We picked a door and Hashem knocked on it. After a brief pause, the door was opened by a middle-aged woman clad in a long, white dress and black *hijab*.

"Welcome," she said. "Who is here?"

Hashem explained that I was a journalist and was trying to learn the opinions of regular Iraqi people. The woman was delighted by this and allowed us in. Her apartment was small. The tiny entryway also served as the play area for a six-year-old girl, who rode her tricycle back and forth in the cramped space. On the right was a small bathroom with a squat toilet and bucket shower; on the left was a kitchen and single bedroom, and straight ahead was a living room furnished with two small couches and a coffee table.

"My name is Houdaka Kadem Ramaden," the woman told us as we entered. I almost tripped over her daughter. Houdaka laughed and kept talking, explaining how her family had been affected by

Ba'ath Party purges in the early 1980s, a time when the United States, under President Reagan, supported Saddam.

"I'm from Iraq, but my family is originally from Iran generations ago," she said. "When Saddam went to war with Iran, my brother was taken from his college. He was first in his class in the secondary school, but Saddam didn't let him continue in his studies because he said 'You are a follower of Iran.' Because of that Saddam wouldn't let him finish his college. You know, he's very educated, but he just sits at home without any job. He speaks English and many languages, but was forbidden from being a translator by the government of Saddam. Sometimes, he works as a taxi driver."

Her husband, Jassim Farhan, emerged from the bathroom, a burly man with sad eyes and wearing a sleeveless white undershirt that showed his girth. He sat next to her on one sofa, and Hashem and I sat on the other.

I asked them what they thought of their current situation.

"My daughter is named Miriam, but if I have a son, we will name him Bush," Houdaka answered quickly. "And I will name every child after that Bush, too."

"When I have a son, I will give him the name of my family," her husband added, "but his first name will be Bush."

"So," I clarified, "his name will be Bush Jassim Farhan?"

"Not just Bush," replied Houdaka, "George Bush. George Bush Jassim Farhan."

"But how can you say that?" I asked. "Do you think the situation is so good right now?"

"My country is destroyed and burned," Jassim said. "It's not easy to fix. We must give Bush more time to fix these things and build new buildings. We must give him more time because he needs the time to prove what he said."

"And do you think Bush is trying to fix things?"

Jassim shifted in his chair, thought, and responded. "It's true that it's not safe to go outside and it's true that we have no electricity in this building, and we have no water in this apartment because there is no electricity to pump the water. But Mr. Bush said in front of the whole world that we will have democracy in Iraq and I think he will prove it in front of all the world, but he needs time. There is no one as bad as Saddam. There is no one else who will come to Iraq and free us from Saddam. You know, Saddam was very, very, bad and no one who comes to Iraq can possibly be as bad as him."

I asked them about their daily lives, their jobs, and their daughter's education. Jassim told me he had just returned to his job at a cigarette factory that morning. There, they met people from the American occupation authority. The Americans handed out 20 dollars to each of the employees, he told me. It was their first pay in three months. "I have a new boss, too," Jassim said. "Our old boss was a relative of Saddam and a member of the Ba'ath Party. America fired him and put in another boss who didn't work in the Ba'ath Party."

"And how do you feel about the new boss that America put in?"

"He's very great," Jassim said. "Actually, it was the workers in the factory who chose him in an election, not George Bush or [recently named U.S. Administrator Paul] Bremer." He explained that the workers had voted out their old Ba'athist supervisor, from Saddam's Tikriti tribe, and voted in one of their coworkers in a tremendous display of workplace democracy.

"What about your daughter?" I asked. "I see she's home. Are you worried that she's not going to school?"

"It needs to be safe before we can send her to school," Houdaka responded. Miriam, having abandoned her tricycle temporarily, giggled shyly in her mother's lap. "She hasn't been to school in four months. There are so many accidents, fires, and kidnappings. When we stop hearing about these things, we will send our daughter to school. When we see police on the streets, we will send our daughter to school.

"It's not just me alone," she added. "All the people of Iraq like safety. I am afraid to go outside of my house. Maybe I will be killed. Even the little children have guns now. I hope the American people will take away their guns, but they need time and we will have to wait to be safe."

I could tell that Miriam was getting antsy. She wanted to play. So I put my microphone in front of her mouth and asked her to say something. She laughed and said: "Who is Saddam? I shit on Saddam, I'll rip him to pieces."

I asked her mother what Miriam does at home most days. "We teach her to read and to sing songs about Imam Hussein and Imam Ali," she said, referring to the two most important figures in Shia Islam. "She's very smart and she learns very fast. Sometimes her friends come over, and they can play together in the apartment, but not very often. They're not able to go out, either."

I asked Miriam if she would sing her favorite song for us. I gave her the microphone so she could sing like a six-year-old diva:

We've entered the Republican Palace
We saw [Vice President] Ezzad al-Doori
Wiping the floor
Hold on!

Saddam is telling [his wife] Sajuda
Pick up your things, poor woman
We've got to go

Sajuda tells Saddam
Let's turn up the boiler and hide the dollars in the hot water

Miriam smiled and her parents laughed and clapped for her. "You must stay for lunch," Houdaka insisted, as we got ready to leave. Hashem explained that we wanted to visit other people that day as well. In any case, I wasn't sure if they even had any food. Under the circumstances, it would have been rude to accept.

As we walked down the dark stairwell, we stopped to knock at other apartments, but no one else allowed us in. They told us at their doorways that they were sorry, but because of the lack of security in Baghdad, they were not letting strangers into their homes. Finally, on the first floor, as we were about to leave the building, a door opened. A young Kurdish woman with dark skin and free-flowing hair said we could come in to ask a few questions.

The large apartment opened into a spacious front room with several couches and tables. A mounted photograph of the Golden Gate Bridge in San Francisco graced the most prominent wall.

"That's where I'm from," I told her. "San Francisco. It's a beautiful city."

The woman said one of her uncles had fled Saddam's regime in the mid-1980s and settled in California. Slowly, over the years, he was bringing his entire family across the Atlantic to America. She gave me her uncle's name and address in San Diego. "When you get back to America, can you get in touch with him and tell him not to give up?" she asked. I promised I would, and we were directed to sit down at the couch closest to the door. When we sat, she went into the kitchen to get us tea.

I turned on my tape recorder and asked her to introduce herself for the microphone.

"My name is Nasreen Ali," she said. "I am twenty-six years old. Before the war, I used to be a nurse. I used to have a job, but now it's all stopped because of the war. It's a bad situation."

"But," I protested, "the hospitals are open and patients are going inside. It seems nurses are needed now more than ever, especially with so many people being killed and injured in violence on the streets."

"They asked me to come back to the hospital," she conceded. "But how am I supposed to get there? There is no public transportation now and the streets are unsafe for a woman. There are killings and kidnappings even in the daytime."

"I understand," I responded, recalling my earlier reporting. "I went to al-Yarmuk Hospital, and a patient had just been stabbed to death in the emergency room."

"That's right," she said, "and it's not the only case. I went to al-Kindi [another government hospital] to ask about a friend of mine who is a doctor. He disappeared during the war. And while I was there a car attacked the hospital. The people in it just opened fire with machine guns . . . it's not right."

"How is the situation overall?" I asked. "Is it better than before the war, or worse than before the war?"

"Before the war, it was better," she answered. "Now the women can't go out of their homes. Even in the morning we can't go out. There are no doctors and on the street we might get kidnapped."

"How do you see Iraq in five years?" I asked. "In 2008, will it be a democracy or an Islamic state or another Ba'athist government?"

"How can we think about the future—five years coming—when we live with no safety today? We expect there will be new buildings and modern life in the future, but we know America will not do it from their own pocket, but from the Iraqi pocket. They are taking the oil. We sleep and we don't know what's happening during the night, if you know what I mean. How can you think about the future when you don't know anything about today?"

It occurred to me that this was the first time anyone I had interviewed had mentioned Iraq's sizeable oil reserve. This resource was not front and center in the Iraqi consciousness. "What would you say to George Bush if he arrived right now? Would you allow him into your house?"

"If he came here!" she said. "I would tell him he is a criminal man. Saddam was a bad man and Bush is a worse criminal than Saddam."

Again, this was the first time anyone I talked to had expressed this opinion. "What makes Bush a worse criminal than Saddam?" I asked.

"Bush killed many people, including Iraqi people, in this war," she said. "He insisted to enter this country. He told Saddam, 'Leave in forty-eight hours or I will go inside Iraq.' He said this on TV, and he killed many people without any reason. He always talks about democracy, where is the democracy? The American people have democracy, but they don't have the democracy to change their government. Is that right or wrong? As an American person, what do you think?"

"What do I think?" I asked. "For myself, I don't like George Bush much, but you know, we've had George Bush and before that we had Bill Clinton and before that we had George Bush—the other one—and before that Ronald Reagan. And during that whole time you had Saddam."

"Okay, so what?" she argued. "Jewish people control America. If one Jewish person said 'yes' for Bush and all the American people said 'no' for Bush the Jewish person will overrule all the other American people."

That was an argument I had heard many times in other parts of the Middle East, especially in Jordan, with its large proportion of Palestinian refugees. Thousands of miles from America, I knew, it seemed like a reasonable argument to many Arabs. What else could explain America's lock-step approval of Ariel Sharon's government? Clearly, there must be some conspiracy.

"It's not like that," I said. "There are a number of reasons why

America is always supporting Israel, but remember that it is the Christians, not the Jews, who are in control of America. George Bush is a Christian, Dick Cheney is a Christian. Donald Rumsfeld and Colin Powell are both Christians and so is Paul Bremer." As in most situations of this type, I didn't reveal my own Jewish heritage.

I thanked Nasreen for her time and promised again to contact her uncle in San Diego. I promised to urge him to keep trying to get her a visa so she could move to the United States, a nation that she hoped would lift her out of the poverty it had brought upon her when it bombed her country.

"Is this what you were looking for?" Hashem asked as we drove back to the Dulaimi.

"It is what it is," I told Hashem, smiling. "People are who they are. They disagree with each other. It makes it difficult for a journalist when things don't break down neatly like you want them to."

Hashem didn't seem to understand what I was saying, so I added, "It was great. Exactly what I wanted. Different ideas from different people about the current situation."

"So we'll work again tomorrow?" he asked.

"I don't think so," I answered. "Kael will probably want to work with you again tomorrow, but I'm probably going to leave soon. I'm sad about it, you know, and I feel like it's the right thing to do."

We promised to keep in touch. He gave me his e-mail address. Internet cafes using satellite connections were just starting to pop up around Baghdad. "Please write to me if you need anything. Anything at all," he said.

I gave him my best, and got out of the car at my apartment building.

———

Raphaël was in the apartment, enjoying a beer while playing chess with a man named Naseer, a middle-aged architect and poet. The two of them had become close friends in the last few weeks and had taken to hanging out together. Naseer was about as pro-war as any Iraqi could get. "The Americans can do whatever they want and we will be happy," he would say. "So long as we don't have to deal with that bastard Saddam Hussein. They can take all the oil they want and we won't care. They have liberated us. Before the war, it would have been impossible for me to come to your house and play chess with you. It would have been forbidden by Saddam."

"You know, Aaron, I have learned a lot from Naseer and from the other people I have met here in Iraq," Raphaël said. "I have met a former Iraqi fighter pilot who dropped many chemical weapons on the Kurds during the Iran-Iraq war. And you know what? His airplane was a Mirage. A French airplane. I have to tell you, when I get back to France I am going to do a lot of writing and speaking. I cannot believe that the French government, which has sold so many weapons to Saddam Hussein, did not have the dignity to remove him from power. You know, Jacques Chirac would have been perfectly happy with another twenty years of Saddam Hussein."

I smiled weakly and said nothing. I was tired of this discussion. It had gone on for more than a month now and it was always the same. Still, something else had changed. Through listening to the arguments of Raphaël and James, and the stories of hundreds of Iraqis, I had developed my own analysis of the situation.

"The taxi will be coming tomorrow at seven in the morning," Raphaël told me, looking up from the chess game. "I have obtained a free ride with a reporter from *Le Figaro*. You know, it will be back to Jordan for me. You are coming, darling?"

"Yeah. I'll be there," I said.

The next morning the taxi came to pick us up. It was a boxy yellow Japanese car, circa 1985. As we crossed Iraq's western desert back to Jordan, new arguments regarding the situation in Iraq began to form in my head. When we got to Amman, I went to an Internet cafe and wrote an open letter to my colleagues back home.

The letter, read, in part:

To whom it may concern,

I believe in radio that furthers peace, social equality, and human rights. It's why I report for Pacifica. I know that Pacifica is a radio station where the people come first. But looking back on the last year of news coverage at Pacifica (including my own work from the United States, Europe, the Middle East, and South Asia), I have to ask myself—did Pacifica adequately cover the needs, hopes, and dreams of the Iraqi people?

The long-term prognosis for the future of Iraq right now is not necessarily rosy—anything from a puppet American dictatorship, to a theocracy, to a civil war could be in the offing and there is still almost no electricity in most of the country. There are day-long lines for gasoline for cars, and the water is so bad there is the possibility of an epidemic of cholera in Baghdad. But while this is true, it is also true that most all of what was bombed were clearly "regime targets," the ministries, the armaments, etc. This actually showed enormous restraint by the Americans as Saddam had put heavy weaponry into almost every school, library, and civil institution, effectively making most of his people involuntary human shields. And there is no way the Americans could possibility be as oppressive as Saddam, who did not allow the Shi'ite religion to be celebrated, who gassed more than 5,000 Kurds and forcibly resettled more than 100,000, who imprisoned people at a moment's notice, who had spies everywhere, and who did not hesitate to assassinate his political opponents, including some of Iraq's leading religious figures.

My biggest fear now is not that the Americans have bad intentions for this place (stealing the oil money and giving contracts to big

American companies is a given but a cost I believe most Iraqis don't care about as they figure there will be more left for them to live on than under Saddam). No, my biggest concern is that the Americans don't know what they're doing. The Civilian Affairs department of the U.S. military—the effective government—is woefully under-staffed. Recently, they allowed a seven-story telephone-switching center to burn down rather than spend their resources to put out the fire. Parents are afraid to send their children to school because the streets are unsafe even during the day. Many people have been un-able to return to work and the economy is a disaster after 25 years of war and sanctions.

What does this mean for mission-driven news? News designed to promote peace and human rights?

Looking back, I believe Pacifica did not show solidarity with the Iraqi people in its broadcasting but instead showed solidarity with the Ba'athist dictatorship of Saddam Hussein. It did so by down-playing the gross human-rights violations of the regime in an effort to build support for the antiwar movement. Instead, I believe that a radio station committed to social justice must report on the human-rights records of all governments in the world, especially those as brutal as that of Saddam Hussein. Solutions put forward to avoid war on Pacifica's airwaves should have focused on nonviolent ways to remove Saddam Hussein and promote democracy and human rights in a postwar Iraq.

Over the years Pacifica has expressed solidarity with the people of East Timor, South Africa, Nigeria, and Burma who have been suffer-ing under the brutal reign of oppressive regimes. I believe the Iraqi people deserved the same solidarity against dictatorship under Sad-dam Hussein.

By the same token, George Bush has made a war that promises democracy and human rights to the Iraqi people. I believe Pacifica should report on whether these promises are delivered or whether an

American puppet dictator is installed. The humanitarian situation in Iraq is a mess and needs to be reported, as do the United States and UN efforts (or lack of effort) to improve the situation.

In the future, I hope that as Pacifica strives to promote peace and social justice, it also shows solidarity with the people of North Korea and Syria, for example, offering peaceful alternatives to war that promote human rights in those countries rather than propping up dictatorial regimes.

In solidarity,

Aaron Glantz

PART TWO

THE OCCUPATION
DRAGS ON

WELCOME TO IRAQI KURDISTAN

The letter did not have the desired effect. Instead of starting a debate within the progressive media, it was largely dismissed (with a few scattered voices saying I had been bought off by the CIA). On my return to the States, most of my colleagues told me the same things my editors had told me when I was in Iraq: that they didn't dispute the truth of what I said, but that those truths were readily available in the mainstream media in the United States and therefore should not be the focus of the progressive press.

I protested.

"That's not true," I would say. "The mainstream media says Saddam Hussein was a criminal and so the war was justified. I'm not saying the war was right. I'm just saying that to oppose the war is not enough. We need to promote a third option—one with no war and no brutal Saddam regime. Are we in favor of human rights or not? If we are, then we must produce stories that promote human rights, even if we happen to point the finger at the same person George Bush is attacking. Otherwise, if we are successful, if we prevent the war and Saddam stays in power, we are dooming the Iraqi people to a dark future."

"So what would you suggest instead?" the question would inevitably come. "What is the solution that leaves us with no war and no Saddam dictatorship?"

"I don't know," I would have to concede. "But this is where the progressive media comes in. We can be a clearinghouse for ideas on this topic. We can invite antiwar activists onto the radio to debate how to get rid of dictators like Saddam using peaceful means. We can have a debate on our own terms, about human rights, rather than just reacting to whatever George Bush says and does."

After a month of taking this up with nearly everyone at my radio network, I gave up. I would not be able to generate change within Pacifica without taking my arguments to a more public, confrontational level, and that was not something I wanted to do. So I simply went back to work. Over the next five months, I traveled to South Korea, Vietnam, and Indonesia to report for Pacifica. When I got back to the United States in January 2004, I talked to my editors about the possibility of returning to Iraq. I wanted to see how attitudes had changed since the euphoria that had followed the fall of Saddam Hussein, and I craved a chance to travel throughout the country, beyond just Baghdad and its surroundings. Since no one else was on the ground, they were excited about the idea.

When I returned to Iraq, I decided to pass through Turkey in the north, rather than through Jordan as I had before. I wanted to see Iraqi Kurdistan, which had possessed its own government since the Western imposition of "No-Fly Zones" after the 1991 Gulf War.

The development was not appreciated by the governments of neighboring Syria, Turkey, and Iran, which all had their own sizeable, largely oppressed Kurdish populations. Before the war, both borders to Iraqi Kurdistan were closed. (The Turkish army had even imposed two of its own bases in northern Iraq, and the Turkish parliament had approved a plan to send its own, separate invasion force to the country if the Kurds in the north declared independence.)

When I arrived in Diyarbakir, Turkish army tanks and humvees still patrolled the streets and demonstrations in favor of Kurdish nationalism remained mostly banned. Officially, martial law had been lifted, but Kurdish radio and TV stations were still regularly shuttered and Muslim scholars remained barred from giving their sermons in Kurdish.

But despite the Kurdish conflict, Turkey's border with Iraq was open. The Kurds in northern Iraq hadn't declared independence, and so Turkey allowed commerce to flow across the Habur border crossing to northern Iraq, with the queue of trucks waiting to cross the border going back almost 100 miles. I took a bus from Diyarbakir to the border and caught a taxi there that took me across for just $12. Customs on the Turkish side of the border were perfunctory.

When I reached the other side, I saw what the Turkish military was afraid of. Unlike Iraq's western border with Jordan, which was manned by American soldiers, the northern border with Turkey was manned by Kurdish militiamen loyal to the Kurdistan Democratic Party. The sign at the border read WELCOME TO IRAQI KURDISTAN, in English and Kurdish. The giant mural of Saddam Hussein that used to grace the border had been replaced by a building-sized painting of the founder of modern Kurdish nationalism, Mullah Mustafa Barzani, the father of one of the two current Iraqi Kurdish leaders, Masoud Barzani.

The Kurdish border guards didn't stamp my passport. Since they didn't officially have a country, they weren't allowed to stamp. Instead, they gave me a paper to put inside my passport and told me that if I lost it I could be arrested for crossing the border illegally. My Turkish-Kurdish taxi driver drove me to the other side and dropped me off at a taxi stand for Iraqi Kurdish taxi drivers. I paid the Iraqi driver $35 to drive me two and a half hours to a cheap hotel in the regional capital, Arbil. James had told me he would be waiting for me there.

By the time I reached Arbil, it was 11 P.M., and in the main part of Iraq (formerly "Saddamistan" but now "Bushistan," I would joke) it would be unthinkable to be out on the road so late at night. But in Kurdistan, the situation was different. As my Kurdish driver drove past the smiling portrait of Mullah Mustafa Barzani and south toward Arbil, we passed innumerable checkpoints. All of them were manned by *peshmerga,* or Kurdish militiamen (literally "after-death men"), wearing the traditional black-and-white *kaffiyeh* on their head to keep warm, and holding Kalashnikovs.

As we approached each one of them, the driver would put on his blinkers and present his ID card along with my American passport and we would be waved through. This was how it worked in Iraqi Kurdistan. When I arrived at Arbil's Fareed Hotel, I noticed that there was a picture of Kurdish Democratic Party leader Masoud Barzani where Saddam's would have been in years gone by.

"Is James Longley here?" I asked the desk clerk, showing my passport. "I'm his friend." It suddenly struck me that I knew only one word in Kurdish, *spas,* or "thank you." I would need to get a translator fast.

After some confusion, the clerk realized who I was talking about and called James down from his room. My friend came bounding down the stairs. "*Habibi,*" he said, opening his arms for a hug. "It's good to see you. Welcome to Howleyr!"

"Howleyr?" I asked as he helped me carry my belongings up the stairs to my room.

James explained: "That's what the people who live here call this city. You have some things to learn, my friend."

"So how is the situation?" I asked.

"*Yani*, [You know] things are pretty good," he said. "As you can see, it's quite different up here than in the south. Have you eaten?" he asked as he put on his coat. "Let's go get something to eat."

We walked to the front of the hotel and hailed a cab. Midnight, and there were still taxis to hail. This was definitely different from Baghdad. "There are a few spots open late," James said. "Mostly the city closes down about ten."

"It's amazing," I said. "You know, there's something that really strikes you when you cross the border and you see that big portrait of Barzani and then you see all those *peshmerga* on the road here. And everyone speaks Kurdish everywhere you go. It's totally different from southeastern Turkey. Everyone is Kurdish there, too, of course, but all the signs are in Turkish and the Turkish flag is everywhere. There are all those Turkish tanks and humvees everywhere and for the most part everyone speaks Turkish when they order a sandwich. I understand now what freedom for Kurds looks like."

The taxi dropped us off in front of a row of late-night *shawarma* shops. James paid the driver the going rate of 1,000 Iraqi *dinar* (75 cents) and thanked him in Kurdish. We sat down and ordered our sandwiches. James returned to the topic of Kurdish autonomy.

"The thing is," he said. "Kurdistan is not so free." He explained that the western half of Kurdistan, which included Arbil, was ruled by Masoud Barzani and his Kurdistan Democratic Party (KDP), while the eastern half was ruled by Jalal Talabani and his Patriotic Union of Kurdistan (PUK). Both organizations were controlled by their leaders, who maintained control through their own *peshmerga* armies.

"Have you heard of the *asayeesh*?" James asked. "The *asayeesh* is the *mukhabarat* [Arabic for state security police] of Kurdistan. It's not as bad as under Saddam Hussein, of course, but it's still there. The first thing you should do tomorrow is go to the *asayeesh*." If I didn't register and obtain a paper of permission from the *asayeesh*, James said, no one would be interviewed by me and I would be asked to leave the Fareed Hotel.

"Don't worry about it," James said. "It's just formalities. But still, it gives you an idea of the way things are run here."

We finished our sandwiches and took a taxi back to the hotel. We walked up to our room and James flipped on the TV. "Have you discovered Channel 2 yet?" he asked. Channel 2 was a Saudi satellite-TV station that broadcast English-language films (edited for sex but not for violence or language) with Arabic subtitles. "This will be your savior," he predicted. Unfortunately, when James turned it on, Channel 2 was broadcasting an Arabic knockoff of American reality TV. The show, *Big Brother*, put a dozen men from across the Arab world in a house in Riyad. In each episode one of them would be voted out of the house.

"This always seems to happen," James said sighing. "There was one of these in Russia when I lived there. The channel started off showing really good movies, but then it started producing cheap Russian knockoffs and I stopped watching."

We changed the channel a few times, but there wasn't much on. There were the two Iraqi-Kurdish television networks, Kurdistan Television (KTV) and KurdSat, which were run by the Kurdistan Democratic Party and the Patriotic Union of Kurdistan respectively. They were the main stations broadcasting in Kurdish to most homes, and they essentially served as political mouthpieces for the two ruling factions. The evening news on KTV, for example, was primarily a summary of what party leader Masoud Barzani had done that day.

There were also Arab satellite news channels like al-Arabiya and al-Jazeera, along with a few Turkish-broadcast channels strong enough to reach northern Iraq. There was also a channel specializing in classic Egyptian films from the 1970s. James liked that station. Since so many Egyptian filmmakers studied in Moscow, he said, the style of movie-making was similar to that of the Russians.

But we were too tired for an Egyptian movie musical. James clicked off the television and we went to sleep.

The next morning I woke up and caught a taxi to the *asayeesh*. In the sun, I could see the basic layout of the city. An ancient fort on a hill marked the center of town. Otherwise, the city was perfectly flat, with houses spreading out in concentric circles away from the old fort. The *asayeesh* was in one of the outer circles, on the city's southern edge. The driver dropped me off in front.

Two older Kurdish men with Kalashnikovs and traditional baggy *sharwal* pants greeted me at the door. Since I didn't speak a word of Kurdish, I introduced myself in Arabic: "*Ana Sahafee Amreekee,*" I said; I am an American journalist.

The registration went pretty much as I expected: lots of sitting around in front of innumerable bureaucrats with large mustaches who took my passport and copied down my essential information into a dizzying number of thick ledgers. After being shuffled from one office to another for hours, I was presented with a yellow piece of paper to give to the hotel and a purple piece of paper with my photo on it. That would serve as my press pass.

Emerging from the *asayeesh,* I decided to walk back to the hotel. In late February, the air in Arbil was already warm enough that a sweater wasn't required. As I walked past juice stands, kebab restaurants, bookstores, *locum* shops, barbershops, and clothing-and-produce bazaars, there wasn't a hint that I was in Iraq.

Kurdish was the only language spoken on the streets and written large on shop windows. Signs on government buildings proclaimed KURDISTAN HEALTH MINISTRY and KURDISTAN MINISTRY OF EDUCATION. The Kurdish national flag—with a giant golden sun backed by green, white, and red stripes, could be seen on all the government buildings, on the main streets, and on many shops. There wasn't a U.S. soldier in sight. It was an autonomy won through a decade of cooperation with America.

"It was decided to work with the U.S. for that purpose," Shukr Piro Sinjo, head of the Iraqi Kurdistan NGO Network, explained to me the next day. "The Kurds were a strong player in the game. They sacrificed for that purpose. The U.S. has to recognize that our people sacrificed, and they should pay more attention to our concerns."

Sinjo and other Kurdish officials were concerned that the Americans were ignoring northern Iraq as they doled out money for reconstruction. Under the United Nations' oil-for-food program that was in effect when Saddam was president, Kurdish authorities in the north received a portion of the oil money for civic projects.

"We were in the middle of renovating the sewer system when the United Nations left," another Kurdish reconstruction official, Phillip Petrus, told me, "but then when the United States took over we had to stop. Since the end of [the United Nations oil-for-food program under resolution] 986, we have not gotten a single dollar for reconstruction. We try to talk to Bremer and his associates, but they don't talk to us. We are waiting. We have gained so much with the end of the Saddam regime, so we are patient. But we will not wait forever."

"Maybe," I suggested, "the Americans are taking your support for granted. Maybe they don't help you rebuild the sewer system in

Arbil because you are not killing the American soldiers. Maybe they are using the reconstruction money to stop the insurgency."

At the negotiating table in Baghdad, Washington was demanding that Masoud Barzani and Jalal Talabani disband their *peshmerga,* which had for 80 years fought successive Arab Iraqi governments. But so far, Barzani and Talabani had refused. They demanded that Kurdistan be responsible for its own defense and they wanted a share of Iraq's oil revenue to pay for it. They also demanded that the oil-rich city of Kirkuk be included in their jurisdiction. The city had been a Kurdish one until Saddam Hussein embarked on a campaign of ethnic cleansing while Iraq fought Iran in the 1980s.

"Maybe they don't want a strong Kurdistan," Phillip Petrus said. "That is not for me to speculate or question. I say only that we are waiting and that we would like to fix our sewer system."

But there were other people who took nationalism quite seriously, and the fighting in Baghdad and the February bombing of the Arbil offices of the KDP and PUK seemed to have intensified the desire to be separate from Iraq. As I arrived in Arbil, Kurdish activists traveled to Baghdad to present the U.S. Administrator, Paul Bremer, with a petition signed by 1.7 million Kurds, more than a third of the country's Kurdish population. The petition asked for a referendum on independence for Kurdistan.

Meeting the activists who were behind this petition was among the first things I wanted to do in Kurdistan. I wanted to learn if Kurds were going to "make a move" toward independence or if they were willing to ride their alliance with America wherever it led.

I asked Istifan Braymook, the Assyrian Christian receptionist at my hotel, if he would be interested in working with me as a translator for $25 a day. Since he was making $80 a month working at the Fareed Hotel, he agreed almost instantly.

Like so many people in Kurdistan, Istifan was underemployed. Highly educated and fluent in English, Kurdish, Arabic, and Assyrian, he had previously worked for a number of the Western NGOs and United Nations agencies that sprouted up in northern Iraq after the 1991 Gulf War. But when the U.S. military toppled Saddam's Ba'ath regime on April 9, 2004, many of those organizations closed up shop or moved to Baghdad, leaving Istifan to work as a receptionist.

On our first day of work, I told Istifan I wanted to learn more about the petition, and he suggested we take a taxi to the offices of the ruling Kurdistan Democratic Party and ask them.

"But I thought this was an independent petition," I said. "I thought this petition was pushing Barzani and Talabani to ask for more. Barzani and Talabani are asking for federalism. These people want a referendum on independence."

"You have to understand the way things work here," Istifan responded as he hailed a taxi. "Everything is organized by the KDP, even if it seems to be in opposition. At the very least, Barzani has to give his permission." If no permission was granted, it followed, the *asayeesh* could be asked to step in and stop it. It was perhaps fitting, then, that the KDP was housed in an old Ba'ath Party office.

Indeed, the *peshmerga* outside the KDP offices knew exactly where to send us. They suggested we go to the Kurdistan General Federation of Trade Unions, which was housed in a giant building on the other side of town. Half an hour later, we arrived at the trade union office and showed my purple *asayeesh* paper to the *peshmerga* out front.

Inside, we found the offices nearly empty. Again, photos of Masoud Barzani could be found on the walls, along with maps of "Kurdistan." On the maps, Kurdistan spread out to include large swaths of Turkey, Syria, and Iran. It met the Black Sea at Trabzon and the Mediterranean at Iskenderun.

At the Kurdistan General Federation of Trade Unions we interviewed Handrian Ahmed, a young man who had headed up the petition drive in Arbil. At first his words were uncomproming: "We have to get independence in our country, so that none of the calamities that happened to Kurdish people under the previous regime will ever happen again."

I asked him about the Kurdish leadership: "So what do you think about the fact that your leaders—Mr. Masoud Barzani and Mr. Jalal Talabani—are not even speaking about independence anymore? They only talk about federalism and how Kurds want federalism."

"Independence is an idea we must keep alive," he told me. "It may not be the right time now. Mr. Barzani and Mr. Talabani are fighting hard for our people, but we must still talk about independence so that someday we can achieve it. Federalism is important to our people, but only as a step on the way to having our own Kurdistan."

Such a declaration might bring a regional war, though. Over the weekend, a senior member of the Turkish army's general staff, Ilker Basburg, had warned that his army would not tolerate an ethnic federation in Iraq—let alone independence. Earlier in the year, Turkey's prime minister, Recep Tayip Erdoğan, had declared that his government would oppose Kurdish autonomy "even if it was in Argentina."

If Turkish politicians wanted, it would not be hard for their army to make trouble in northern Iraq. The Turkish army already maintained two bases there, one of which was right in the center of Arbil.

Officially, the Turkish base housed a multinational force that was established in 1996 after a terrible war broke out between the PUK and the KDP. At issue were control over Arbil and dispensation of customs duties imposed at the Turkish border. The battle was a bitter one—so bitter, in fact, that Masoud Barzani ended up calling on Saddam Hussein for help. When Saddam's tanks rolled into Arbil, Jalal Talabani's PUK was forced to withdraw and Barzani's KDP declared victory, as Saddam's agents hunted down and killed dozens of opponents of his regime. (This was not the first time Kurdish leaders had made such a request of Baghdad. In 1970, Jalal Talabani convinced the Ba'ath government and then–Vice President Saddam Hussein to give air support in a war against Masoud Barzani's father, Mullah Mustafa.)

After Saddam intervened, the Western powers stepped in and brokered a peace treaty between the two Kurdish factions. The agreement put forward a system of revenue-sharing between the KDP and the PUK and imposed a peacekeeping force on the region, composed of American, British, French, and Turkish soldiers.

After tensions eased, elections were held, with the KDP winning all the seats in the areas its *peshmerga* controlled and the PUK winning every seat in the area controlled by its militia. The European and American forces left northern Iraq, but the Turkish forces remained—rebuffing many requests by Kurdish leaders that they should withdraw to their border.

After talking to Handrian Ahmed, Istifan and I hailed a taxi and headed toward the Turkish base. A walled structure covered with barbed wire, its most visible feature was a five-story watchtower. Either ironically or purposely, it had been built just a block away from the *asayeesh* headquarters. We walked up to the heavy steel door that marked the entrance to the base. I knocked, and after a moment a soldier slid a panel to the side, revealing his face.

"What is your business here?" the soldier said in Turkish.

I told him in Turkish that I was an American journalist who had some questions. I handed over my press pass. He asked me to wait for a moment, closed the metal panel, and walked away.

After a few minutes, his senior officer appeared, my American press pass in hand.

"We don't have any time to talk to you now and we won't in the future!" the commander screamed in Turkish through the small steel window. A junior officer translated his words simultaneously into Kurdish for Istifan's benefit.

The senior officer threw my press card into the dirt. We asked for his name and he refused to give it. He waved his arms: "Get lost! I never want to see you again!" With that, he slammed the steel window shut.

Such were relations between Turkey and Iraqi Kurdistan, I thought.

A few days later, I got another reminder of relations between Turkey and the Iraqi Kurds. I walked to a cafe a few blocks from my hotel, with the goal of listening to my interview recordings and writing a story on Kurdish nationalism, but I ran into a communication problem.

I realized I didn't know how to ask for coffee in Kurdish. But I knew how to ask in Arabic. "*Aku khahwa?*" I asked. The cafe owner, a young man who had received his schooling since the establishment of Kurdistan in 1991, gave me a strained look.

So I asked in Turkish. "*Kahve varma?*" At this, a look of concern entered his face. "Where are you from?" he asked in halting English. I told him I was American and took out my passport and my paper from the *asayeesh,* but he was still skeptical. Clearly, I looked like I could be a Turkish spy.

He walked away.

Confused, I sat down and took out my minidisk recorder and headphones and started to listen to my interviews while I waited for my coffee. But the cafe owner had not gone to make coffee.

When I looked up, three burly, Kalashnikov-toting *peshmerga* were staring down at me. They motioned for me to gather my stuff and come with them, and I did, walking just a few steps down the block so as to be out of view of the cafe.

The *peshmerga* asked to see my papers. I showed them my passport as well as my purple paper from the *asayeesh.* "You don't speak Turkish?" one of them asked.

"Only a little," I said. That satisfied the *peshmerga,* who escorted me back to the cafe. They spoke briefly to the owner, who then insisted on giving me free coffee.

Eventually, the Turkish military left Arbil. In December 2004, the army abandoned the base. But as of this writing, the Turks continue to maintain another base closer to their border, in Dohuk. That base is said to hold about 5,000 soldiers.

.7.

PESHMERGA IN CONTROL, REFUGEES IN CAMPS

For the most part, I was treated well in Iraqi Kurdistan. The vast majority of Kurds in Arbil broke out in wide smiles when they heard I was American. I took taxis and walked the streets of the city late into the night without a care about my safety.

Internet cafes had sprouted up, connecting Kurdistan to the wider world through the miracle of satellite technology. After I sent my story from an Internet cafe near the old city, I would walk through an open-air produce market a few blocks from the hotel, purchase some oranges or *locum* for late-night snacks, and buy a fresh-squeezed kiwi or some pomegranate juice for less than 25 cents before heading back to the hotel.

Other aspects of life in Kurdistan were relatively comfortable, too. On the streets of Arbil, new cars proliferated. Nice cars, too: Mercedes, BMW, and other high-end European brands, which had started to flood across the mountainous Turkish border in trucks immediately after the United Nations lifted its sanctions on Iraq the year before. The cars were cheap—no more than $3,000 for a used luxury car that surely would go for at least $20,000 back in the States. Rumor had it that the cars were cheap because they were all stolen from the streets of Europe and stripped of their identifying features before being sold in Iraq, where no one would be able to track them down.

When we hailed a taxi, Istifan refused to ride in anything but a Mercedes. "You will let me pick the car?" he would ask each time, fearful that I would hail an old hunk-of-junk from the sanctions period. "Why shouldn't we ride in comfort? It is the same price for the trip as one of those old cars we have been stuck with for so many years."

There was a certain spring in most Kurds' step—they were happy in the knowledge that Saddam was finally gone.

But despite the change in attitudes, most aspects of daily Kurdish life hadn't changed much in the 11 months since the regime's ouster. Electricity was available for only three hours a day, and telephone services weren't much better than in Baghdad (really a terrible indictment of the PUK and KDP, which had ruled independent of Saddam since 1991). Unemployment and poverty remained high, and—despite press reports to the contrary—most of the hundreds of thousands of Kurdish refugees who lost their homes under Saddam continued to languish in camps.

There certainly wasn't much of a dent in the population of Benslawa Camp. Located just outside of Arbil, the sprawling community of more than 50,000 Kurds was almost as large as it had been before the war.

"Only two percent of the refugees have been able to return

home," the camp's mayor, Rafat Abdel Mohammed Amin, told me the day Istifan and I traveled to Benslawa. We arrived in an orange-and-white Mercedes taxi.

I asked Rafat about the date of the camp's construction. "We constructed this camp after the 1991 war," he said, "but most of the people who live here have been without homes for much longer. These people, like most refugees in Kurdistan, are refugees from al-Anfal."

Al-Anfal was the massive campaign of ethnic cleansing Saddam launched in the late 1980s. At the time, the Iraqi army was locked in the long war with Iran. Europe and America feared Iran's new ruler, Ayatollah Khomeini, so they backed Saddam with arms and food aid, but the Kurdish guerrillas had other ideas.

"I was a *peshmerga* at that time," Benslawa's mayor explained. "During the daytime we would fight for the Iraqi army. Then in the evening when the army was sleeping we would sneak away to the mountains and shell their positions. We wouldn't let them sleep. Our goal was to liberate Kurdistan and get our freedom." Saddam did not take kindly to this activity, so he unleashed a reign of terror in the Kurdish countryside—forcibly depopulating thousands of Kurdish villages where the guerrillas could seek shelter. That's how Mayor Rafat lost his home.

"I remember that day very well," he told me. "They came one morning, Saddam's police. They brought bulldozers to destroy our house the moment we left it. Then they gave us a tent to live in. We were completely surrounded by checkpoints of the Iraqi army."

Between 1987 and 1989, Saddam's military destroyed at least 2,000 Kurdish cities and villiages. Kurdish refugees were transferred to internment camps, where they often died of sickness and starvation. Some were taken in trucks to the south of Iraq, where many were executed. According to Human Rights Watch, prisoners were frequently lined up and dragged into pre-dug mass graves.

Other Kurds were shoved into trenches and shot where they stood; still others were made to lie down in pairs, sardine-style, next to mounds of fresh corpses, before being killed. Two years after George W. Bush's invasion of Iraq, most of these mass graves still haven't been exhumed, so it's impossible to come up with an exact figure of those killed. Human Rights Watch now conservatively estimates that 50,000 Kurdish civilians were killed. Kurdish political parties in Iraq put the number at 182,000. Both say the Anfal campaign meets the legal definition of genocide.

Somehow, Rafat, told me, he had escaped. He lived in the mountains for years, carrying a Kalashnikov for the *peshmerga* of KDP leader Masoud Barzani. He fought in the 1991 uprising against the regime, and when the stalemate resulted in the creation of the Kurdistan autonomous area, he helped construct Benslawa Camp.

I asked Rafat what he thought about America. "You know," I said, "at the time when Saddam committed these atrocities he was backed by the United States against Iran."

I noted that President Reagan had largely ignored reports that Saddam Hussein was using chemical weapons against the Iranian army and domestic Kurdish insurgents. I also noted that as the gas rained down, Donald Rumsfeld had traveled to Baghdad and shaken hands with Saddam Hussein. I showed him a Reagan press release that read: "While condemning Iraq's resort to chemical weapons, the United States finds the Iranian regime's intransigent refusal to deviate from its avowed objective of eliminating the legitimate government of Iraq to be inconsistent with accepted norms."

"How does it make you feel," I asked, "that at that time the United States was calling Saddam the 'legitimate government of Iraq' and now they have gone in and removed him?"

"The U.S.A. supported Saddam because they thought this relationship would benefit them," the mayor responded nonchalantly.

"Every country does this. Then they changed their mind. They wanted to remove Saddam, so they started a war against him."

You could say the same, I thought, for the Kurdistan Democratic Party of Masoud Barzani. At various times, they had fought alongside America, Iran, and even Saddam Hussein when it came to dislodging the rival Patriotic Union of Kurdistan from Arbil. I wondered what the future would hold for the U.S.-Kurdish alliance.

One thing that was obvious, though, was that the U.S.-Kurdish alliance did not extend to helping improve the condition of Kurds living in refugee camps. After saying good-bye to the camp's mayor, Istifan and I turned our attention to the camp itself.

Thirteen years after the camp's construction, refugees in Benslawa still lived along dirt roads with packed mud and canvas tarps serving as their roofs. Their walls were made of stacked cinderblocks donated by the United Nations. They had no plumbing, their only water coming from United Nations–installed central water and toilet facilities. Their local government didn't seem to provide them with anything, and neither did the United States.

My particular interest was to find refugees from Hallabja. Because Saddam's use of chemical weapons there had become such a powerful image used to rally support for the war, I thought it was particularly important to turn on my microphone and let the survivors speak for themselves.

After some asking around, we found such a family living in a one-room cinderblock home. "My name is Aftow Khafood," an elderly woman told us. She was clad in a black headscarf and a long black dress with long sleeves. "I'm from Hallabja."

Unlike the homes of other families in the camp who had installed doors made of crushed olive-oil tins, Aftow's home had no door at all, but simply a gap in the cinderblocks that allowed people to enter and exit. Their roof was a canvas tarp. "There are three of us living here," she explained, "myself, my [14-year-old] daughter, and my husband. Before the war, he used to work for the Kurdistan Democratic Party guarding against Saddam Hussein, but now that the war is over, they dismissed him and he has no job, so we have no money."

I asked her to reconstruct the day she lost her home: March 16, 1988, the day Saddam Hussein doused the city with deadly chemicals, killing more than 5,000 civilians.

"The wind was blowing the other way," she answered. "So we survived. We tried to escape. We travelled on foot for seven days and seven nights toward Iran. It was in the mountains and there was snow and no roads—only some *peshmerga* to help us."

"The *peshmerga* helped you get to Iran?" I asked.

"Yes," she said. "The *peshmerga* had a lot of information about the troops and the land mines on the border. That's how we went. We kept asking them 'When will you get a car?' but they didn't have one. They just helped us find the way on foot to Iran." She said her family had lived in Iran for four years until after the 1991 Gulf War and the creation of the Kurdish autonomous area. "After that," she said, "we came here and we're still in these tents."

"But," I asked, "Hallabja has not been under the control of Saddam Hussein for more than ten years; why haven't you gone back?"

"They have destroyed all our houses," she responded. "So how are we supposed to go back? We want them to help us go back there however they can. Either build us a house or give us some aid so we can build our own house. But they don't give us anything, so we stay here."

I asked a political question. "Hallabja," I said, "is famous all over the world. George Bush has made this war in the name of Hallabja and Saddam's weapons of mass destruction. So how does it feel to you that you find yourself here?"

"I have nothing to say," she responded as her daughter—clad in

a beautiful pink headscarf—moved beside her. "That is politics and
I cannot say anything about that. We would like to improve our situation." Aftow's daughter—like so many residents of Benslawa—
was born in a camp. "When it rains, we are afraid our house will
collapse on our heads. We want to return to our homes and live like
others in normal houses."

"What is your expectation?" I asked.

"We are hopeful that the situation will get better," she answered,
but her voice didn't reveal much hope.

Istifan and I stayed at the camp for most of the day interviewing
other families, but the story was almost always the same. Most families had lost their homes during the Anfal campaign and the Iran-
Iraq war. When the Iraqi army destroyed their homes, they had fled
deep into Kurdistan's inhospitable mountains—sometimes crossing the border into Iran. All were happy that Saddam was gone, but
most were not optimistic about the immediate future. None of the
families seemed to be getting help from anyone.

We also visited with Hussein Qaladi, the Kurdish official in charge
of the camp. A former *peshmerga* with the Patriotic Union of Kurdistan, he wore a dapper suit and tie and had a spacious office with
an expansive map of historic "Kurdistan" behind him. The map included ethnic Kurdish areas in Turkey, Syria, Iran, and Iraq, and it
stretched all the way to the Mediterranean Sea in the west and to
the Black Sea in the north. I thought, "That's all well and good, but
how are you going to liberate your whole homeland when you can't,
or won't, find housing to move your people out of refugee camps?"

But maybe there was a reason the refugees of northern Iraq were
still living in camps. Maybe they were serving a political purpose.
That's what I thought as the PUK's Hussein Qaladi spoke to us
from his high-backed leather chair.

"You can see," he said. "Hallabja is a live witness to all the world that we were sprayed with chemical weapons and are victims of genocide." Is it possible, I wondered, that the KDP and PUK were using their refugees as a bargaining chip? As long as the refugees languished in camps, the terms of the continued suffering of the Kurdish people could be held up before the world to elicit sympathy.

"Has there been any money allocated by the American government for the reconstruction of Hallabja?" I asked.

"I cannot say directly how much it is," the PUK official said, "or even if there is any, but it would be in the money given to the Kurdistan Reconstruction Organization." On my first full day in northern Iraq, I had met with officials from this organization. They had told me they hadn't received any money at all for reconstruction since the UN oil-for-food program ended in 2003.

We thanked Hussein Qaladi for his time and readied to leave. The bureaucrat made his way around his large desk and walked us out to his waiting area, where each of his three female assistants had a document for him to sign. He told us he had a new black sedan and offered to give us a tour of the camp. But we told him we had spent the whole day at Benslawa and were ready to head home.

On our way back to Arbil, I turned to Istifan. "I just get so angry talking to these people from KDP and PUK. Don't they care at all about the conditions for the refugees in their camps? In the media, they make a big deal about the conditions of the Kurdish people, but you can see that they have had control since 1991—for more than a decade—and they haven't done anything for their people."

"Aaron," Istifan replied, "I will tell you something. These people—these *peshmerga*—they don't care anything about the people here. They just care about their own money and their own benefits. You know, in 1996, when the PUK and the KDP were fighting against each other, Mr. Masoud Barzani—the leader of the KDP—invited Ali Hassan al-Majid to his headquarters in Sala-haldin. This man, Ali Hassan al-Majid—your president calls him 'Chemical Ali.' He is the man who gassed the people of Hallabja and organized the genocide of al-Anfal. And Mr. Masoud Barzani invited him to Kurdistan as an ally. It is no surprise that there is no help for the people of Benslawa."

Later I would learn that Istifan's older brother had died at the hands of the KDP. They hadn't killed him on purpose, but they had laid land mines so indiscriminately in his neighborhood that he was killed as he walked down a main street headed to the family home.

Still, some Kurds had benefitted tremendously from the fall of Saddam, and most of them could be found in the oil-rich city of Kirkuk. Unlike other large Kurdish cities like Arbil, Dohuk, and Suleymania, Kirkuk was not part of the Kurdish autonomous region. It had been ruled by Saddam Hussein until the fall of his regime in April 2003.

I wanted to go to Kirkuk primarily to report on the oil industry. Since most of the foreign press resided in Baghdad, the oil fields of Kirkuk were rarely visited—even though they held much of the wealth of the country. So Istifan and I went to Arbil's main bus station and bought two seats in a communal taxi going south to Kirkuk.

Just a few miles out of Arbil, though, the traffic slowed to a crawl. It was the first major checkpoint I had encountered in Iraq—the border between Kurdistan and the old "Saddamistan." As we approached the checkpoint, I saw that every ID card was checked, every truck searched, every engine inspected. The queue took 30 minutes to clear, and I knew it would take even longer on the way home when we reentered "Iraqi Kurdistan."

"You see," Istifan said as we passed through the checkpoint. "We have good security here. They won't let any of the Arab terrorists get through."

Before the war, it had been impossible to cross this border. Now that Saddam was gone, one side represented the area ruled by Kurdish forces and the other side represented the chaotic space controlled by the Americans.

In Kirkuk, the *peshmerga* wouldn't be in control. The Americans would. Or, at least that's what I thought.

Pulling into the vast campus of buildings outside Kirkuk that housed the offices of Iraq's Northern Oil Company, I noticed that there wasn't an American soldier in sight. Instead, there were Iraqi Kurds with Kalashnikovs. They were wearing blue-and-gold uniforms typical of private security guards. Their shoulderpatches read ERINYS-IRAQ.

We walked up to one of the guards, and Istifan said: "Excuse me, this man is with an American radio station and he's wondering if you will talk to him about what you do here and what this Erinys is?" The man refused to comment but told us that his superior could be found in an office up the road.

I already knew a little about Erinys. A friend back in the States, who ran a website on corporate accountability, had sent me a packet of information on the company. So I already knew that the American authorities had awarded the company a contract worth over $80 million to provide security for Iraq's vital oil infrastructure. The company didn't have much of a reputation and appeared to have gotten the contract through personal connections and, some critics have charged, through bribes.

Pulitzer prize–winning journalist Knut Royce had written a series of stories for *Newsday* that detailed shady aspects of the deal. According to Royce, soon after this security contract was issued,

Erinys started recruiting many of its guards from the ranks of Ahmed Chalabi's former militia, the Free Iraqi Forces, raising allegations from other Iraqi officials that he was creating a private army.

Chalabi has the distinction of being one of the least-liked people in Iraq. Scion of one of Iraq's most politically powerful and wealthy families until the monarchy was toppled in 1958, he had been living in exile in London when the U.S. invaded Iraq. The chief architect of the umbrella organization for the resistance, the Iraqi National Congress (INC), he was once forced to flee the Kingdom of Jordan in the trunk of a car after being sentenced to prison for fraud in connection with the collapse of the country's bank.

An industry source familiar with some of the internal affairs told *Newsday* that Chalabi had received a two-million-dollar fee for helping arrange the contract. Chalabi, in a brief interview, denied that claim, as did a top company official. Chalabi also denied that he has had anything to do with the security firm.

Yet Chalabi's INC was deeply connected to Erinys. For example, a founding partner and director of Erinys Iraq is Faisal Daghistani, the son of Tamara Daghistani, for years one of Chalabi's most trusted confidants. The company's Baghdad attorney was Salem Chalabi, Ahmed's Chalabi's nephew.

This information bounced around my head as Istifan and I walked up to the oil facility's main checkpoint. I expected that this would be the place where we would find an American contractor or a wealthy Iraqi exile.

Instead, we were greeted by a giant Kurdish man named Mamand Kesnazani. When we entered the checkpoint's office, he was reclining in a high-backed leather chair. We introduced ourselves, and he shook our hands and then leaned back, placing his feet on top of his desk. He ordered us tea with a wave to one of his subordinates.

"What are you interested in?" he asked in English.

"My name is Aaron Glantz and I'm a reporter for Pacifica Radio in the United States," I said, choosing my words carefully. "I'm interested in the security that's being provided for the oilfields here. You know, Iraqi oil is a big issue in America. So I thought I'd come and talk to the people providing the security."

"You should talk to Mr. Nasser," he responded. "He's in charge of the media here."

"I know there are people assigned to talk to reporters," I responded. "But I want to get the real story of the security and I know from experience that the only people who answer truthfully are the people who actually do the job."

"Without the tape recorder?" he asked.

"That's right," I said, putting my microphone away. "Just basic information."

"Well," Kesnazani said, "there's not much to say. Ninety-five percent of us are *peshmerga* from the PUK. We came to Kirkuk with the American army last April. We secured the oilfields. We've been guarding them ever since."

I laughed at the story's simplicity. Another reward to the Kurdish leaders for their support. Unlike his subordinates, who had donned the blue-and-gold uniform of Erinys, Kesnazani had not even bothered to change his uniform. He still wore the checkered black-and-white headscarf and *sharwal* typical of *peshmerga* fighters.

"I've had a lot of bosses this year," Kesnazani continued as he ordered another round of dark Iraqi tea. "First it was the PUK, then the U.S. Army came with Kellogg, Brown, and Root. That's Dick Cheney's company," he said, smiling. "Now the company has changed again to this company called Erinys, but it's always the same people—the PUK *peshmerga*."

"So you have to be a *peshmerga* to work here?" I asked.

"You don't have to be a *peshmerga*," he responded, still smiling.

"It's just that almost all of us are. Anyone can work here—technically speaking."

"But there must be some foreigners working here?" I asked. "People who aren't *peshmerga*. Are they your bosses?"

This, I learned was a sore subject. The top wage for a rank-and-file Kurd who guards the oilfields was $120 a month, hardly a living wage, but better than nothing in a country that had an estimated 75-percent rate of unemployment. By comparison, Kesnazani said, their supervisors, many of whom were white South Africans, earned an average salary of $5,000 a month.

"They said they had to teach us how to fight," a Kurdish guard chimed in from the door of the office. "They taught us hand-to-hand fighting and how to use more advanced weapons than just the Kalashnikov. We already knew how to fight," he said. "Saddam's regime taught us how to fight in his army and the *peshmerga* taught us how to fight Saddam Hussein. Then KBR [Kellogg Brown & Root] taught us how to fight for the Americans."

"What do you think of the South Africans' training methods?" I asked Kesnazani.

"They're a bit strange," he replied.

The South African trainers interested me because of published reports I had read about Erinys trainer François Strydom, who was killed in Baghdad on January 28, 2004. His colleague Deon Gouws was seriously injured in the same blast. The two men, in addition to being Erinys trainers, turned out to have been members of South Africa's secret police in the 1980s under the apartheid regime.

Strydom was a member of Koevoet, a notoriously brutal counterinsurgency arm of the South African military that operated in Namibia during the neighboring state's fight for independence in the 1980s. Gouws is a former officer of the Vlakplaas, a secret-police unit in South Africa. According to South Africa's *Sunday Times,* Gouws received an amnesty application from the Truth and

Reconciliation Commission after admitting to between 40 and 60 petrol bombings of political activists' houses in 1986 as well as a car-bombing that year that claimed the life of KwaNdebele homeland cabinet minister and ANC activist Piet Ntuli and an arson attack on the home of a Mamelodi doctor. I explained some of this to the *peshmerga,* but they weren't interested.

"What's important," said Kesnazani, "is that we guard the oilfields, but they get paid. That's not fair."

When Istifan and I got back to Arbil that night, I went to the Internet cafe to do more research on the foreign fighters. Like the South Africans, thousands of ex-military men from around the world were flocking to Iraq to find jobs that they couldn't get in their home countries. Derek William Adgey, a Royal Marine from Belfast who was jailed for four years for helping the Ulster Freedom Fighters, was hired by Armor Group, a British company, to guard Bechtel employees. (He was subsequently suspended when the *Belfast Telegraph* published details of his past.)

Former members of the British military, I learned, were getting top dollar in Iraq—as much as a $250,000 a year, which was about three times as much as they could earn in Britain—from terrified American businessmen working in the country.

John Davidson, who runs Rubicon International, a British security company whose interests in Iraq include contracts with BP and Motorola, told the newspaper *The Scotsman* that they preferred to hire former members of Britain's special forces, like the Special Air Service (SAS).

"The SAS are extremely well-trained, low-profile, not waving flags. They go about things in a quiet manner, they are the crème de la crème," he told the paper.

Meanwhile the South African Police Services' elite task force, a division of 100 men who accompany senior politicians like President Thabo Mbeki, were facing an even more severe crisis: as many as half of their employees were asking for early retirement in order to go to Iraq. The $5,000 monthly salary for these men is equivalent to about six months' pay at home.

"What is alarming is that members of specialized units are resigning. It will have a negative effect to lose that experience—it takes at least a year to train them," Henrie Boshoff, a military analyst, told *The Sunday Independent* newspaper in South Africa.

As for myself, I was less concerned about the geopolitics of these contracts than about what it meant to the situation around me. As I left the Internet cafe and walked across a wide square toward my favorite late-night juice stall, I remembered one of the things Mamand Kesnazani had said. As time went on, and the country became more dangerous, his observation would seem more and more prescient.

"For the $5,000 a month they pay one of these South Africans, they could hire thirty or forty Iraqis to do the same job," he had explained. "How hard is it to guard an oilfield? Everyone in Iraq is trained with a gun. He has the gun whether or not he has a job. Why can't we be trusted with the security of our own country?"

It was pretty ridiculous, I thought, especially since the Kurds were willing to work for four dollars a day.

8

CHANGING ATTITUDES
ABOUT TERROR

I came to feel at home in Iraqi Kurdistan, with its relatively peaceful atmosphere and friendly people. Istifan and I had long, relaxing lunches in clean restaurants, and I would take long walks at sunset around Arbil's old city walls and through its markets, buying fresh *locum,* fruits, and nuts. I made frequent trips to the neighborhood barber for a shave and haircut. I would have enjoyed staying there much longer, but it seemed that every day a new piece of news came that mandated I move to Baghdad. Usually that news involved a major attack or explosion.

Just a week after my arrival in northern Iraq, a series of terrible explosions struck Shi'ite religious celebrations in Baghdad and Karbala. At least 143 Iraqis were killed in the attacks and more than 200 were wounded. Suicide bombers attacked Shia Muslims as they observed Ashoura, the holiest day on their calendar. Ashoura commemorates the death in battle of Hussein, the third Shi'ite Imam, in AD 680.

In Karbala, there was an explosion in the center of the city as well as explosions on a road used by Shi'ite pilgrims leading to a shrine. It was the worst attack during the first year of the occupation. The Bush Administration blamed Jordanian fundamentalist Abu Musab al-Zarqawi, a Sunni who they maintained had ties to al-Qaeda, but Washington provided little proof of this and such comments were not given much credence in the Arab world.

Since I was in northern Iraq at the time of the bombing, I experienced the attacks and their aftermath primarily by watching television. That evening, al-Arabiya gave a lengthy interview to Grand Ayatollah Hassen Fatlallah, a respected Iraqi cleric living in Lebanon. He offered this analysis in comments broadcast via satellite throughout the Middle East:

Someone is planning to divide Islam in this world. Someone is interested in starting a war between the Sunni and Shia. We know that America has a project in the Middle East, a project to control all the governments, to ensure all the regimes in the Middle East are controlled one hundred percent by America, but that will not happen because no matter how many people they kill and shoot, this will never be like Lebanon with brother killing brother. We can't prove that America has participated in these explosions, but I don't think it's Zarqawi or al-Qaeda. We know that the Americans are treating our people very badly. They have to leave immediately and the CIA has to know that they cannot put the Shia in a place to fight the Sunni.

It was a different rhetoric from the year before, when clerics had called for cooperation and negotiation with Washington as a way of achieving liberty and sovereignty.

Al-Qaeda, which like most terrorist organizations is usually quick to claim responsibility for its acts, sent a statement to the London-based newspaper *al-Quds al-Arabi* denying involvement.

I knew the bombings were big news, and my editors back home requested a story, but I was a full day's drive away from Baghdad. So I did the best I could. The next day, Istifan and I went to Arbil's main bus depot and bought two seats in a communal taxi to Kirkuk, the closest city with a sizeable Shi'ite population.

As our cab made its way through a *peshmerga* checkpoint on the edge of town, we talked about the other major suicide bombings since Saddam's fall from power. There was the August 19, 2003 truck-bombing of the United Nations headquarters in Baghdad that killed UN envoy Sergio Viera de Mello and 22 others; the August 29, 2003 car-bombing in Najaf that killed 75 people including Ayatollah Mohammed Baqir al-Hakim (of the Tehran-backed Supreme Council for Islamic Revolution in Iraq); and the twin suicide bombings of Kurdistan's two governing factions in Arbil on February 1, 2004. "These attacks," I said to Istifan, "are different from all the other explosions and attacks we've seen. The rest of them are all against the American army and contractors like Halliburton and Bechtel. They are targeted against the occupation itself. You could say the attacks against the PUK and KDP were political, and maybe the attack on al-Hakim. But these attacks in Baghdad and Karbala, you really have to ask: Who can benefit from such carnage?"

Istifan was not swayed by my speech. "These terrorists," he said, "you cannot try to see any kind of logic in their actions. If they are al-Qaeda or the Ba'ath, then you just have to know that they hate the Shia and the Kurd and want to stop them from gaining power. I know you are looking for negative things with America, but you need to understand. These terrorist monsters are not logical."

Since the U.S. government had failed to provide any hard evidence about the perpetrators of any of the bombings, the cases remained essentially unsolved, and we couldn't settle our argument. "Time will tell," I said. "We'll just have to wait until the truth emerges somehow."

In the meantime, all we could do was "get reaction" to the bombing—talk to people and get their perspective. When we got to the taxi garage in Kirkuk, we caught a second taxi and asked the Kurdish driver to take us to the city's main Shi'ite neighborhood.

The driver gave us a funny look, as if we had asked him to take us into a firestorm. "Why do you want to go there?" he asked. Istifan told him I was an American journalist covering the bombings in Baghdad and Karbala. The driver asked for a steep rate ($1.50) given the danger, and we accepted.

Kirkuk's Shia neighborhood is a poor one, a slum, populated mostly by Shi'ites forced to move north from their ancestral lands in the 1980s by Saddam Hussein, who was simultaneously forcibly resettling the area's native population, the Kurds, to the south. It was a neighborhood without sidewalks, one that barely had pavement, where chickens and other livestock walked in the streets. It didn't feel like the rest of Kirkuk at all. More like a village in India.

We walked up to the first shop, a small fruit stand where a few young men sat around smoking cigarettes, owing to the paucity of customers. The proprietor was a young man named Ali Adnan Adwan. The 25-year-old Shi'ite told me that he'd graduated from law school a few months before the war, but that with limited telephone service and intermittent electricity it was hard to run a law practice, so he'd started a fruit stand.

"The people who don't have jobs will go to anyone with money and explode themselves," he offered. "A taxi driver told me there are people willing to pay $250,000 to potential suicide bombers."

Almost a year after the fall of Saddam Hussein, official statistics put the unemployment rate in Iraq at over 75 percent. "Of course some people will take money to explode themselves," Ali explained.

"That way their family and their grandchildren will be able to live well in the future."

The shopkeeper mentioned that George Bush had recently gotten $87 billion extra from American taxpayers to spend in Iraq. "They have spent so much money on their military," he told me. Less than 25 percent of it had been spent on reconstruction. "If some of the money went to unemployed Iraqi people," he said, "there would be fewer bombings."

As our interview continued, a crowd began to form, some watching, some seeking an opportunity to speak to the foreigner. Among them was a young man in long black robes, and the crowd parted for him. He sat down next to me. "My name is Muftar al-Hassan Romathey," the young man told me. "I own the video store a few doors down." More important, he said, his father was the representative of Shi'ite cleric Muqtada al-Sadr in Kirkuk.

"The Americans encourage these bombings in order to be sure that they will stay here for a long time," he said, noting that the bombings occurred on the same day the country's new interim constitution was scheduled to be signed. "When these steps finish, they will have to leave this area," he told me, "and for this reason they are encouraging this terrorism." The young man told us that this was the message of Muqtada al-Sadr, and he invited Istifan and I to walk with him to his video store. Inside the store, he turned on the television and popped in a video-CD of Muqtada al-Sadr's latest sermon in the southern city of Kufa. This was how the cleric spread his message to the masses, Muftar told me. In every Shi'ite neighborhood, each one of Sadr's sermons could be purchased for less than the price of a taxi ride.

I recalled that this method—distributing tapes to regular people on the streets—was a key method of resistance used by the African National Congress during its struggle against apartheid in South Africa. I told the young man this, and he was pleased. "Would you like some of Sayyed Muqtada's speeches?" he asked, and indicated that he also had many of Muqtada's father's speeches in stock. Muqtada's father, Grand Ayatollah Mohammed Sadiq al-Sadr, had been executed by Saddam's regime in 1999 after arguing for the dictator's overthrow in Friday prayers.

I respectfully declined. Looking around the store, I saw that the clerics' speeches weren't the only products in stock. Hollywood fare also proliferated, including a disturbing number of Martin Lawrence movies.

The time was getting late. Istifan nudged me. We needed to get back to "Kurdistan" before it turned dark. I agreed it was time to go, and we said our good-byes. We hailed another taxi to the bus depot and then bought two seats back to Arbil. "You see, these people are so ignorant," Istifan said as we sped north. "They think the Coalition forces would kill all these people. There is no reason, no fact, behind this."

I agreed with him, but I had to add something. "Look," I said. "I don't think the U.S. government bombed the Ashoura celebrations. But what's interesting to me is that these people no longer see Americans as their protectors but as their oppressors." I added, "It's easy for people to start thinking this way when America doesn't bring any of these alleged foreign terrorist masterminds to an open trial with evidence of guilt presented in a way the Iraqi public can see. In the absence of hard evidence, Iraqis have to go with their gut, and these days it seems to me that gut is often anti-American."

"Well, you won't find any of those things said in Kurdistan," Istifan responded. "In Kurdistan, we respect the Coalition forces. We know they are here to protect us."

It was time to leave the north and head toward Baghdad. Every day, my editors were writing me to ask how much longer I planned to stay in Kurdistan. A good reporter was needed in Baghdad.

James was also planning on a trip back toward Baghdad, where he would resume work on a number of films, including one on the movement of Muqtada al-Sadr and another about a small boy, one of the few Iraqis who suffered from the AIDS virus.

So we said good-bye to Istifan and the Fareed and went to Arbil's main bus station, where we paid $10 for two seats in a communal taxi and headed for the capital—through Kirkuk and then the northern end of the Sunni triangle. Since I had left, James had begun to work with my old translator, Nadeem Hamid. Eventually, he had moved into Nadeem's home, where he lived with his family. This would be our first destination.

"Can you drop us at Palestine Street?" James asked the taxi driver in Arabic as we arrived in northern Baghdad. Nadeem's house was not far, and the driver agreed. We turned left at a monument to the slain ayatollah, Mohammed Baqir al-Hakim, near Mustansuriye University, but the taxi couldn't take us all the way to Nadeem's house because a whole section of Palestine Street had been turned into a used-car lot. Five- and ten-year-old Mercedes, BMWs, and Renaults were selling for $2,000 to $3,000—cars that would have sold for ten times as much in the States.

James and I dragged our bags through the used-car lot and walked a few blocks through the middle-class neighborhood to Nadeem's home, a two-story brown stucco structure on the corner. We opened the gate and entered an intimate garden space behind a brown stucco wall.

Nadeem was home when James knocked on the door at mid-afternoon: "Aaron, oh my God!" he greeted me. "How are you!?" We kissed on the cheek a half-dozen times and he ushered James and me into his home. Inside, there were a small kitchen and pantry and a sparsely furnished living room with cushions to sit on. James's and Nadeem's rooms were in the back, along with a small bathroom. Nadeem's older brother, an engineer named Waseem, lived upstairs with his wife and two children, but they had a separate entrance.

The sun was going down and there was no electricity, so the house was quite dark. James turned on the stove to make some dark Iraqi tea for the two of us and Nescafé for Nadeem. When we finished our drinks, Nadeem suggested we go out to eat. Most nice restaurants by now had installed backup generators. We hopped into Nadeem's new, used Mercedes and drove off toward Zeuna Street, a middle-class shopping street not too far from his home.

As we opened the door to the restaurant, air conditioners blasted from a half-dozen windows. There were at least four televisions, all with their satellite dishes tuned to Lebanese music channels on which scantily clad women danced for the camera. This establishment had a powerful backup generator.

"So how is the situation?" I asked Nadeem as we ordered pizza and Pepsi along with traditional Middle Eastern side dishes.

"Oh, God, it's bad," Nadeem said. "It gets worse and worse all the time. You know, I will never want to have Saddam back. But the Americans—I don't know. Before the war, we used to go out and party until four in the morning and then sleep all day. Now there's nothing to do. I haven't seen a girl in months."

"How's your band?" I asked, remembering that his boy band had gotten connected with some British promoters immediately after the fall of Saddam.

"We haven't done anything in months," Nadeem responded, sipping his Pepsi while scanning the restaurant for girls. "The deal with the record label fell through. There's so much to do now, we don't have time."

I could tell it was a sore subject, so I let the matter drop. Nadeem and James discussed what they would film next. We finished our meal, got back in the car, and drove a few blocks to a mobile-phone store. This was a major innovation of the past year. Under Saddam's regime, mobile phones had been banned. Foreigners who arrived carrying them had them confiscated.

Now, the phones were a hot commodity. Almost a year after the fall of Saddam, the U.S. occupation authority had done little to rebuild the country's telephone grid, but it had moved quickly to erect cell-phone towers—at least in Baghdad. At the cell-phone store, I learned that the occupation authority had granted Illinois-based Motorola (through an Egyptian holding company named Orascom) a two-year monopoly on mobile-phone service in the capital. The monopoly meant that the SIM card to start service was quite expensive—$90, compared to less than $10 in neighboring Turkey or Jordan. That didn't count the cost of a phone (which I already had) or the service (which I would have to pay for by buying $20 scratch cards). I scoffed at the price, but like any Iraqi who wanted a telephone, I was forced to pay it.

When we got back to Nadeem's house, his friends were waiting. Like Nadeem, most of them were students at nearby Mustansuriye University. There was Ahmad Ayyad, a former member of Saddam's feared *fedayeen* who now worked as a translator for the BBC. He had fallen in love with one of their journalists, and they were preparing for a marriage that would allow him to obtain a visa to travel back to London.

Another friend of Nadeem's told me he loved American country music like Garth Brooks and Toby Keith and often approached American soldiers at a nearby base to ask them if he could borrow their music.

Then there was Ali Zekki. A short student with a slim mustache and a leather jacket, Ali served as the butt of most of his friends' jokes, most of which were pretty infantile. "He's a fag like Ali Zekki!" was the most popular one, with its many permutations. For example, "Hey, Aaron, if you're looking for some, you should try Ali Zekki." The butt of many jokes as a kid, I identified with Ali Zekki, but I knew it wasn't my place to intervene.

I relaxed and listened. Late at night, Nadeem gave me his bed to sleep in. The next day I moved to downtown Baghdad, to a hotel called Aghadir, where many independent journalists were staying. The price was $20 a night, breakfast included. My room had a window overlooking Sa'adoon Street, one of Baghdad's main drags. It was a 15-minute walk from the Palestine Hotel, but I didn't like it because at night I was alone.

At night, I would walk a few blocks down Sa'adoon Street to Karada, the biggest market street in Baghdad. It was this street that James had complained was deserted in the days immediately after the war. But the first time I walked the streets in the evening on my second visit, most of the shops were still open at eight o'clock.

I felt perfectly safe among the cafes, Internet cafes, clothing emporiums, ice-cream shops, barbershops, kebab restaurants, and produce markets that lined the street. There was a buzz of activity representing a city that was alive.

Then, at precisely nine o'clock, the Americans turned off the electricity. The streetlights went off and most of the shops shut. A few opened again moments later after they revved up their backup generators, but for the most part the evening was over. It was nearly pitch black and I didn't feel safe anymore. I walked back to the hotel.

This haunting darkness was an especially big worry for me. Because of my deadline, I had to go to the Internet cafe each night to send my story back to the radio station. Entering Baghdad's dark streets with nightly gunfire in the distance, I felt I was taking my life in my hands each and every time. It was an entirely different feeling than I'd had in Kurdistan. I found myself wishing for *peshmerga* on every corner.

I was spooked further when—less than a week after I moved into the Aghadir Hotel—a car-bomb exploded just two blocks away, destroying a small hotel called Mount Lebanon and laying waste to an entire city block. When the bomb exploded, eight stories of my hotel shook, the windows rattled, some of them shattered. A fire started at the end of the hallway and was quickly put out. I grabbed my work bag and ran down to the hotel lobby along with my neighbor in the building—a British filmmaker named Julia Guest. She piled into a car with a bunch of other camerapeople. I ran across the street with another American journalist I didn't know and we hopped n a taxi—though the bomb site was just three blocks away.

When I got out of the taxi it was red everywhere. Red fire coming from all the buildings, red sirens coming twirling down the road. I lifted up my camera to take a photo of an American soldier on top of a tank controlling traffic. He pointed his machine gun at me and screamed "No reporters!" I put my camera down as an ambulance rushed by. Then a man grabbed my hand. "You got to get out of here," the man said, "they're shooting foreigners." He turned out to be Ahmad Ayyad, Nadeem's ex-*fedayeen* friend. I had met him just a few days before. He grabbed my bag and we walked quickly together back to the hotel. Other more experienced journalists began to return from the bomb site, and a crowd gathered in front of the communal TV in the hotel lobby as images came in on al-Arabiya. Everyone watched even though they had seen the same events firsthand. (Now the Arabiya reporter we were watching is dead—shot the next day by U.S. troops when they fired and missed a car that had run one of their checkpoints.)

An hour passed. I chatted with another reporter who was staying at the hotel. Outside, an Apache helicopter went by. Then another. Then a tank.

Arabiya reported casualty figures. Most of the victims, it was said, were Iraqi civilians who lived in the adjacent buildings, but a few victims were foreigners, including two British contractors. In Washington, George Bush's spokesman Scott McClellan faced reporters and linked the bombing to September 11th. He blamed foreign terrorists and pledged to stay "on the offensive" in the war on terror.

More time passed, and at around 10 P.M. Julia and I and a few other journalists walked the three blocks to the bomb site. Things had calmed down. Two American tanks guarded each nearby intersection, but we were allowed through when we showed our press passes. Inside the bomb zone there was a crater that took up much of the block. A gaggle of photographers and cameramen circled around like vultures over a corpse. I might have been one of them, but I had left my camera at home just to be on the safe side. Family members of the victims wanted to enter the area but U.S. troops pushed them back. Julia tried to keep back her tears.

When I got back to the hotel, and then when I went to a restaurant next-door for some late-night chicken kebab, I noticed that no one was watching the news. Both places had switched their TVs from the news channels to the American-run al-Iraqia station, which had cut away from the bombings to broadcast a soccer game between Iraq and Saudi Arabia. To be honest, I wasn't much for news, either. I was happy that folks around me were watching sports.

When I returned to the site the next day, the area had become a media circus. Peter Jennings of ABC News was refereeing an argument between his Iraqi driver and an American soldier (the driver claimed the soldier had pointed his gun at him, an allegation the soldier denied. Jennings, who had missed the incident in question, sided with the soldier). Fox News was there, too. Their correspondent was doing a live, on-air interview with a U.S. Army spokesman. The spokesman was wearing regular combat fatigues, but the Fox News reporter, alone among the hundreds of journalists, soldiers, victims, and onlookers, was wearing a bulletproof vest and full body armor.

The whole area was surrounded by American tanks and armored personnel carriers—one of which, equipped with a bulldozer, was clearing debris away from the 30-foot crater left by the bomb. U.S. military patrols on the streets of Baghdad were up—and the White House pledged a stepped-up effort to stop their enemy.

I climbed past the tanks and the cameras and around piles of blown-up cinderblocks and long iron rods and found a carpenter, Mohammed Qassim Ali. His home, next-door to the hotel, had been destroyed in the blast, but, thanks to God, he said, his family had survived.

He denied that the explosion had come from a bomb strapped to the car (which seemed the obvious explanation given that there was a gigantic hole in the ground under a destroyed automobile). Instead, he insisted that an American missile had come from the nearby Palestine Hotel, where many military contractors were staying.

"We put the responsibility for this on the American troops," he shouted into my microphone, explaining that he had lost his hearing after the blast. "They want to make a lot of explosions so they'll stay longer. This is something we don't want. We want them to go back to America. We will serve and protect Iraq. We want them to leave." This was the story of almost every Iraqi witness of the attack on the Lebanon Hotel. Indeed, it was the general opinion of most Arab Iraqis about almost every bombing Washington blamed on "foreign terrorists." Almost everyone I talked to claimed to have seen a missile and suspected an American or Israeli conspiracy.

At the same time, the number of attacks on Americans continued to rise. In the 24 hours after the bombing of the Lebanon Hotel, at least two more American soldiers were shot and killed. In northeastern Iraq, three journalists working for a U.S.-government-run TV station were also shot dead.

As I walked away from the remains of the Lebanon Hotel, an old name came to the surface. "We wish we had Saddam Hussein," one man said, pointing at a giant hole blown through his apartment. "Only he can heal the Iraqi people."

9

AMERICA BECOMES
THE ENEMY

Since Nadeem was working with James, he couldn't work as my translator. So he asked his older brother Waseem if he would be willing to work with me. Waseem was more settled, with a wife, two children, and a regular job as an electrical engineer, so he wouldn't be able to work long hours. But he was completely trustworthy—and in a country with rising anti-American sentiment, it was important to my personal security that I work with someone who wouldn't abandon me in trouble or trade me for cash.

Our first workday together was March 18, 2004—the day after the bombing of the Lebanon Hotel. My goal was to make a report that explained the anti-American sentiment I had reported previously. Our first destination was the offices of the Iraqi Human Rights Organization. They were co-sponsoring a week full of events highlighting human rights under American occupation in concert with International Occupation Watch, an organization founded by the San Francisco–based pacifist group Global Exchange.

Given the prewar silence of Global Exchange and other Western left-wing organizations about the human-rights abuses of Saddam's regime, I approached the event skeptically. I was likewise concerned about the record of the Iraqi Human Rights Organization. The group claimed to have operated continuously since 1960—before the rise of the Ba'ath Party. What kind of human-rights organization, I wondered, was allowed to operate under the regime of Saddam Hussein?

Still, an e-mail announcement said that Iraqis who'd experienced the abuses of the occupation would be in attendance, along with representatives of the new Iraqi Ministry of Human Rights, which had been appointed by the Bush Administration. It seemed like a good opportunity to learn about American-Iraqi relations. I hopped into a taxi and asked the driver to head toward the old Justice Ministry building. The Human Rights Organization was next door. Waseem would meet me there.

At the event, the American-appointed official spoke strongly. "We are not satisfied with the way things are going and we want change," he told me. His name was Sa'ad Sultan Hussein, a lawyer for the Iraqi Ministry of Human Rights. He spoke in a long-winded, jargon-laden style typical of bureaucrats. He declared that America was holding more than 8,000 Iraqis in Abu Ghraib prison, formerly Saddam's most notorious lockup. He said almost none of the prisoners had been charged with any crime and none had been allowed to see a lawyer.

"The main problem that the Iraqi people suffer from is random capture by the U.S. military," he said. "They are disappeared and nobody can tell where they are or the reason for their capture. They don't even allow families and relatives to visit them. That's against the Geneva Convention, which says families must be allowed to meet the prisoners and see them."

He talked some about the exact terms of the Geneva Convention and accused the U.S. military authority of lying to Iraqi officials: "Paul Bremer said the same thing in a memorandum of understanding," the lawyer told me. "He said the family must be allowed to meet the prisoners and also the same memo said there should be lawyers for the prisoners and fair trials. Now everything that's happened is one hundred percent against that memo."

"So what are you going to do?" I asked.

"After pressure from the minister of human rights, we won a very small success. There is some hope that this ministry will be able to open offices in the prison in order to see how the people live there. What's their condition? How are the interrogations? Inside Abu Ghraib prison, we will witness all the conditions of the prisoners and whether they were able to see their family. We will see the treatment they receive and see if they are beaten or tortured."

"How are the conditions now?" I asked.

"I cannot give a point of view," he said, "because actually I haven't seen any of the prisoners deeply. So far, I have just seen what they wanted me to see. We haven't entered the room of interrogation and we didn't witness any interrogations. For the moment we cannot say we are satisfied. When we open the offices, we will be able to see everything. Then I will be able to tell you what happens."

The official told me he expected they would be able to open their office in Abu Ghraib within the next two weeks. Over the next two months, and well after graphic photos of prisoner abuse became public, I would check with him regularly to see if they had opened the office, but the answer was always the same: "We hope to soon."

Regular Iraqis at the event spoke less hopefully about action from the American authorities, and they showed visible frustration at the ministry's lawyer for not taking a harder line, often shouting at him during his presentation. An elderly Shi'ite man who quaked as he spoke told me that his 20-year-old son had been captured by the Americans during the invasion a year before. His story was typical:

> The Americans picked him up but nobody knows where he went. I don't know where he is. I went to the Green Zone [U.S. military headquarters]. After that I went to Um Qasr near Basra to a prison run by the Americans and the British forces. I described the situation and when they checked in their computer they told me my son's name was in their record. When I asked them, "Where is he?" they told me "We can't tell you now because it's against our security rules."

"Your son," I asked, "was he a member of the Ba'ath Party or an important part of Saddam's government?"

"No," the old man quavered. "He was only in the army because Saddam made everyone go to the army. I don't know why they didn't tell me where he is."

Others had similar stories. A farmer complained that American soldiers had accidentally shot his young son during the invasion and taken him away to a hospital. The son had never been heard from again.

A resident of Sadr City, Mohammed Awad Jobur, told me how the U.S. military killed his mother during a routine patrol of his neighborhood. "At 12:30 in the afternoon the American troops came to a school near our house asking the guard of the school to open the door," he recalled. "The guard of the school didn't answer so they just turned and opened fire on my home. They killed my mother and my son lost his leg."

At the time of our interview, there had been virtually no attacks on American troops in Sadr City. Mohammed told me he should be exactly the type of person to favor the American army, since he'd served 23 years in Saddam's hated Abu Ghraib prison, but that this wasn't his position.

"The American soldiers treat us worse than animals," he told me. "Even animals have more rights than us." Jobur said that the American military had come to his home later and admitted they made a mistake. They told him they would pay him $3,000 in compensation, but the money hasn't come.

"Yesterday's bombing [of the Lebanon Hotel] was terrorism and I can't support it," he told me. "But I want you to know that I hate the Americans now. They won't even compensate me for the loss of my house and my family. I need money. So maybe if someone comes to me and offers me money to kill the American troops I will think about it. I don't think I would do it but I'd think about it."

As a journalist, I knew the best way to get information on an issue was to get out in the field on my own rather than rely on stories from those who bothered to come to a press conference.

I asked Waseem if we could travel north to a small village called Abu Siffa. A few weeks before, the *New York Times* had reported that the U.S. military stormed the village and took all the adult men to Abu Ghraib. One of the tried-and-true tricks of reporters is to follow up on someone else's work, and that is exactly what I proposed to do.

At first Waseem was resistant. He had never heard of the town, and when I told him that the *Times* report said it was near Balad, in the heart of the Sunni triangle, he bristled. "Those people," he said, "they hate Americans. They are very much from the former regime."

"I know," I said. "But if they are being rounded up and taken to Abu Ghraib we should go and try to find out what happened and why."

Again Waseem protested.

"Let's say this," I bargained. "At the first sign of trouble, we turn back to Baghdad, no questions asked. If at any point you feel unsafe we can return right away."

"Okay," Waseem acceded reluctantly. We drove off to Abu Siffa in his newly bought 1996 BMW.

On our right on the highway out of Baghdad was a gigantic walled area that went on for miles. Waseem explained that before the war it was one of Saddam's bases. Now it was an American military base, and the Americans were expanding it—making it one of what would become the U.S. military's 14 permanent bases in Iraq.

A moment later, we were stuck in a traffic jam. A large convoy of U.S. Army supply trucks were traveling north on the highway toward the base's main entrance and they were receiving a full U.S. military escort. They occupied only one lane of the freeway, but American humvees blocked Iraqis from accessing any lane, "for security reasons," and traffic slowed accordingly. I picked up my camera to take a picture of the American traffic jam, but Waseem told me to put it down, saying: "They will think you have some kind of gun and shoot us."

When the Americans pulled into their base, traffic quickened again. At the exit for Balad, we turned off the freeway and stopped in town to ask for directions. Waseem asked me to wait in the car. In this part of the country, Americans were very unpopular.

Nothing happened, though, and as we got farther away from the highway, I relaxed. I remembered the trip to al-Mufwrakiyya village in the south months before. It was wonderful to get out of Baghdad, with its Los Angeles–style pollution and congestion. Here, as in al-Mufwrakiyya, the land was lush. The air was clean, and date palms and citrus trees swung in the wind. We were near the mighty Tigris in the breadbasket of Mesopotamia. We saw two children playing on the side of the road.

"Salam walayekum!" Waseem shouted from his car window. "Is this Abu Siffa?"

The children answered that, yes, this was the village we were looking for. "Did you have some problem with the Americans here?" Waseem asked.

"Yes, we did," one of the children answered. "They took the people in the morning. We had already gone to school. The Americans went house to house, and all the men who were still in the house were taken to prison."

"Have the men returned?" I asked.

"Just two," he said. "Two of them returned five days ago." We asked the boy if he would take us to meet the newly returned, and he got into our car.

Inside the village, the houses were spacious. Blessed with excellent land to farm and good relations with the former regime, the people of Abu Siffa had grown wealthy. The boy introduced us to his father, schoolteacher Nasser Jassem Hussein, one of the town's few remaining men.

"They took eighty-three Iraqi men from our village," he explained. We were sitting on small plastic stools in a public square on the banks of the Tigris. Nasser's wife served tea. "That includes three lawyers, ten secondary-school teachers, and sixty-seven farmers, fourteen of whom were more than sixty years old. They also took three children under sixteen."

A young man, 15-year-old Ahmed Itar Hassen, was one of two to have been released. He sat nervously next to Nasser. In a moment, we would hear his story.

"Have any of them been charged with crimes?" we asked the father.

"None of them has been charged with any crime," he answered. "None of them has a lawyer and we haven't been able to visit any of them in prison. The soldiers said they were looking for weapons, but all they found was a few Kalashnikovs, and everyone in Iraq has one or two."

"What did they tell you?" I asked.

"They were looking for a specific man who was very important in the Arab Ba'ath Socialist Party," Nasser said. "But they didn't know his face. They just knew his name, so they took all the men from here so they could see if they were him or not."

Eventually, Nasser said, the Americans located the Ba'ath Party officer, but they nevertheless kept nearly all the men of the village in custody.

"Are you a member of the Ba'ath Party?" I asked.

"Of course," the teacher answered. "But not a very big member. We're all members of the Ba'ath Party here, but that doesn't mean we're involved in the resistance. When Saddam was president, we wanted to farm, and now the Americans are here and we want to farm."

I asked Nasser why he hadn't been arrested and he made allegations of theft that I would hear again and again during my time in Iraq but would never be able to prove. The Americans, he said, "took three million Iraqi *dinar* [$2,000] from me. That's why they didn't bomb this house. I knew the Americans were going to attack the village and when they will leave. But even though I gave them three million Iraqi *dinar,* they took two pickup trucks from me. I had to pay one and a half million *dinar* [$1,000] for each one to get them back."

Such allegations of theft were denied by the Americans, and I was unable to confirm whether they were true. But across Iraq I would hear the same story again and again. My own feeling, which I came to slowly, was that the Americans probably seized large sums of cash when they found them, thinking they were being stock-piled for the resistance. But with Iraq's banks looted after the war and the whole financial sector in complete collapse, most Iraqis kept their life savings in cash at home, meaning that any wealthy man would have a large stash of cash.

We turned our attention to the young man, Ahmed Itar Hassen, who had just returned after almost four months in prison. A dark-skinned boy who looked older than his 15 years, Ahmed wore a polo shirt and windbreaker. He wasn't old enough to grow the thick mustache typical for Iraqi men, but he did have teenage fuzz between his nose and upper lip.

"Can you explain what happened when the Americans came?" I asked.

"It was three in the morning," he said. "It was raining, and I was handcuffed in the rain outside the door of my house along with my four brothers and two of my uncles. A lot of my relatives were taken because we were living in this same area. They searched the place and they just found one Kalashnikov."

Ahmed told me that all 83 villagers were kept outside in the rain for hours before being taken to a U.S. base near Samara, a one-hour drive to the north. "We were there for six days," he said. "We just waited in an open field without any roof, without any warmth. It was just like that."

"When you say you were staying with nothing, do you mean you were staying in a tent, or do you mean that you were staying with nothing at all?" I asked.

"We had nothing at all," he said. "We were without any tent, without anything. We were exposed to the sun and the rain and everything else."

"What were the bathroom facilities?" I asked.

"We would go in the open area," he said. "When someone asked for the toilet, the Americans just took him far from the group and told him to go outside, just like that."

"And did you have any interaction with the Americans over those six days?"

"They didn't tie our hands," the boy said. "We would just walk around talking with our relatives, and the area was just like this public square, but with barbed wire. At night, though, the soldiers threw little stones at us when we tried to sleep. Maybe it was just for fun."

"How often did they do that?" I asked.

"Every day. They didn't allow us to sleep. As soon as we would go to sleep they started to throw these stones."

In the daytime, Ahmed said, the soldiers would shout at him for hours, while an Egyptian translator looked on. "He didn't translate all the shouts they made," Ahmed said. "They would shout things, and then they would finally get to a question and then the translator would translate the question."

"And what were the questions?"

"They gave me a rocket," the 15-year-old said. "And they took a picture and I was supposed to say 'This is mine.' They kept shouting at me and they wouldn't stop shouting at me until I said 'This is mine.' I kept saying 'No, it's not mine.' I never gave in."

Ahmed's interrogation story, while severe, seemed light by the standards of the occupation. In its February 2004 report on conditions the prior year, the International Committee of the Red Cross (ICRC), which had been allowed to inspect Iraq's prisons, found that detainees had been whipped, tied down on their backs with cables, kicked in the testicles, hung on iron bars of the cell or from windows or doors, and burned with cigarettes. Several people held by Iraqi police under American occupation told the ICRC they had been made to sign statements that they had not been allowed to read.

Ahmed said that after six days in the open field he was taken to Abu Ghraib prison, where he was kept for 25 days. "They kept me in a very small cell," he said. "It was one and a half meters by four meters. I got my own cell because I am a child."

It was a cell in the same prison where Saddam held political prisoners during his reign.

Ahmed said that for 25 days he was not allowed to exercise, was never allowed to go outside. He said he never saw the sky. "I couldn't get out of the cell. My only time out was when I took a bath. The American soldiers would take me out and wash me directly with very cold water and then put me back in the cell."

"Can you describe, more broadly, how you were treated?" I asked.

"At night, they put a dog in the cell in order to frighten me," he said. His response was almost nonchalant. In two months, photos would surface from inside Abu Ghraib showing exactly this practice.

"It was a wolf dog," he continued. "Usually the police use this kind of dog. Every night one of the soldiers would enter with his dog. Every night, a different soldier would enter with a different dog. Then a Japanese man came from the Red Cross and asked me about the situation. I told him about the dog and then the Americans stopped bringing the dog."

Ahmed said that a few days after the Red Cross visit, he was transferred out of Abu Ghraib and into a different facility for juvenile offenders. The 15-year-old had spent almost a month in the notorious prison. He said he was never allowed to see a lawyer, was never charged with any crime, and was allowed only one visit—from his mother, who gained access to the prison by bribing an Iraqi policeman.

We got up from our seats and walked around the village, arriving moments later in front of Ahmed's home. The entire front of the house was riddled with bullet holes. The front of what was still standing, anyway: a larger weapon had destroyed whole sections of the building. It looked hollow.

Ahmed introduced us to his mother. A beautiful woman in her mid-forties, she was clad in a shiny black velvet fabric, her head covered under a velvet *hijab*. Her name was Rejan Mohammed

Hassen, and she told us the American soldiers had taken all four of her sons. Her husband was already dead.

"First thing in the morning, they took us from the home," she explained. "They just took us from the home and asked us to stand around. When we asked why, the Americans started to beat the women and forced us out. After that, two tanks came to our house and started to shoot using the machine guns on top of the tank and then two missiles from the cannon at the head of the tank. After one hour, they allowed us to return to our home. Everything is destroyed now: the television, the radio, the satellite—everything—it's all damaged."

Even though much of the front of her house had been destroyed by the tank, Rejan told me she was still living in the house with her daughters. "We have no other place to live," she said.

"One of your sons has returned from prison this week," I said. "Do you know where the rest of them are?"

"They're in Abu Ghraib, but I haven't been able to see them," she said, beginning to cry. "I couldn't find my son [Ahmed, just released] in any kind of American prison. But then he was transferred to an Iraqi prison because he was very young. So I bribed the Iraqi police with 100,000 Iraqi *dinar* [$65] and I was able to see him."

"How has life been," I asked, "with all the men in prison? Who works the fields now?"

"I started to work by myself," she said. "I had been depending on my sons but now I'm working by myself in the fields. It's very hard for me because I didn't use to do this. I had to learn everything."

"Is there anything else you would want to add?" I asked. "Anything you would want to say to people listening to the radio in America?"

"It's just an occupation," she said. "There is no freedom. There is no anything. Everything they say about democracy and human rights. It's all a lie."

As we prepared to leave, Rejan invited us to lunch inside her destroyed home, but Waseem insisted we decline. We had to get back to Baghdad before dark, he explained.

On the way home, I reflected on the similarities and the differences between this trip to Abu Siffa and my journey a year earlier to al-Mufwrakiyya in southern Iraq. Like Rejan's home, the homes of al-Mufwrakiyya's villagers had been destroyed by American firepower. But in al-Mufwrakiyya, the villagers saw their suffering as necessary to achieve the removal of Saddam Hussein; what was the purpose of this raid on Abu Siffa? There was a high-ranking Ba'athist in the village who was organizing attacks on the Americans, but the U.S. military didn't know who he was. So they raided the village, destroyed homes, and took away all the men.

When I got home and searched the Internet, I read a new report from the human-rights group Amnesty International. It catalogued 15 confirmed incidents of house demolition across Iraq and noted regular reports of torture and beatings perpetrated on prisoners in U.S. custody. The report also alleged that prisoners were subjected to sleep deprivation, hooding, and bright lights.

What was the point of all this? When questioned by human-rights groups, the commander in charge of the raid on Abu Siffa, Colonel Nate Sassaman, initially indicated that the raids and detentions were necessary for "national security." But after two months, U.S. forces admitted that the detainees were only guilty by association because they lived in the same village as the Ba'ath official. Nevertheless, only one of the men had been released, so the mothers and children were missing their husbands and fathers, the school was missing its teachers, and the fields were left untended.

What were the Americans hoping to achieve this way? What kind of society were they hoping to build?

.10.

FUNDAMENTALISTS
UNITE

The mounting anger at and suspicion of America's intentions still hadn't spilled over into more widespread support for armed resistance. The inclination of those wronged, I noted, was to complain of being wronged by the Americans rather than to call for retaliation. There still seemed to be a certain amount of the feeling I had found immediately after the fall of Saddam Hussein: Whatever America's intentions, it wasn't much use to fight them. It would only result in the destruction of the Iraqis' own homes and cities.

This attitude was apparent when Waseem and I visited a number of Baghdad mosques on Thursday, March 18. The next day would be the one-year anniversary of George Bush's war to oust Saddam Hussein. Since it would also be a Friday, I assumed many an imam would be giving a sermon on the topic, and I told Waseem I wanted to get as wide an array of views as possible, both Sunni and Shia.

Driving around the city, though, it became clear that the clergy was not as political as I expected. As we arrived at each mosque, I would wait in the car as Waseem went inside to speak to the imam. Most of the time he would emerge a few minutes later and explain that the imam did not plan to give a political sermon and refused to comment to the press.

When we did get an interview, it was from a religious leader of the more extreme variety. In the Sunni stronghold of Adamiya, for example, we were granted access to the imam of the Allah Akhbar Mosque.

"I told him you were French," Waseem told me, winking, as he walked out of the mosque. "It makes things easier here." I was happy to get the interview, but from my seat in the van I scolded him, saying it wasn't a good thing to lie—since it could cause trouble if we were found out. I was willing to stretch the truth, I told him, but not lie. "For example, you could say I work for the French public radio," I said, "because that's true. I don't usually work for the French, but I do freelance sometimes. You could also say that I work in Turkey. That's also true, and I have a Turkish press pass to prove it. But try not to lie."

Waseem sighed. "Aaron," he said. "Trust me, around these people it's easier if you're French." He flashed a smile and threw open the car door. "C'mon," he said. "They're waiting."

They were waiting, indeed. A half-dozen young men escorted us into the imam's office, a large, sparsely furnished room with old couches along its sides and faded Arabic calligraphy on the walls. They introduced us to the preacher, Sheik Ma'an Hassen al-Janabi, served everyone Pepsi, and sat down opposite us on the other side of the room.

"What does he want to know?" Sheik Ma'an asked Waseem.

"He wants to know about what has changed in the last year, since America invaded, and if you'll be speaking about this at Friday prayers."

"Yes," the sheik said thoughtfully. Leaning back into his couch, he launched into a long monologue of vagaries. "When someone starts a war," he said in the voice of a sage, "many people are sacrificed no matter who they are—whether they are Sunni, Shia, Kurd, Arabic, foreigner—it's all the same. The church is destroyed along with the mosque and the *husseiyni* [Shi'ite mosque]."

"Let's speak specifically," I said, trying to narrow things down a bit. "Compared to before the war, how many people are coming to your Friday prayers? Is it more or fewer?" I was trying to find out if he thought his influence had increased since the fall of Saddam.

"The number of parishioners gets bigger each week," he said. "Thanks to God the Iraqi people have returned to God and their belief in Him. The terrible things push people back to their faith."

"When is there the biggest turnout?" I asked.

"The funerals," he said gravely. "The biggest turnout is at the funerals. The funerals are very big and the dead are very many."

He tried to drive his point home. "The dead are as many as the number of new cars on the street and the new satellite dishes you see."

He made a bitter joke: "It's as much as the amount of democracy we have received." A year since George Bush launched his war, his country was effectively controlled by an American viceroy and military commander. An Iraqi Governing Council was in place, but that had also been imposed by the Americans. In addition, most of the members of that council were former exiles. No elections had been held.

I wanted to ask a follow-up question, but he continued to talk, his hands gesturing lazily in the air: "I like the satellite dishes when they are in good hands, because if they are in good hands they will cause people to behave better, but right now there is a lot of evil programming coming into the television in Iraq."

Finally, he stopped, and I had the opportunity to ask, "So who is dying? Are they being killed by the Americans? Are they children dying in the hospital because of the dirty water? What can account for all these deaths?"

"All the funerals I've attended are deaths by random killing," the imam responded. "Random killing made by people—no one knows who did it. They just kill and run away. We don't know who did it or the place or the idea of the killers."

"Some say it is people killing for revenge," I said. "You know, because so many people in this neighborhood were connected in some way to the former regime."

"It's not revenge," he said. "I'm not going to point to a person. We cannot accuse anyone in particular of these killings, but now all the men who did this, they all have the same reason. They are outsiders. They are being supported by American intelligence, the Israeli Mossad, Iranian intelligence, and the other groups that have entered from outside our border. As you know, there are no border police [because America dismissed them after the fall of Saddam]. We never saw these things under the last regime, just one or two a year."

It's not our fault. It's a problem that's coming from the outside. This was becoming a standard argument. Probing wouldn't reveal any truths.

The imam continued, but Waseem stopped translating and he looked at me longingly with a sigh that begged me not to ask any more questions so that we could leave. "Would you like another Pepsi or tea?" the imam asked as I gathered my belongings to leave. We respectfully declined and walked back to the van. After we passed the gates of the mosque, Waseem quickened his pace. He was clearly in a hurry to get away.

"I really hate this kind," Waseem said as he turned on the ignition. "You see the way he talked. This is the way of speech of the former regime. Blaming the Iranian intelligence and the Israeli intelligence for everything."

We made a sharp turn over a bridge into Kadamiyya, the oldest and most solidly established Shi'ite area of Baghdad. "Where are we going?" I asked.

"To see a very wise man," Waseem said, clearly unhappy that so far we had only been able to interview someone whose views and experiences differed so vastly from his.

Waseem explained where we were headed: "You know, it was a big problem when my wife and I wanted to get married, because I am a Shia and my wife is Sunni from a very Sunni family. So when I first went to ask her father for permission to marry, he said no. Then I went to this very wise man and he met with both sides of our family and received the permission. He is a very great man."

We pulled into a side street off a bazaar. The front door of the mosque, where the parishioners entered, faced the main bazaar, but the imam's house was on the other side. A few men with automatic rifles stood idly on the corner. They were the cleric's bodyguards.

"Wait here," Waseem said, and rushed into the house.

After a few minutes, he emerged. The clergyman wasn't home, and his assistant had said the imam wouldn't be home for hours. In any case, like most moderate imams, he wasn't giving interviews. Waseem was clearly disappointed. "Shall we go?" he said.

The Last of the Mohicans soundtrack reverberated throughout the van. "What was the name of that imam?" I asked.

"His name is Hussein al-Sadr," Waseem said, getting onto the freeway. "He is related to Muqtada al-Sadr somehow, but he is not like him. He is a very wise man and the representative of Ayatollah Sistani in Kadamiyya."

We drove through Baghdad in silence for a while, except for the classical music blasting through the car. I considered the position of Ayatollah Ali al-Sistani. The 73-year-old cleric was the most respected Shi'ite religious authority in Iraq, but his impact on politics had thus far been limited by the constraints he put on himself. Sistani espoused a school of thought called the quiet *hawza,* which meant he rarely spoke up on political matters, and it was this silence that had allowed him to live when so many other clergymen were killed by Saddam.

Since the fall of Saddam the year before, he had spoken up only occasionally. He condemned all violence—by both the Americans and the insurgency—but his public statements were primarily related to one topic and one topic only: that the future of Iraq could only be decided through free elections and that those elections should be held as soon as possible. Eventually, a slate of Sistani-backed candidates would triumph in elections held in January 2005. In the meantime, though, Sistani held his tongue.

But if Sistani was largely silent, more-militant factions were always happy to speak out. The next day, Friday, March 19, 2004, was the one-year anniversary of the start of the war. Though Waseem and I had failed to find news of any demonstrations, an Iraqi representative of Occupation Watch had told me that protesters would gather in a large traffic circle in front of the Abu Hanifa Mosque, a pro-regime Sunni house of prayer. It was in this same space that Saddam was last seen before going into hiding. He was smiling happily, kissing babies in the middle of the street while U.S. airplanes bombed the country.

When U.S. troops reached Baghdad, they encountered stiff resistance around the mosque, whose minaret and clock tower were crumbling as a result of munitions fired from the barrel of a tank. It was one of the last parts of the capital to fall to the U.S. military.

Parishioners from Abu Hanifa would be at the demonstration, I was told, along with those from neighborhood Sunni mosques, as well as Shi'ites leaving prayer in neighboring Kadamiyya. "It will be a show of brotherhood," the man from Occupation Watch told me, "of a united stand of Sunni and Shia against the American occupation."

When Waseem came to pick me up at the hotel, I suggested we attend the prayer as well as the demonstration. I still remembered the sermon that the pro-regime imam in Fallujah gave right after the war. I told Waseem how that imam had condemned the invasion and occupation as "crimes against humanity" but had nonetheless spoken against attacking the American army.

I knew the imam of Abu Hanifa came from the same political background as did the one in Fallujah, and I wanted to see how much things had changed since the days immediately following the fall of Saddam.

Waseem initially opposed the idea. "I don't think it's safe," he told me. "You know those people." He suggested he go in alone with my tape recorder, but I insisted that as a journalist I had to be able to observe the atmosphere with my own eyes. Eventually, he relented.

At the mosque itself, we gained entry without a problem. Waseem told the guards I was an antiwar American journalist and we were waved in (although our mobile phones, like everyone else's, were held with our shoes at the front desk. There had been a rumor of sorts that someone in Baghdad was planning to bomb something using a cell phone, so the communication devices almost always needed to be left with security outside a public building.

We sat down on the floor of the mosque and prayed, standing and bowing before God at the appropriate times as I had in the mosque in Fallujah. Then it came time for the sermon. It began in the fashion typical of an opponent of the occupation:

"We lost our dignity, our country," the imam, Hassen Ahmed al-Taha, told his congregation. "How could we allow our enemy to invade our homes and hurt our women and children?"

Then he went into a long tirade against the Jews, using the Prophet Mohammed to back up his points: "There is an old story from the Prophet at Medina," he preached. "There were two groups [of Muslims] fighting, and after that the Jews came and made money off them. Don't give in to Jews; when two Muslims kill each other, both of them will go to hell."

Raising his voice into a kind of high-pitched squeal, he said that those Iraqis who cooperate with the occupation are not Muslim and deserved to be killed. He extended this even to those Iraqis who were gathering the destroyed remains of Iraqi tanks and selling them for scrap.

"You have to stop them from stealing the money," he preached. "This is the wealth of your country. You can even kill them, because they stole your money. It's all been witnessed in the holy Qu'ran. There are no people in the world who can live without tanks and aircraft. How can we, as Muslims, deal with these problems? We must fight!"

At that, the congregation poured out onto the street readying for a demonstration. Waseem and I retrieved our shoes and mobile phones. A message came from the mosque's bombed-out minaret: "We're waiting for our brothers from Kadamiyya," it blared. "Then we'll begin our demonstration."

The Shia arrived—about a thousand of them, walking across the bridge over the Tigris that connects Adamiya to Kadamiyya. All of them were followers of Muqtada al-Sadr. They carried posters of their leader, who was depicted in an angry pose, his index finger pointed into the air. They chanted "With our blood, with our soul, we'll fight for all Iraq." This was a new version of the Ba'athist chant, "With our blood, with our soul, we'll fight for Saddam." One sign read NO TO OCCUPATION, another said NO TO DICTATORSHIP. The crowd began to march toward Aritar Square a few blocks away.

I kept scanning the area for U.S. troops, but none emerged. There weren't even American helicopters overhead. There would be no "incidents" at this demonstration, which was in any case fairly small at two or three thousand protesters. At the square, Sadr's representative in Kadamiyya, Shi'ite cleric Hazem al-Araji, stood atop a truck with his fellow imams—guarded by a dozen men holding Kalashnikovs.

"My brothers!" he screamed into a bullhorn. "One year of the occupation has passed. They thought we would just be happy, dancing and singing. No! Today we refuse them, but in a new way—in a brotherhood of Sunni and Shia!"

Araji announced that the imams had formed a Muslim Scientists League, or a League of Clergy. Their demands included cancellation of the interim constitution signed by the American-appointed Governing Council and a refutation of federalism and Kurdish autonomy. They demanded free speech and free expression for Iraqis and called for the law of Islam to be adopted as the law of Iraq, and they resolved together that violence against the occupation was justified.

This was a change. I remembered the words of Sadr's representatives in the days immediately following the fall of Saddam. They were grateful for the dictator's ouster and waiting to see if liberation or occupation was coming. Since then, they had confined themselves mostly to protecting schools and hospitals, dispensing aid to the poor, and meting out justice using their own Islamic courts.

They had even organized elections in Shia strongholds like Najaf, throwing out municipal councils appointed by a North Carolina contractor, Research Triangle International, which had been given $457 million to "identify the most appropriate 'legitimate' and functional leaders" for coalition forces to work with. Elections organized by the Sadr movement had now replaced the people chosen by RTI with governments that represented the people in the area.

But now they seemed to be turning toward direct confrontation: "The young people in Iraq—every one of them is a bomb controlled by an imam!" Hazem al-Araji screamed to the crowd. "And we have our finger on the button. Yes! Yes! We won't give them a chance to sell Iraq. . . . They say we had weapons of mass destruction. We didn't have any nuclear weapons, but just one talk from an imam—Sunni or Shia—is bigger than a nuclear bomb."

The demonstration ended with Araji leading the crowd in a chant: "No to America, no to Saddam, yes, yes, to Islam!"

"Pretty scary stuff," I said to Waseem as we walked back to his van. "These folks want strict Islamic law and no rights for Kurds. They're crazy!"

"You see," Waseem said simply, turning the key in the ignition. Today we would listen to *Barbra Streisand with the Bee Gees.*

"Shall we see if your friend in Kadamiyya will talk to us today?" I asked Waseem. "I would hate to put a story together with just these crazies."

Waseem sighed. "Yeah, we can try, but I don't think he will agree."

Waseem turned out to be right. This time Hussein al-Sadr was home, but he wouldn't grant an interview. Waseem explained to me afterward.

"What can I tell him?" the moderate cleric had asked Waseem. "I can't speak about this. If I say I support the Americans I will be killed, and if I tell the people it was better under Saddam Hussein they won't agree with that, either. It's better if I just keep quiet."

"I guess I'll just have to write down what all these imams said, and then say that more moderate clerics refused to talk," I told Waseem on the way home. "I hope back in America they get the point."

"I think they'll understand," came Waseem's response as he dropped me back at my hotel.

That night, when I wanted to feed my story, there were two American tanks parked in the middle of Sa'adoon Street right outside the hotel. Colin Powell was in town, and there was a bomb scare. I talked to the soldiers about getting through and they told me there was a bomb somewhere in the area, so they had sealed it off. Still, they told me I could pass them if I wanted to risk my life. I walked around the checkpoint to get to the Internet. As I was sending my story a half-hour later, the earth shook and there was a low boom.

PART THREE

WHEN AMERICA
LOST IRAQ

.11.

THE CLOSURE OF
AL-HAWZA NEWSPAPER

The increase in violent insurgency and anti-American sentiment throughout Iraq meant it was no longer safe to live at the Aghadir. I was spooked by the bombing of the Lebanon Hotel and concerned about my late-night walks though dark streets to file my story from Internet cafes. I decided to move back to the Dulaimi, the furnished apartment building where James, Raphaël, and I had lived during our first trip.

When I arrived with my bags to move in, I found that the building had changed a great deal since my first stint there. The 1970s decor remained the same. Fake ivy still wrapped around the ceiling fans and blue back-lighting still emanated from behind the ceiling trim, but while the basic furnishings remained the same, the clientele had changed completely. Gone were the daily wedding processions. The Dulaimi no longer served as a honeymoon suite for middle-class Iraqis. The Australian ambassador had taken over the hotel across the street and had had large concrete barriers erected to protect the building and its surroundings. As a consequence, the Dulaimi was occupied almost completely by foreign journalists and the price had been adjusted accordingly. I would have to bargain.

"The price is fifty dollars a night for a one-bedroom," the owner, Hamza al-Dulaimi, told me as I stepped into his office.

"But last time, I stayed here with Mr. James and Mr. Raphaël from France and the price was five hundred dollars a month," I said. "There were three of us and we had two bedrooms."

"Mr. Aaron," he said kindly. "You must forget that price. That price is over. Do you know how much your old apartment is going for now? Fifteen hundred dollars. Now the rooms have Internet cables and satellite TV. That was not there before. You must talk realistically to me about a price."

Eventually, we settled on a price of $600 a month for a one-bedroom, with a living room, bathroom, kitchen, and a small balcony overlooking the Tigris and the U.S. military Green Zone on the other side of the river. Sitting on the balcony in the evening, I could see a steady stream of U.S. tanks crossing the river and going out on patrol, rattling every window of every house in the neighborhood.

For the rest of my stay in Baghdad, I would live in the Dulaimi—making my own dark Arabic coffee or sugar-filled tea first thing in the morning, enjoying olives with feta cheese and honey for breakfast, and watching late-night Hollywood movies on Channel 2 before turning in to bed.

So far as security went, the building also had the advantage of being owned by the Dulaimi clan, one of the most powerful in Fallujah and the so-called Sunni Triangle. It was highly unlikely, I thought, that the insurgency would bomb its own building.

When I moved in, I had no idea how important that protection would be. Within two weeks of my occupancy, the U.S. government would make a number of decisions that would turn the armed insurgency from a handful of fundamentalists to a national resistance with broad public support.

The U.S. government launched its first broadside on March 28, 2004. On a sleepy Sunday morning, American troops blocked the four roads leading up to the offices of Muqtada al-Sadr's newspaper, *al-Hawza al-Natiqa* (in English, *The Spoken Islamic University*). They entered the paper's offices and presented the staff with a signed letter from U.S. Administrator Paul Bremer that ordered them to close down the weekly paper for 60 days.

When the gates were closed, there was a new lock, marked AMERICAN MADE. A new sign was there, too. It read, in English and Arabic: THIS BUILDING HAS BEEN PLACED OFF LIMITS BY THE CPA—ANYONE WHO ENTERS WILL BE ARRESTED.

In his letter, Bremer said he shuttered *al-Hawza al-Natiqa* because Sadr used it "to provoke violence" against occupation troops. Its editors, Bremer wrote, were guilty of publishing "false" articles.

To prove his point, Bremer cited a February article stating that the destruction of new Iraqi police barracks in Iskandariyah was caused by a missile fired by an American helicopter.

"In the same edition," Bremer wrote, "you published an article entitled 'Bremer is following the example of Saddam.'" In that story, Bremer claimed, the paper had stated that his authority was "making the Iraqi people hungry so that they will spend their time trying to find food and will not have the chance to demand their political and individual freedoms."

"This report is false," he wrote, "and the CPA is doing its best to provide food and medical help for the Iraqi people and to repair the infrastructure of the country and put the fundamentals of political, economic and individual freedoms in place." These efforts, Bremer said, were previously "outside the dreams of the Iraqi people."

This was only the first of the offending articles, however. On August 6, 2003, Bremer wrote that the paper had accused the United States of invading Iraq "not only to remove Saddam and steal Iraq's oil but to destroy the character and civilization of the Iraqi people." Bremer wrote that on August 21 the paper had claimed that the Americans in Sadr City in Baghdad were "fighting Islam and its symbols." That, he wrote, represented "a serious threat of violence against the 'Coalition Forces' and against the Iraqi people who are co-operating with the CPA in the reconstruction of Iraq."

When Waseem and I went to the paper's offices, U.S. military humvees were still parked at all four corners of the intersection, which had a large traffic circle at its center. A U.S. military helicopter flew overhead. A few dozen followers of al-Sadr had gathered there, though none of the paper's reporters were on hand. They had gone into hiding.

As the U.S. military worked to silence al-Sadr, they also built their own propaganda machine. Shortly after the occupation began, the Defense Department had founded a new Baghdad TV station called al-Iraqiya and a new newspaper called *al-Sabah* (The Morning). The State Department had gotten into the act, too, funding a new Iraq service for its pan-Arab radio station *Radyo Sawa* (Radio Together) and a new satellite news channel called *al-Hurra* (The Freedom) which broadcast pro-American Arab news from Virginia.

But until the closure of Sadr's newspaper, the comparisons to Saddam's regime had ended there. Under the Ba'ath dictatorship, no independent papers were allowed to publish. Under American occupation, there were dozens of papers published by nearly every hue of society. Kurds, Communists, capitalists, and Islamists all had papers, as did Sa'ad al-Bazzaz, a former high-ranking official in Saddam's government. Many of them were openly critical of the occupation, and some demanded that the Americans leave.

At Bazzaz's newspaper, for example, the best-known columnist, Majid al-Samarai, had been a popular talk-show host on Iraq state TV before the war (he called himself the Larry King of Iraq) and continued to write favorably about Saddam long after the dictator's ouster. He was not troubled by the U.S. military.

So what was the reason for *al-Hawza*'s closure? To me, it had less to do with the newspaper's content than with the Sadr movement itself. A powerful force across Shi'ite Iraq, Sadr's followers were setting up their own governmental structures, which came up directly against those of the Americans. I wanted to explain this to listeners back home, so I went to meet with Sheik Selim Mejid Jumar, one of Muqtada Sadr's top lieutenants in Baghdad. The wiry cleric in flowing white robes could be found most days of the week in the municipal building of one of north Baghdad's primarily poor Shi'ite neighborhoods, Showle. He was a member of the municipal governing council and had come to power in June 2003 in an election organized by Sadr's forces.

"It wasn't a perfect election," the sheik conceded, "but it was fair. It was overseen by academics and religious people, and one man from every house was allowed to vote. When we were finished we had a local council that represented the people."

He told me that the Americans had called any election premature. After it took over from Saddam, the occupation Coalition Provisional Authority had hired the American company Research Triangle International (RTI) to hand-pick and train local governments to replace politicians chosen by Saddam Hussein and his Ba'ath regime.

Initially, the sheik said, RTI refused to accept the elected slate, but after months of argument an agreement was reached. Of the

21 people appointed by RTI, five got to stay, and the rest of the council were those selected in the Sadr movement's election.

"So now that you are on the local council, what do you do?" It was an obvious question.

"We don't have much power," he conceded. "We are still living under occupation, so the Americans have all the power over us. But as members of the local council we can at least complain to the occupation authority on behalf of the people and tell them that there is no electricity and no garbage service. They don't do anything, but at least we can complain. With God's help the occupation will end and then we will be free."

I thanked the sheik for his time, and Waseem and I walked out of the local council. As we left the building, two Apache helicopters flew overhead. We paused to ask the local U.S.-trained Iraqi guards what they thought of Muqtada al-Sadr and his elected local council.

The first men we spoke to, young men with scruffy beards and Kalashnikovs, refused to talk to us, but their superior—a well-built man in his middle years—was more than happy to oblige. His thin mustache was neatly trimmed and his bluish-gray police uniform was neatly pressed. He was a lieutenant, armed with only a pistol.

"I want to tell you something," he said. "I was in Saddam Hussein's prison for many years. I was arrested by the regime in 1979 during the first uprising against his rule."

"There were many followers of Muqtada Sadr's uncle, Ayatollah Mohammed Baqir al-Sadr, who took part in that revolt," I noted.

"That's right," he said, "and I met many of them in prison. At that time, I was a follower of Musla al-Hakim [a Grand Ayatollah and father of Mohammed Baqir al-Hakim, the assassinated founder of the Supreme Council for Islamic Revolution in Iraq], but I met many followers of al-Sadr when I was in prison and I have a lot of respect for them."

He said there was something he wanted to show us. He reached into his pocket and pulled out his wallet. There, inside his wallet, was a photograph of Muqtada al-Sadr and his father, Grand Ayatollah Mohammed Sadiq al-Sadr.

"This guy," he said, pointing at Muqtada's photo, "he's a kid. He's an idiot and his council is full of idiots. They ride around in their cars all day putting up his poster and screaming *Allah akbar!* But his father—I have tremendous respect for him. He gave his life trying to free us from that bastard Saddam Hussein. I will never forget that."

When I asked why he signed up for the Iraqi Army, the lieutenant told me it was the best way to keep Baghdad safe from looters and thieves, but he added that if supporters of Muqtada al-Sadr forcibly took the municipal building, he would abandon his post.

He explained that there was a difference between the Sadr family and the terrorists he had sworn to fight. "I was in prison with this family," he said, "and even before they were arrested I respected all of them."

On the way home from Showle, Waseem and I got stuck in a typical postwar traffic jam. Such problems were commonplace in Baghdad partially because its sprawling layout put everyone into cars, but also because of a number of factors directly related to the war.

For one thing, American security precautions meant that many of the important streets and freeways of Iraq were regularly closed for hours on end. Some streets had been permanently shut down and could only be used by American troops, foreign contractors, and a privileged few Iraqis with connections to the American authority. Two of these permanently shut streets were main roads to al-Dulaimi. One was a wide boulevard that ran along the Tigris. It was closed because of its proximity to the Palestine Hotel, home to the BBC and Associated Press as well as big American contractors like Halliburton and Bechtel. Also closed was a bridge over the

Tigris that ran close to the Green Zone where the American authority was housed. The closure of both approaches made my trips home exhausting.

Further exacerbating the situation was the lack of electricity. A year after the war, there was still only intermittent electricity in the capital. As a consequence, there were no reliably working streetlights in Baghdad, and traffic regularly ground to a screeching halt.

"It's no wonder the people are killing each other," I said to Waseem as we sat stalled. "In America we would just call it 'road rage.' I can't imagine what would happen if we experienced this back in the States."

We sat, silent. *The Last of the Mohicans* soundtrack was on the car stereo again; Waseem turned it down. "Aaron," he reflected, "do you remember when Colin Powell went before the United Nations and said that Saddam Hussein had mass destruction weapons? We were watching it on television. We were all gathered around the television—my family and some friends—and we were all hoping, praying, *please let there be some weapon of mass destruction.* Please let there be something to justify the invasion, something to justify the removal of Saddam Hussein. After Powell finished, you know, Syria spoke, and then France, and it was clear that the United Nations was not going to vote for war. We wanted so much for there to be some weapons of mass destruction."

Another long pause; the radio played softly as Waseem considered what to say next. "I was arrested," he revealed. "I was put in prison for three years because a neighbor of ours who was in the Ba'ath Party didn't like me. So he just had me arrested, and I was sent to a special section of Abu Ghraib prison. Just like that, they threw me in prison. They didn't need to have any reason or anything. Just like that."

Waseem honked his horn lightly at the taxi in front of us, letting him know we wanted to get by. The taxi moved off to the side slightly as the driver tried to park. Waseem maneuvered the van forward ever so slowly through the traffic jam.

"In Abu Ghraib I was tortured," he said. "They did terrible things. I was shocked with electricity and other things like that. They did it just for fun. They didn't ask me any questions. I wasn't charged with anything, You know I am strong. But there was one thing . . ." his voice started to break. I thought he was going to start to cry but he pulled himself together. I could tell he was seeing the scene in his head.

"In the same area as me there was another prisoner, and they were just tired of torturing him so they brought in his wife and made him sit and watch while they raped her. After that, they brought his small son and made him watch as they raped him. Just like that." I stayed silent, not knowing what would come next. The traffic was letting up now and we were getting closer to the Dulaimi building. I wondered what made Waseem share this personal information with me. Clearly, it was not something he talked about eagerly. It had been hard for him. "I got out when my family paid a bribe," he said. "It was difficult for them to find the money, but there was no other choice."

We arrived at the edge of the compound set up to protect the Australian ambassador. Waseem killed the engine and we shook hands, touching our palms to our hearts afterward in the Arab tradition.

"Tomorrow I'll meet you at your house," I said. "I'll take a taxi. It's silly for you to drive through all this traffic if we're going to end up going to Showle or Sadr City."

Waseem thanked me for the consideration and I got out of his car and was left with my thoughts. As I walked up the stairs to my apartment, I guessed that Waseem's need to share had something to do with American actions against Muqtada al-Sadr, whose family had also been persecuted by Saddam.

At the same time, I knew that Waseem—like most middle-class Iraqis—had no affection for Muqtada and his rabid rhetoric. In any case, things had not turned out the way he had hoped when the Americans invaded, and the situation was about to get worse.

Soon after *al-Hawza*'s closure, all hell broke loose. Within a week, the U.S. military would be at war with almost the entirety of Iraq's Arab population—attacking the Sunni insurgency in the west of Iraq and the Shia followers of Muqtada al-Sadr in the south of the country. The capital, Baghdad, would be Ground Zero in both fights and almost all the goodwill inspired by America's removal of Saddam would be eliminated. In April 2004, America would lose Iraq.

.12.

THE WAR BEGINS

On March 31, 2004, four Americans were pulled from the wreckage of their burning car near Fallujah. Jubilant Iraqis then beat them with sticks before dragging their charred corpses through the streets of the city. Finally, the men's carcasses were hung from the old Fallujah Bridge over the Euphrates River in the center of town. That day also brought news of the combat deaths of five U.S. soldiers who were involved in stepped-up American patrols in and around Fallujah.

Like most people in Iraq, I saw the matter unfold on TV and didn't think much of it. Like most of the people around me, I was disgusted, but although the killings were more gruesome than usual, they fit a familiar pattern.

It was quickly revealed, for example, that the Americans killed were not civilians, but former soldiers contracted to the occupation authority as mercenaries, much like the white South Africans contracted to train guards for Erinys. Their company, North Carolina–based Blackwater Security, supplied workers who, among other things, made up Bremer's personal bodyguard group.

So perhaps I should have listened more closely to the condemnation that came from U.S. Administrator L. Paul Bremer, a stocky longtime associate of Henry Kissinger, who didn't speak Arabic and seemed perennially exhausted by his work. At a graduation ceremony for Iraqi police cadets, Bremer vowed revenge: "Their deaths," he said, "will not go unpunished."

Still, I didn't think much about the dragging deaths in Fallujah. Almost every day, it seemed, a soldier or foreign contractor was killed in Iraq, and each time it brought a bellicose statement from Washington. Angry words came with the attacks on Shi'ite pilgrims at Ashoura and the bombing of the Mount Lebanon Hotel, but U.S. authorities never did anything radically different afterward. They just stepped up their patrols, arrested more people, and incarcerated them at Abu Ghraib without trial.

I asked Waseem if, to underscore this point, we could make the rounds at Baghdad's hospitals. There we could report on the grisly violence that affected most Iraqis every day.

In al-Yarmuk Hospital, which the Americans had attacked during the war, we found Ma'an Desere in the emergency room. The white-haired Sunni Arab wore a wispy beard and a checkered black-and-white *dishdash*. He stood over his son, who was hooked up to an oxygen tank, his chest full of bullet holes. "He was hit by somebody," the old man said. "I don't know who."

"If he's a man, he should come and face me and I will drink him up!" the old man screamed, gesticulating as if firing a machine gun. "Only a woman would hit you and run away. Cowards! They stopped the car. They hit my son and left."

In the year since the Bush Administration took over Iraq, Baghdad's city morgue had registered more than 5,000 deaths—more than double the tally in a typical year under the Saddam regime. The figure didn't even include those killed in fighting between insurgents and American forces, since resistance fighters didn't usually take those bodies to the morgue.

The head of the gunshot ward at this hospital told me was treating 80 victims a day. He said most of the deaths came during armed robberies. "It's all because of the U.S. and England," Ma'an Desere continued to rant, standing over the body of his dying son. "All of these things have been done by America and England. Our enemy is America. This," he said, pointing at his son, "is because of them." He said he had a message for the Americans. "There is God," he screamed, pointing his finger at the sky. "We're standing with God. No one can face him. Not Bush. Not America. God is stronger than all of them."

I wanted to keep talking with Ma'an, but Waseem grabbed my elbow and led me out of the gunshot ward, thanking everyone for their time. "The situation is about to get dangerous," he said. "I know these people."

As we walked down the main hallway of Yarmuk Hospital, we saw a small group of young nurses off in a corner, smoking. "Let's find the most beautiful one and talk to her," Waseem requested, smiling.

"And your wife," I asked, "she won't mind?"

"It is only for looking, not for touching," he said. "There is nothing forbidden in looking at a beautiful woman."

I told Waseem he could pick the nurse. As we approached, we could hear that they were talking about violence—not the dragging deaths in Fallujah, but the type of violence that had come to affect the everyday lives of all Iraqis.

The most beautiful among the nurses was a 22-year-old woman named Taleibet Tamrir, so Waseem asked her to relate what had happened. "A neighbor of ours was kidnapped," she said. "Her car was stopped and the kidnappers got into the car. She is an old woman who wears the veil. We don't know where she is now."

Kidnappings had become common in Iraq since the fall of Saddam Hussein. With unemployment high and law enforcement weak, ransom was seen as an easy way to make money.

Indeed, in Taleibat's neighborhood kidnappings had become so common that the same day, the nurse said, "there was a woman who was walking to the bank. She was walking home at around six in the evening. She screamed and her captors let her go. She was lucky—she could have been killed."

"Are you scared to go to work?" I asked.

"Yes," she said. "Before the war, I would come on my own, but now my father drives me to work in the morning and home in the afternoon. Otherwise I don't go out."

I was still going out, though. Not at night, when the lack of electricity and the dark streets made me feel unsafe. But during my time off during the day, I enjoyed walking up Karada, the main street that ran past the Dulaimi. It was a ten-minute walk from the Tigris, although the actual approach to the river was blocked by an American checkpoint (the other side being the Green Zone). Still, I needed exercise, so I walked along the street past a lovely restuarant with a romantic garden where people could eat lunch, past a herd of sheep being slaughtered on the sidewalk, and past two American tanks that were holding up traffic (the soldiers were ordering strawberry ice cream). A bit farther along I hit a refrigerator-and-microwave shopping district, then a leather market with ten shops selling genuine leather, then a CD store where I picked up a Barbra Streisand album to give to Waseem.

On my way back, I bought groceries—six liters of bottled water (with only intermittent electricity to run the treatment plants, the tap water was still not clean), mango juice, coffee, tea, sugar—and for breakfast, *lavas* (flatbread), cheese, honey, and olives. I planned to sit on my fifth-floor balcony overlooking the Tigris, and also Baghdad's smoky al-Durra oil refinery, the next morning.

I was also happy because I had a new roommate, Andy Berends, a documentary filmmaker from New York and a good friend of James from their college days. He was a quiet man who would sit in a chair listening to music on headphones before bursting out with a wry comment that would cause those around him to laugh as well. His arrival cut down the monthly rental costs and gave me some company.

Despite the closure of *al-Hawza* newspaper and the killings in Fallujah, everything seemed to be going along about the same as it had been. What I hadn't counted on was the plans Washington had for al-Sadr and Fallujah.

While Waseem and I were making the rounds at al-Yarmuk Hospital, U.S. officials were promising revenge in the Green Zone. At a regular press conference, Paul Bremer's spokesman Dan Senor promised reporters that the American mercenaries killed in Fallujah "did not die in vain. The Coalition, Americans, and others came here to help the people of Iraq," he said. Unlike Bremer, Senor was completely unflappable. Built like a football player, with a wide chest and flat-top haircut, he seemed to enjoy praising America at thrice-weekly press conferences, at one of which he said, the Coalition:

> came to help Iraq recover from decades of dictatorship, to help the people of Iraq gain the elections, democracy, and freedom desired by the overwhelming majority of the Iraqi people. These murders are a

painful outrage for us in the Coalition. But they will not derail the march to stability and democracy in Iraq. The cowards and ghouls who acted yesterday represent the worst of society.

Senor was followed to the podium by the U.S. military spokesman, Brigadier General Mark Kimmitt. "The Coalition is stepping up its offensive tempo to kill or capture anti-Coalition elements and enemies of the Iraqi people," he said. The Marines—a more ruthless fighting force than the Army—were being called back into Iraq to lay siege to Fallujah. They were getting ready to invade.

"It's going to be deliberate," the general said of the coming attack. "It will be precise and it will be overwhelming. We will not rush in to make things worse. We will plan our way through this and we will reestablish control of that city and we will pacify that city."

Watching television, I couldn't help but remember my trip to Fallujah with Raphaël a year earlier. At that time, there was a great diversity of opinion in the city about the Americans. Some people were happy about the fall of Saddam, others—who had benefited under the former regime—were angry. Everyone was unhappy about the lack of electricity, clean water, and other essential services. I wondered if the pro-Saddam imam who preached against violence back in May was still speaking out for peace.

No mention was made at the press conference of Muqtada al-Sadr or the closure of his movement's newspaper, a situation I found odd since Bremer's confrontational stand against Sadr seemed like a major departure from his administration's earlier policy of negotiation. It also seemed odd since, despite all their angry rhetoric, Muqtada al-Sadr's movement had yet to call for armed resistance.

That would change a few days later, though, when the U.S. military arrested one of Sadr's chief advisors, Mustafa Yakoubi, and announced a warrant for Sadr's arrest in connection with the killing of a pro-American ayatollah the year before. The warrant itself was suspect. Defense Secretary Donald Rumsfeld would say only that it had been issued by a "courageous Iraqi judge" whose name was withheld for security reasons. The trade association of Iraqi lawyers and judges said the document had no legal standing. On the streets of Baghdad, most everyone saw the situation the same way: America had decided to take out al-Sadr.

With that in mind, I was most interested in one of Paul Bremer's explanations, which was carried on the BBC. I thought of Muqtada Sadr's elections, traffic police, hospital guards, and Islamic courts. "He's effectively attempting to establish his authority in place of the legitimate Iraqi government," Bremer told reporters. "We will not tolerate that."

Accused of a murder (which he may or may not have ordered), his newspaper shuttered, his organization deemed illegal, Muqtada al-Sadr declared *jihad* and urged his supporters to "terrorize the enemy." Observing a sit-in at one of Najaf's holiest mosques, the cleric said that street demonstrations had become pointless. It was the first time he had urged his followers to opt for armed resistance.

Sadr's revolt was ferocious. Thousands of his followers—young, poor Shi'ite men—took to the streets across the center and south of Iraq. They carried Kalashnikovs and rocket-propelled grenades. They called themselves the *Jeysh al-Mehdi*, a name that referred to the Imam al-Mehdi, whose arrival religious Shia believe will remedy the world's evils and establish a new world with only one religion and one government. They quickly defeated the Spanish army, which occupied the holy city of Najaf, and battles raged through Baghdad, Amarah, Nassariya, Karbala, and Kuwt. In Basra, Iraq's second-largest city, Sadr's militia briefly seized the governor's office.

Since I was in Baghdad, the easiest thing for me to do was go to

Sadr City, which was just east of Waseem's house near Mustansuriye University. Hospital officials had told the Arab media that more than 75 Iraqis and 10 American servicemen had died in the last 24 hours. With a sense of danger, I hailed a taxi whose driver I did not know and rode it to Waseem's front door. His wife Yisrah, an educated engineer who dropped her career when the couple's first child was born, served us breakfast. Then we got into Waseem's maroon van, and he drove toward Sadr City.

On the State Department–funded *Radyo Sawa* we heard American authorities downplay Sadr's uprising. *He has only a few thousand diehard followers,* we were told; he would be eliminated immediately. We knew these statements were false.

As we approached the entrance to the sprawling slum, we saw dozens of American tanks parked up and down the main streets, blocking most access points. "If I feel anything at all, we leave, that's it," Waseem said, trying to maneuver his van around the tanks. "These people, they have no education. They will do anything—just like that."

"Okay," I agreed. "First, we should go to the hospital. That should be the safest place to be. There, we should be able to find out who was being killed."

Waseem sighed and twisted the wheels of his car around another bend, turning off the radio. We pulled up next to el-Ubaidi Hospital, which had been guarded by al-Sadr's forces for months. Iraqi women in black *chador* and young Iraqi men ran in and out of the hospital. Every so often, a group of Sadr's followers would parade out of the hospital with a coffin, singing songs of martyrdom.

When we reached the receiving area, the receptionist told us that we could not enter the hospital. We would first have to get permission from the ministry, she said, a process that could take days.

As we wondered what to do, an Iraqi cameraman from CNN showed up with a young sheik from al-Sadr's office. The man from the Sadr office was not more than 25, with a large black beard and wearing a black turban. He ordered the hospital officials to let the CNN cameraman in, and Waseem and I followed with his permission.

Inside the hospital, we found Sadr's followers in complete control. A group of young sheiks stood at the entrance, and they directed our group toward the hospital director's office. We walked quickly. There, the head of the hospital, an older doctor with a graying mustache and wearing a white lab coat told us that dozens of gunshot victims had entered his hospital since hostilities had erupted. He did not yet know the number of the dead.

The young sheik from al-Sadr's office got up. It was time to go to the next location—the gunshot ward. He raced through the hallways of the hospital at breakneck speed. When we reached our destination, he pointed at a teenager whose gut was covered with bandages and said that we should interview him. This was the only patient I would be allowed to interview.

"What is your name?" I asked cautiously.

"Ali Hussein." He could barely speak the words. I noticed he was being fed by two IV tubes, both entering at his stomach.

"How old are you?"

"I am fifteen years old." He looked much younger. Like so many Iraqi boys who grew up during the sanctions period after the 1991 Gulf War, his growth had been stunted.

"Do you have anything you want to say?" I asked.

"I was standing in my doorway and I was shot," he said, lifting his head up ever so slightly to see who was asking the questions. "It was an American bullet."

"What do you think about the Americans?" came my question. It felt gratuitous, but this is the job of a reporter.

"I don't have anything to say to the Americans. It's just between them and God." His head collapsed back onto his hospital bed.

I looked around. The other victims seemed very similar to Ali Hussein. Most of them were young boys, who seemed always to run outside curiously at the slightest abnormal noise. The American soldiers probably shot them, I thought, thinking they were fighters.

When you are a soldier in a war zone and you see a young boy standing in your peripheral vision, you don't have time to notice whether he's armed. You just shoot. I felt sure that none of the boys in the hospital were fighters. Sadr's warriors wanted to be martyred, to fight to the death.

As we left the hospital, another casket was carried out, this one without much ceremony. Just a few weeping women and men walking alongside.

The CNN cameraman turned to us. "We're going to the police station. Do you want to come?" We accepted.

A half-dozen tanks and armored fighting vehicles guarded the Iraqi police station closest to the hospital. Iraqi Police Lieutenant Jasseem Mohammed told us the U.S. Army had retaken it from Sadr's forces that morning. He said that Sadr's forces had looted his offices. The young sheik from Sadr's office objected, saying the police had no proof that it was Sadr's forces who looted the station, but his statement was disregarded by everyone present.

The extent of the looting was almost comical. The lieutenant stood in a bare room with absolutely no supplies, not even a desk or file cabinet. Sadr's forces had taken everything.

Another member of the Iraqi police listed what had been taken from the weapons storeroom, which was also completely bare. "All my guns have been stolen," he said. "Sixty-one Kalashnikovs, sixteen hundred Kalashnikov bullets, eleven hundred pistol bullets, four bandoliers, and four walkie-talkies. Also they took five pistols and six Kalashnikovs that were being held as evidence of criminal activity—and two ceiling fans."

We said good-bye to the CNN cameraman and the sheik from al-Sadr's office and walked back to Waseem's car. Outside, the air throbbed with the loud hum of the idling tanks. Amidst U.S. soldiers in body armor and Ray-Ban sunglasses were many young children. With nothing else to do, they played soccer among the tanks. When they saw a journalist walk by, they abandoned their game and crowded around me, chanting the name of their leader, Muqtada al-Sadr.

Waseem was already in the van, eager to leave. I got into the car and we drove off. "Where now?" Waseem said, as we drove out of Sadr City.

"I don't know," I said, thinking. "I think we need one more perspective. Maybe Mustansuriye University. It's near your house, and Sadr's support there is strong. But they're students, so it's not so dangerous."

"Okay," Waseem sighed. I knew he wished he was done for the day.

When we arrived at the university, a pro-Sadr rally was already in progress. Hundreds of students marched through the center of campus. Their chant, translated, meant: "The dead want a brave people, so we won't follow the law of Bremer."

The students had a list of demands. They wanted the arrest warrant for Muqtada al-Sadr to be revoked, and his advisor Mustafa Yakoubi to be released. They also demanded that *al-Hawza* newspaper be allowed to reopen. The demand letter ended, "You must accede to these demands or . . ." Nothing followed the ellipse.

I asked the student at the head of the demonstration what the ellipse meant. "We will act according to the situation that we face," he replied. His name was Wassam Mehdi Hussein, and he was the head of the Islamic Union of Iraqi Students. I asked him if he stood by al-Sadr's declaration of *jihad* against the occupation. "Of course," he replied. "We will use any means, peaceful and violent."

"This week," I said, "marks the first time a lot of Shia have fought the Americans since the beginning of the occupation. Before this, the war has mostly been from the Sunni in places like Fallujah and Samara. In fact, the Americans are sealing off Fallujah as we speak."

At this observation, another student demonstrator stepped forward. He gave his name as Ali Mohammed.

This violence only started when the Americans closed *al-Hawza* newspaper and arrested Yakoubi. We don't want to fight the Americans. We are very grateful to them. They are very dear to us because they released us from Saddam. But at the same time we want them to do something for humanity. A lot of people are suffering from hunger and sitting at home having no work. These things make the situation bad and then we turn to explosions. We want to respect them and we want them to respect us.

Such respect didn't appear to be immediately forthcoming, though. When I got home in the afternoon and flipped on the TV, I saw footage of American Apache helicopters attacking several neighborhoods in Baghdad—both Sunni and Shia. Instead of moving to broker a peace, the Americans had escalated the hostility.

.13.

APACHE HELICOPTER
STRIKES

From the news reports of larger outlets, it was difficult to determine the exact location of the helicopter strikes. But the televised footage was spectacular, and when I learned that one of the helicopters had been used against Sadr's forces in Showle, I asked Waseem to call Sheik Selim, a member of Showle's local council who was active in Muqtada al-Sadr's movement.

"Hello, Sheik!" Waseem yelled into the phone as we left his house the next morning. Cell-phone connections in Baghdad were never good. After an exchange of pleasantries, Waseem asked if it would be possible for us to meet.

"It has been a terrible night," the sheik replied, "and I am still washing the dead. Maybe some other time." The phone cut out.

It had indeed been quite a night. Not only had the Americans unleashed air power in residential neighborhoods, but Sadr's forces had built on their early successes in Najaf and taken the cities of Karbala and Kufa—giving the young cleric control of most of Shia Islam's sacred sites. In Fallujah, a massive U.S. air assault had begun.

I asked Waseem to call Sheik Selim again, but his phone was off.

"He probably doesn't want to say anything over the phone," Waseem noted. "Since he's a member of the local council, the Americans have his phone number. They could be tracking his location every time he speaks on the phone."

"Well, let's just go to Sadr's Showle office," I suggested. "We can ask them what's happened."

Waseem wasn't crazy about this idea. A grown man with a wife and two children to look after, he was acutely aware of issues of safety. When I had shown up at his home that morning he had suggested we stop working for a while. I countered that times of crisis were when honest reporting was most needed. Now I argued that given the events all around us, heading to Showle was the safest option—considerably safer than the alternatives of driving to Najaf, Karbala, or Fallujah, journeys that would include long, unsafe stretches of highway.

As we drove toward Showle, Waseem and I experienced a rare phenomenon: There was no traffic. Everyone knew we were entering a new era of violence in Iraq, and most Iraqis, like Waseem, preferred to stay at home and watch to see exactly what form the violence would take. In the car, Waseem told me he had pulled his two children out of school.

"For how long have you pulled them out?" I asked.

"We will have to wait and see," he replied. "It depends on the situation."

Then, gunfire. First we heard it faintly, but as we traveled through the Sunni stronghold of Adamiya it got louder and louder.

Waseem switched off the radio and we both strained our ears, try-ing to figure out what was happening. The only gunfire came from AK-47s and other light arms. No tanks or helicopters, which seemed to indicate no Americans.

Waseem circled around in his van until we saw them. It was a fu-neral. Hundreds of supporters of the resistance were firing their guns into the air. Waseem parked the van across the street from the Abu Hanifa Mosque, where opponents of the American occu-pation had gathered and preached resistance on the anniversary of the start of the war. From this parking spot, it would be easy to speed across the bridge that linked Adamiya with Shia-dominated Kadamiyya if a quick getaway became necessary.

Waseem paid a parking attendant 250 *dinar* (15 cents) to watch the van and we walked quietly toward the procession. I did my best not to draw any attention to myself. With my Semitic features, mustache, and button-down shirt and slacks, it was easy for me to blend in on any Iraqi street, provided I didn't open my mouth. So I remained silent, carried my minidisk recorder in my pocket, and placed a special concealed microphone in my ear.

Waseem saw somebody he knew. "Abu Yassir!" he yelled, mo-tioning for me to join him in the middle of the procession. "What happened?"

"You know how the Americans come through here each night in their hummers," the man said. "Every night we attack them, and last night was no different. But this time after we attacked their hummer, the Americans came with Apaches. They tried to kill the resistance fighters but these men are very fast. They just hit and run away. So they only killed one boy—a twelve-year-old who was standing unarmed in front of the mosque watching like it was a football match."

So the body being buried today was that of a 12-year-old boy. With this information in hand, we rushed back to the van. I looked over my shoulder as the resistance brought bodies into the mosque. At its head were a group of imams, most of them young, chanting slogans of martyrdom.

"You hear the way they speak?" Waseem said as he turned on the ignition. "It is the same voice that you can hear on the TV from the imams of Hamas in Palestine. They are using this voice for the cameras—for al-Jazeera and al-Arabiya—to link their struggle to the Palestinians. To them, a martyred child is good, because it makes America look like Israel." Waseem sneered as he drove away.

In Showle, the municipal building had been abandoned by the local council. There were a few guards outside. They told us no one was inside. We would need to go to the Sadr office.

In the streets of Showle, the anger was palpable. On the main street leading to the Sadr office, a cheering crowd had gathered around the smoldering remains of an American military vehicle. Waseem rolled down his window. He refused to allow me to leave the van or speak in English.

"We're from Radio France," he told the crowd. "What happened here?"

"What's happened here is against the Americans," a young man responded. "We want them to leave Iraq."

"But what happened?" Waseem pressed.

"I don't follow Muqtada, I just want the Americans to leave," he responded. "A few young people just lost their patience, so they did this, but the real thing didn't begin yet."

"Yes, but what *happened*?"

"After last night's battle," he said, "the Americans came to the hospital to take one of the wounded men. When they tried to arrest him, other people resisted. That's when we destroyed this hummer."

Another young man jumped in front of my microphone. "The

Americans go round and round and make us uncomfortable," he said. "So our brothers in the *mujahadeen* attacked their car. They block the street, always checking us, and a lot of people are in prison, including Sheik Yakoubi. We want them to release the prisoners—from Sheik Yakoubi on down. These are our demands."

"I heard there was a helicopter attack last night," Waseem interrupted.

"Yes," the first man said. "They hit the mosque with the Apache."

"Who was in the mosque?" Waseem asked.

"A lot of wise men," he said, "and people who were carrying weapons against the Americans. But the Americans didn't just hit the mosque. Their Apache also hit the apartment building next-door. Three people were killed, and all of them were women hiding in their home."

"Thank you very much," Waseem said, and we were off to the Sadr office, an old Ba'ath Party headquarters that had been plastered with posters of Muqtada al-Sadr, his slain father, and his slain uncle. When we explained that we were journalists, we were quickly shown into the waiting room.

"You have a camera?" the young men in the Sadr office kept asking, anxious for publicity. Many of them were sheiks in white turbans. All were under 30 years old. Waseem and I waited among them until a door opened and we were shown into the office of an older black-turbaned man, Sheik Nasser al-Sa'adi. He had a long black beard graying in parts, and angry eyes.

We asked him about the Apache attack.

"For two days the people who normally live regular days took part in peaceful demonstrations," Sheik Nasser said, the anxious-looking young sheiks having gathered around him. "Then the American troops started shooting the people and a lot of people got killed."

He portrayed his followers as complete innocents and said the Apache had fired even though Sadr's followers did not fire a single shot. This didn't seem possible to me, so I changed the subject.

"In Washington," I said, "George Bush has compared Sayyed Muqtada to Hassan Nasrallah of Hizbollah. What do you think of that?"

"We are defending our country and demanding rights for the people," Sheik Nasser responded quickly. "Any good man—like Hizbollah's Hassan Nasrallah and Muqtada al-Sadr—any decent man in the world should feel very proud of us. The Americans are making the people angry by using the Apache helicopter and killing people in their houses, killing the innocent. We have a picture of a child whose face is disfigured by the bullets."

"Why do you think America has chosen this time to attack al-Sadr?" I asked, eager to get the perspective of an older, more experienced person in the Sadr movement. "They have said he is a criminal for killing Ayatollah Khoei, but that was a year ago. They have decided to close the newspaper now and arrest Yakoubi. Why now?"

"There is some kind of political game going on now," Nasser said. "They made this confrontation before the hand-over of political power [June 30] in order to delay it. If you notice, now they begin to say that they will have to stay for a long time to keep the security." This seemed far-fetched to me, but another, somewhat similar analysis was possible: that the U.S. military had attacked al-Sadr in advance of the June 30 hand-over in an effort to prevent him from taking part in any future Iraqi government.

I changed tack, asking the sheik why the local council had been abandoned after the Sadr movement had worked so hard to take control of it through elections.

"First, the elections were a long time ago, before all this," Sheik Nasser said, indicating the American attacks. Clearly, he was following al-Sadr's edict: that the time for peaceful organizing was over and the time for armed struggle had begun.

"Now," he continued, "everything is clear. The decent men didn't want to sit on the Governing Council. They are traitors. They're only serving to gain personal wealth and position."

Once the occupation is over, he said, "History will remember who stood where. The Arab people stand for their history and we will recall where these Governing Council people stood and where the decent people were standing."

After we had thanked Sheik Nasser and shaken hands with all the young white-turbaned sheiks, Waseem and I were led out of Sadr's compound by a few of his young, armed followers.

Back at Waseem's house, we flipped on the TV to al-Jazeera. We learned that Iraq's most respected cleric, Grand Ayatollah Ali Sistani, had weighed in. In a carefully worded statement, Sistani said that Sadr's cause was righteous, but that there was no reason to resort to violence. It was a significantly softer statement than the ones coming from Washington and from Iraq's Bush Administration–appointed interior minister, Ayad Allawi, a former Ba'athist turned CIA asset who had run a Pentagon-funded organization dedicated to promoting a military coup in Iraq before the fall of Saddam Hussein.

In remarks broadcast live on al-Jazeera, Allawi compared the violence unleashed by al-Sadr to the suicide bombings of al-Qaeda. He said both forces wanted to "stop Iraq from heading toward democracy and liberation," and that they would be stopped.

Upon hearing Allawi's remarks, Waseem sat bolt upright, scowling with disapproval. "They can't just put them together like that!" he screamed at the TV. "You know, I really hate Sadr, but he is nothing like bin Laden, he's just a little crazy, that's all."

But Allawi's comments were important. He was being groomed by the U.S. to hold a higher position of power, and therefore his comments could be seen as coming straight from Washington. Since the fall of Saddam Hussein, the United States had appointed Allawi to more and more important positions—first to a seat on the Governing Council, then to the office of head of the Interior Ministry. Finally, on June 30, 2004, Allawi would be appointed prime minister.

The most interesting comment, however, came from the Americans themselves. Faced with the initial success of Sadr's forces, who had taken control of most of southern Iraq, Defense Secretary Donald Rumsfeld and Chairman of the Joint Chiefs of Staff General Richard Myers called a press conference. Myers was asked what had contributed to the upsurge in violence, and his answer seemed to confirm a thought that had been brewing in my mind: that the United States had provoked Sadr to violence.

"What contributed to this was our offensive action," Myers told the assembled reporters. "[We] shut down his newspaper. Went after one of his lieutenants, Yakoubi, and it was not unanticipated or unexpected that we would find some resistance to that. They think they can stop progress for twenty-five million Iraqis. That's not going to happen."

What was unclear, though, was why the United States had suddenly decided to try to kill al-Sadr after dealing with him as a legitimate political force for over a year. One theory was that Bremer was afraid that the cleric's success in infrastructure projects and the popularity of his anti-American rhetoric would allow him to assume greater power after the planned June 30th hand-over of sovereignty. Another theory, equally plausible, was that the criminalization of al-Sadr was linked to Israel's assassination of Hamas leader Sheik Ahmed Yasin, which had occurred at approximately the same time. The Bush Administration had supported that assassination, and Bush himself regularly linked Sadr with Hamas and Hizbollah, groups that Sadr spoke of in increasingly glowing terms.

Regardless of the reason, the attack on al-Sadr had been a huge miscalculation. "They think they can kill al-Sadr just like that," Waseem said as we turned off the TV, "but what they don't understand is that by attacking al-Sadr they make him very big. Now all the people will rally for al-Sadr. Not for al-Sadr exactly, because in any case most people don't like him, but they will defend their brother against the foreigner."

At the Dulaimi later that afternoon, I got a phone call from Nadeem Hamid, Waseem's brother, with whom James had been living for months.

"Do you have room for James?" he asked.

"Of course," I answered.

"Stay where you are. We'll be there soon," Nadeem said definitively as he turned off his phone.

An hour later, Nadeem arrived with James and most of his belongings, which they had thrown together very quickly. After we lugged the bags up the stairs, James had trouble making sense of them when it came time to unpack.

"Some friends of Nadeem began talking to him about the risk of having an American living in his house," James said in explanation, but none was needed. The atmosphere on the Iraqi street had deteriorated alarmingly in just a few days. It was as though a giant *"click"* had occurred in the minds of the vast majority of Iraqi people. Whatever they thought of al-Sadr or the Sunni resistance in Fallujah, they would not stand for a war against such a large portion of their own population. We offered James the couch and he accepted gratefully.

As he settled in at the Dulaimi, James explained that what most frustrated him was his inability to continue to go out and film. It was no longer safe for him to make his movie. He told the story of what had happened the last time he had tried to film one of his regular subjects, a young AIDS patient, and his family in a farm south of Baghdad:

> Nadeem and I drove out to the family's farm, as we had done so many times in the past. But this time the family seemed downcast and not so happy to see us. When we sat down with them they told us that a group of men had come to them, men they didn't know. They claimed to represent the Iraqi resistance. They said they knew that an American had been coming to their house to film, and they threatened to kill me if I came there again. They also threatened to kill the family, because they had allowed me to visit them as a guest. In Makhmudia this has been a growing problem, not only for foreigners. According to the family, Iraqis have been captured and killed there simply because they were strangers in the area, and suspected of being spies for the Americans. One Iraqi man who operated a roadside soft-drink stand was killed simply because he made conversation with the American soldiers who stopped there.

James dropped onto the couch and threw his hands in the air. "I blame America for this completely," he ranted. "All of this was entirely predictable. It is an entirely predictable result of the policies they put in place and the actions they took. America attacked Fallujah. America attacked al-Sadr, and now there is nowhere to work."

James stared for a while up at the fake ivy and ceiling fan above his head. He wanted to rest but was so aggravated that he returned to his rant.

"It goes back to even before that," he continued. "The failure to prevent looting, the failure to protect civilian infrastructure, the failure to understand Iraqi cultural norms, the rounding up of whole families and sending them to Abu Ghraib, and so much more. Now, because of this long list of failures, I can't work anymore. I blame America!"

A year before, I would have argued with James, urging patience with the occupation, suggesting that maybe the situation would improve. I would have argued that the former regime's brutality could not be swept aside without some death and destruction. But now, James got no argument from me. Everything I had worried about in the early days of the occupation had come to pass. A year into the occupation, the streets were still unsafe and there was still only electricity a few hours a day. Most of the water in the country was still dirty. Hospital officials complained that they hadn't received regular deliveries of medicine in months. There was no doubt that, on a functional level, the country had worked better under Saddam Hussein.

Now, on top of that, the Americans were destroying, once and for all, their status as liberators.

With James settled in, our little one-bedroom apartment became quite a mess. With the streets outside so dangerous, we spent more and more time at home. Andy started smoking, and dirty ashtrays began to populate the apartment. We all started drinking, and I drank too much. Unable to exercise and frequently intoxicated, I put on weight. My dreams became increasingly grotesque, my headaches more frequent, and I started to worry about my own sanity. I was fairly sure that I would be able to behave responsibly and avoid becoming a victim of violence, but I was less sure about the state of my brain, and this led to even more drinking—often while watching an inane movie on Channel 2, trying—without success—to relax.

.14.

IT'S NOT SAFE
TO GO OUTSIDE

As I spent more time at home, I began to notice a change in the clientele of the two hotels and one furnished apartment building adjacent to the Dulaimi. In the early days of the occupation, when the Dulaimi had been filled with Iraqi newlyweds, these more expensive hotels were occupied by foreign aid workers and journalists. Now the aid workers were leaving and the Dulaimi was full of journalists. The nicer hotels, meantime, had filled up with mercenaries, older former soldiers with Australian, white South African, and South American accents who were paid to guard contractors who stayed at still-nicer hotels that were barricaded inside the Green Zone.

The mercenaries could be found most evenings sitting around the dining rooms of these hotels, or sitting poolside, drinking beer, with automatic weapons slung over their shoulders. Even though they were paid big money to guard the contractors, they didn't have to do much work. They simply told the contractors that it wasn't safe to go out and work, and that it would be better to wait for safer times to engage in reconstruction.

I never talked to these mercenaries, though their proximity to the Dulaimi caused me to worry that the area would become a target of the resistance. The situation had become so polarized between the Iraqi people and the occupation forces that mere proximity to the outsiders could result in death. This could be clearly seen in the relationship between U.S. troops and the people. It was no longer possible to simply walk up to American soldiers and talk to them as I had done in the early days. They had their own bunker mentality, and the only way to really gain access to them was to become embedded. Given such a choice, I decided to focus exclusively on the Iraqi people, trying to capture as much of their hopes and dreams as possible, and striving for the maximum diversity in viewpoint among the Iraqi public—a goal that was admittedly difficult under the circumstances.

All of this was before the United States Marine Corps opened a massive air assault on Fallujah. After the first few days, hospital officials reported that more than 200 Iraqis had died. In the lobby of the Dulaimi, al-Jazeera was on almost non-stop and the employees of the building—nearly all of whom had family in Fallujah—crowded around the television, trying to learn something about their loved ones.

While the U.S. and British press broadcasted reports almost exclusively from government press conferences and embedded journalists, al-Jazeera broadcasted live from inside Fallujah. Their correspondent, Ahmed Monseur, was almost everywhere, it seemed. One moment he stood atop one of the city's clinics relaying the latest Iraqi casualty figures in real time. The next moment he was inside the clinic showing images of dead Iraqi women and children. Later, he would be at the site of a former mosque destroyed by an American air strike.

"A fine thing your country has done," said a voice from behind me. It was Hamza al-Dulaimi, the owner of the building. "Two of my cousins are dead in this bombardment. Can you tell me why they are dead?"

I offered my condolences. "I would love to interview you about this," I suggested. "It would be a way for your voice to carry back to the people in the U.S. Maybe that way they could make George Bush stop this."

He agreed to the interview, but added in a quaking voice, "I don't think the American people can do anything about Bush, but I thank you for the opportunity. Maybe my voice will carry somewhere where it will do some good."

We walked into his office, where we had initially negotiated my room rate. He asked one of his employees to bring us tea. He told me again that two of his cousins, both men, aged 25 and 31, had been killed.

"And were they carrying guns?" It was an important question. The Bush Administration claimed that each of its attacks was carefully targeted at terrorist cells.

"No," Hamza said. "They were just civilian people. They stayed inside their home because Mr. Bremer gave them an order. He said 'If you stay in your house you will be safe.' They stayed and did not do anything. They are just a civil family. Then the bomb came down on their house. Two killed and five injured."

U.S. Administrator Paul Bremer had announced a ceasefire in Fallujah that morning, saying that humanitarian aid would be allowed in and civilians would be allowed to leave. Negotiations were to take place between respected clerics and U.S. Marines, but as I talked to Hamza, American helicopter attacks continued. Hamza told me that after two days, his dead family members still lay in their living room.

"For two days," he said, tears welling up in his eyes. "For two days they put ice from the refrigerator over them. Two days, they spent two days rotting in the house and now he [the head of the family] is looking to bury them in his garden. Maybe he will put them in the garden now. But he can't put them there yet, because if he goes outside he will be killed. Everybody who goes outside his house, maybe the military of America will kill him. This is a difficult thing. You know, you are living with two guys who were killed and five injured. What can you do?"

Hamza started to sob. I tried to change the subject to a matter more political and less personal.

"I was struck by the fact that Bush attacked Fallujah and the Mehdi Army without any approval from the Governing Council," I said. "Bush did this, and after that the Governing Council made some statements, but—"

"I'm sorry for this word," he responded. "But they are rubbish. This group, they take money from Mr. Bush and so they are rubbish."

"So you don't have any faith that they will be able to make some solution?"

"No," he said. "We hope so of course, but I think there is no solution for this case. Mr. Bush won't give up and the *mujahadeen* say 'We will keep our resistance for al-Fallujah.' So there is no solution."

"Has the invasion of Fallujah changed the way you think about the Americans?"

"I think everyone in Iraq hates the American people now," he said. "Because before Saddam fell down, many people in America were going out of their houses and saying 'We do not want war.'

Why is there nobody demonstrating now to say 'No' to what America is doing in Fallujah. Why? Why does nobody demonstrate like before and say 'Stop this war that's killing civilian people?'"

"Anything else?" I asked. The emotion was such that I had to end the interview, lest we both break down crying.

"Please if you can help the civilian people inside Fallujah then anyway please help them because we are very tired and we have lost many, many civilian people inside," he said. "I hear from my cousin, maybe five hundred people have been killed, nobody helped them. They cannot get to treatment. We have just one hospital, a small one, and it is impossible to get to. Take this voice, please help us."

I turned off my tape recorder and rose to shake Hamza's hand in a sign of our shared humanity and respect. I had turned to walk up-stairs to my room, when I saw an image on al-Jazeera that made me fear for my life. The network was broadcasting Friday prayers live from a mosque in Abu Ghraib, the last stop on the road to Fallujah before American checkpoints blocked the way. The mosque was overflowing, and the imam, Sheik Hared Adari, was reading a *fatwa,* or religious edict, supported by Iraq's Sunni religious authority.

The edict forbade Iraq's citizens from helping foreigners of any type, especially Americans, and further forbade the purchase of any American or British products.

"In these days," the imam preached to a chorus of *Allah akbars,* "there will be a great victory for Fallujah and for all of Iraq and the entire Arab nation. Go to them, this is a battle of history, the bat-tle for all of Iraq. The *mujahadeen* who are fighting, they welcome death! They want to be martyred!"

Tensions were running high everywhere. Even members of the U.S.-appointed Governing Council increasingly sounded anti-

American. Mohsen Abdel Hamid, the head of Iraq's largest Sunni political party, the Iraqi Islamic Party, offered to broker a peace deal between the U.S. military and the people of Fallujah. When Washington rejected his offer, he threatened to quit the body.

Other members of the U.S.-appointed Iraqi government followed suit. The country's minister of human rights resigned "in protest of the practices of the Americans." Tribal sheik Ghazi al-Yawar, who would later be named president, told reporters, "We hated Saddam for punishing people collectively. We will not tolerate whoever we thought was our friend to do the same."

Even millionaire businessman Adnan Pachaci, one of the country's most pro-West politicians, stated: "It is not right to punish all the people of Fallujah. . . . We consider these operations by the Americans unacceptable and illegal."

Despite strong statements from some members, the Governing Council never took up a resolution condemning the twin attacks on Fallujah and al-Sadr. A few council members, like Ayyad Allawi, openly backed President Bush. The rotating head of the body, Kurdish leader Masoud Barzani, supported America.

"We have a joke about the Governing Council," Waseem told me the next day as we drank tea together, discussing what to do next. "The Governing Council is like a woman. Every month it bleeds away a little bit."

After some discussion, Waseem and I decided that our best option for reporting was to head to Diala, on the eastern edge of the Sunni Triangle. Like Fallujah, Diala was a center of armed resistance, with U.S. patrols there regularly coming under attack. Diala would be safer than Fallujah, though, not only because it was being left out of the current assault, but also because it was the hometown of Waseem's wife, Yisrah.

"I told you that my wife comes from a very Sunni family," he said. "So we will take the whole family together to Diala and see her family. It will be safer this way. No one, no matter how much of a resistance man he is, will harm us if he opens the van and sees a woman and two young children. Besides, my wife will enjoy seeing her mother and father." So we all piled into the van and drove out of Baghdad, east toward Diala, with Waseem's family in tow. It was a dangerous journey.

While battle raged in Fallujah, militants in Baqouba, near Diala, had forced down a U.S. OH–58 Kiowa helicopter. So we were all relieved when we arrived at the home of Waseem's father-in-law, a former general in the Iraqi army under Saddam Hussein, who welcomed us with open arms.

"There are a lot of people who joined the Ba'ath Party as young men simply because it was the thing to do," Waseem had confided to me on the way there. "My wife's father is one such person. Over the years, they saw that something was very wrong, but there was nothing they could do, so over time they kept doing their jobs and moved up, trying not to hurt anyone." Waseem's father-in-law was also missing three fingers on his right hand—an injury sustained while fighting in the Iran-Iraq War.

With a public and honorable history, Waseem's father-in-law, General Farouk Mu'adan, had become an important power broker in Diala after the fall of the Ba'ath regime. His history in the Iraqi army earned him the respect of the resistance, while his distance from Saddam's brutality earned him the respect of the Americans. Working with a powerful local sheik, he was doing his best to broker a truce between the resistance and the local American military commander.

"We have a problem," he said, "which is that the American military goes door to door and captures people for cooperating with the resistance. This causes more people to join the resistance and makes it more difficult for us to make a peace here."

The general said community leaders had proposed that the Americans suspend their patrols in Diala and offer jobs in the reconstruction effort to local residents. In exchange, he said, former Ba'athists like himself would do everything in their power to stop attacks on U.S. troops.

"And what did the Americans say?" I asked.

"The local commander is a nice man," General Farouk responded. "I really think he wants peace and to do good things for the Iraqi people, and I see that he sees the wisdom in our proposal, but when he goes back to Baghdad to talk to John Abizaid [the commander for all of Iraq], Abizaid always overrules him. So we get nowhere and there is no peace."

General Farouk also said the American assault on Fallujah had made it more difficult to reach a settlement in Diala. "Under these circumstances, you cannot blame anyone who shoots the Americans," he said. "You cannot say he was wrong, because he is under occupation and they keep rolling and rolling and rolling with the Apache helicopter and the tanks. All these things make the man uncomfortable, restless. He just boils and boils and boils. What do you expect? There must be some kind of resistance."

I agreed with him completely and told him so. He invited us to an expansive lunch of broiled fish, rice, and a myriad of side dishes. It was the best meal I had eaten in months, I told him. General Farouk smiled happily.

"We hate the American army," he said seriously. "We hate the occupation, but we love the American people. Can I ask you a question? How can the American people, who are so generous, make life so difficult for the people of Iraq?"

"I don't know," I said honestly. "It has been a long time since I have been in the United States for more than a few days. For most of the last few years I have been traveling. But I know that in America there are a lot of different types of people who think different things. Not everyone supported Bush in this war and not everyone supports him now."

"Yes, I know," the general said. "But what I don't understand is this: Before Bush made the war, there were many people in the streets of America saying 'No to war.' At that time, we wanted to get rid of Saddam. We said maybe we would wait to see what America would do. Now, America is occupying our country. Where are all the Americans who are against the occupation? Why are there no demonstrations like before the war?"

I told General Farouk I didn't know the reason for the lack of street demonstrations in the U.S. I told him that I regularly got e-mails from Pacifica listeners thanking me because no one else was reporting what I was, a statement I found somewhat odd since I didn't feel like I was doing any investigative journalism, but merely reporting the obvious. "People in America really don't know the truth about what's happening in Fallujah," I guessed. "All the American journalists are embedded with the U.S. military. So there are no accurate news reports. People in America don't have the information they need to protest."

Farouk shook his head in a gesture of sadness, picked a fish bone out from between two of his teeth, and invited me to wash my hands. Lunch was over.

In addition to talking to Waseem's family, I had an itinerary of interviews I wanted to make before leaving for Baghdad later that afternoon. Because Diala was smaller than Baghdad, it was easier to travel and easier to secure appointments. It was safer, too, because we would travel the city with Waseem's brother-in-law. Since his family was well known and well respected, it was unlikely that any harm would come to us. We would have a full day of work.

Our first stop on this tough tour was at the offices of the Sunni-dominated Iraqi Islamic Party, whose leader had threatened to quit the Governing Council over the siege of Fallujah. Their offices were in an expansive building with a large grass field in front. As everywhere, there were armed guards at the door, but the relaxed atmosphere put me at ease.

Waseem asked if we could speak to the appropriate representative, and we were led past a group of men drinking tea and watching the news, to a small desk in the back. After a short wait, the head of the local office appeared. He gave his name as Musla Ibrahim. He offered us tea and we accepted.

I asked him why, given the popular outrage over the U.S. attacks on Fallujah, the Governing Council had been unable to muster a resolution condemning the siege.

"The Governing Council didn't make any important statement about the situation or the people who believe in Muqtada al-Sadr," he responded. "It's because the Governing Council didn't want to lose the support of the man on the street, but the Governing Council also is in contact with the occupation force."

"So what will happen?" I asked. "If the Governing Council is unable to say anything at all with one voice, who will give voice to the Iraqi people?"

"There is a sense between all the Iraqi people," he answered, "between the Sunni and the Shia, that wasn't there before. Before, they said it was only the Sunni who resist and that the Shia walk in a more political way, but what's happened now is that Muqtada al-Sadr has changed the facts. Now the Sunni and the Shia both resist the occupation."

"So you support the armed resistance?"

"No," he answered, ever the politician. "We don't accept violence and we have twenty-five thousand members in our party in Diala alone. They obey us and will not raise a gun while we're talking about policy."

"What about al-Sadr?" I asked. "Some people say if the Americans leave there will be a civil war between Sunnis like yourself and the followers of Muqtada al-Sadr and the other Shia."

"Nobody touched al-Sadr until the Americans closed *al-Hawza* newspaper," the Sunni politician responded, "and about that I was very surprised, because the Americans always talk about freedom of opinion and democracy. As long as nobody was handling a gun it should have been acceptable. Now al-Sadr has picked up the gun, but only after he was attacked."

"So what do you think should happen now?" I asked.

"I think the Americans should calm down," he said. "They must take care. We want the transfer of power from the Americans to the Iraqi people and I have heard it will be on June 30. The settlement of the country will come this way through the rule of the Iraqi people themselves. In the meantime, they should rethink the offer of Dr. Mohsen Abdel Hamid to mediate this dispute. He is a very respected person and the people of Fallujah will listen to him. It's just up to the Americans now."

As we left the offices of the Sunni Iraqi Islamic Party, I pondered the comments of their officer. A year after the fall of Saddam Hussein, the future of Iraq was still almost completely in America's hands. Despite the widespread revulsion at the U.S. military's current actions, there was still no force large enough or popular enough to articulate a vision that posed an alternative to the status quo.

The Governing Council was a particular mess. Not only had it been silent on Fallujah, it had scarcely opened its mouth about the American crackdown on the movement of Muqtada al-Sadr. For analysis on this, we drove toward the local offices of the Supreme Council for Islamic Revolution in Iraq (SCIRI), whose leader, Abdel Aziz al-Hakim (brother of the slain ayatollah, Mohammed Baqir al-Hakim), sat on the Bush-appointed Iraqi Governing Council.

The head of SCIRI's local office, Zaid Saadi, welcomed us and offered us tea. When we told him we had drunk tea earlier, Pepsi was brought. Saadi was a thin man in his late 40s with dark skin and a thick beard. He offered this analysis of the Sadr movement: "They are civilian people. They're workers, students, and teachers. When they join the Mehdi Army they think they are better than before. They think otherwise no one will give them their rights."

He said to truly understand the anger of the poor young Shi'ite men who make up the Mehdi Army, one would have to look at the environment they grew up in. He cited 13 years of tough United Nations sanctions on Iraq which brought the country's education system to a screeching halt.

"Thirteen years ago, from the entrance of Iraq into Kuwait to the fall of the former regime, there were a lot of people who were uneducated," he noted, "who didn't finish secondary school. And because of the situation, our secondary school is nothing compared to those of other countries. At that time, the teachers were only paid one or two dollars a month. That's nothing. So they only worked three days a week and spent the rest of their days working as garbagemen or construction workers. What kind of education can you have in such an environment?"

"So you think the rise of the Mehdi Army can be traced to the UN sanctions?" I asked.

"Absolutely," he said. "Even for religious things—just a few of them know how to wash before praying and some of them don't even know the words for prayer. If they don't even know the religion itself, what can you expect of them, this kind of guys?"

His response typified that of the middle-class Shia, I thought. In this, it was similar to Waseem's. There was nothing but contempt for al-Sadr and his followers, but at the same time there was a feeling that the blame for his excess lay elsewhere—with Saddam's brutality and America's overheated response.

"You can build me a school," he continued, "and you can build me a mosque and you can build me a highway, but what can you do for me—the person that's been damaged during all these years? The Iraqi person was finished. Nobody worried about that, not even the UN. We want to build up the person. That's why I cannot come at him from the other [American] side. I cannot enter from that side because he will tell me we are from the same place, that we are the same people, and it will be true."

As we readied to leave, more Pepsi was offered, but we refused. We didn't have time to stay and talk, since we wanted to get back to Baghdad before dark. As we drove by Diala's municipal building, Waseem's brother-in-law mentioned that the local council was a frequent target of resistance attacks, since its members were appointed by the North Carolina contractor, RTI. Minutes later, as we dropped him off at home, we heard a familiar low boom. We turned on the radio. The municipal building had been attacked by a rocket-propelled grenade. A nearby American humvee had fired back at the fighters. We'd just missed it.

Back in Baghdad, I joined Waseem for dinner in his family's living room. We listened back to some of the interviews, doing exact translations of the Arabic. Afterward, over tea, Waseem told me he was thinking of quitting.

"You know, Aaron," he said. "The situation has become very bad. You are my friend, but now I don't know about this work. It is dangerous and I have to think about my wife and my children. I don't know. Maybe I will have to take a gun to fight if things continue. I don't know."

This was the surest sign yet that the situation had deteriorated significantly. I didn't need to remind Waseem that he and his family had prayed for the American invasion. I knew it was already front and center in his mind. "We will always be friends, I hope," I said.

Then Waseem called his brother Nadeem, who drove me back to the Dulaimi.

That Friday, the one-year anniversary of the end of Saddam's regime, passed without fanfare. In Paradise Square, where Saddam's statue had been toppled, U.S. military vehicles went on patrol, tearing down posters of Muqtada al-Sadr and blasting a message over loudspeakers in Arabic that anyone entering the area would be shot. When they finished, the soldiers blasted rock music from the speakers as parishioners left a nearby mosque. The tactic had become a part of U.S. military exercises.

Wire services reported that in Fallujah U.S. troops were blasting AC/DC's "Hell's Bells" and other rock music at full volume from a huge speaker. Unable to advance farther into the city, an Army psychological-operations team hoped a mix of heavy metal and insults shouted in Arabic—including, "You shoot like a goat herder!"—would draw gunmen to step forward and attack. But they hadn't had much luck.

.15.

AMERICA'S MASS GRAVE

After a few days cooped up in the Dulaimi, I was going stir-crazy. More important, I needed to tell the stories of the people of Fallujah and the followers of al-Sadr. What were they doing? What were they thinking? What did other Iraqis think of them? I couldn't find the answers to any of these questions from inside the guarded compound. I needed to get out.

Since Waseem wasn't willing to work under the current security situation, I approached one of the professional translators who frequently hung out in front of a journalists' hotel down the street.

His name was Kadem and he was a friendly man who lived in one of Baghdad's poorer Shi'ite neighborhoods. His English was excellent, but he rarely had work because of his history as a minder in Saddam Hussein's Ministry of Information. During Saddam's reign, Kadem would be assigned journalists to escort around Baghdad. He would set up interviews with permitted individuals, provide "official translations," and make sure the responses of all the journalists' sources were dutifully reported to his superiors. For this service, Kadem was rewarded. The regime allowed him to study Russian in Moscow at a time when most Iraqis were forbidden to leave the country.

James refused to work with him. "People can just smell the Saddam regime on him," he explained. "These former minders have a sleazy feeling about them. Everyone can tell they used to be Saddam's secret police. So your sources won't trust you."

But I didn't have many options. Also, I figured people from Fallujah, who had largely benefited under the foreign regime, would be less angry than most about the presence of a former government minder. So I walked over to the journalist hotel and negotiated a deal. I would pay Kadem $25 a day when we worked together. In addition, I would have to hire a driver, since Kadem didn't own a car.

The first day we worked together, my roommate, filmmaker Andy Berends, came, too. The U.S. military had briefly paused its assault on Fallujah and told residents they could flee the city if they liked. Tens of thousands of residents did just that, loading themselves into cars and busses and heading toward Baghdad. Andy, Kadem, and I got in the car and traveled west toward the city's Sunni suburbs, where support for the resistance was strong. We would try to talk to some of the refugees.

We found what we were looking for almost immediately. After asking about refugees at a few neighborhood stores, we came to a suburban-style ranch house in a neighborhood populated by officers of the former regime. More than 50 refugees had been taken into this house. They had fled as a family after a wedding celebrated under American bombs.

"We called it a challenge wedding," the head of the family stated, beaming, his finger in the air. "My daughter was getting married to my nephew, and we had to celebrate that. So we challenged the Americans and said 'We will defeat you no matter how much you bomb us!'"

Kadem introduced Andy and me as European journalists and we were welcomed profusely. Pepsi was brought, and a dozen chairs were set up on the front lawn. The men sat down ready to talk to us, and the children crowded around, intrigued by the commotion. The women were instructed to stay indoors in accordance with custom.

Once we were all seated, the head of the family introduced himself as Fakri Amash Abdullah, or abu Zaid. A heavyset man with a graying beard, he was dressed in loose-fitting, head-to-toe Islamic garb whose color was a faded blue.

"On Monday the American forces surrounded the city and they circled it completely so that no one could go out and no one could go in," he began. "So we decided as a family that we would have to do the wedding inside the city. We went to the house of one of our relatives and we celebrated there. We were in the Golan quarter."

"And how did that feel?" I asked. "To be performing such a wonderful thing as a wedding while all around the Americans were bombing?"

"Of course, it was very difficult psychologically," he answered. "We are living in a situation where we don't know if a rocket is going to fall on me right now where I'm sitting. The situation became so bad that we couldn't sleep—how can you sleep? You say your prayers and you try to sleep, but there are wounded people on the streets and no one can pick them up and put them in the hospital. Sometimes, the ambulance would come and the Americans would hit the ambulances."

I interrupted. "The Americans were shooting ambulances?" I asked, skeptically.

"Yes," he said, "so the people started putting white flags on their cars and taking injured people to the hospital and even those cars became targeted."

I wouldn't have to wait long for confirmation of this rumor. Soon I would receive photos of bullet-riddled ambulances, and testimonials from doctors, hospital officials, and relatives of the dead. At the time, though, I tried to change the subject back to a topic on which abu Zaid could offer his firsthand observations: his daughter's wedding. He was more than happy to oblige.

"For our wedding, we had six or seven cars," he said. "We had the wedding inside Fallujah. The bombing was already happening. But we could not cancel our celebration because it was an Islamic celebration. It was a challenge celebration. We took the bride from her house and drove her to the groom's house. We were determined to carry out the wedding. 'What ever will be will be,' my uncle said. There were some other weddings at the same time. Beautiful weddings. There was another wedding that was broadcast by al-Jazeera that was also during the time of the bombing."

"And your wedding was not bombed?" I asked.

"No, thanks to God, no," abu Zaid replied. "But one of my relatives was killed. When the electricity went out and he went outside to turn on the generator, an American sniper hit him and he was martyred."

"It sounds very scary," I said.

"Of course it is scary and it is terrible," he said, "but we believe in God. Whatever God decided for us will happen and we can't change our destiny."

I thanked abu Zaid for speaking with us. "Is there anyone else who has lost someone?" I asked. There was a brief discussion among the men, and then a young boy in a brown-and-tan polo shirt was pushed forward. He looked shell-shocked by recent events, and looked at me through vacant eyes. He gave his name as Yusuf Fakri Amash, 11 years old.

"And did somebody you know die?"

"Yes," he said. My journalistic composure, already rattled by recent events, was at its limit. I wanted to cry.

"Ahmed," he said. "Ahmed was in my class. He was younger than me. He was standing next to the wall of the secondary school. He was trying to cross the road and he was hit by a bullet."

I did my best to hold back tears. I couldn't imagine what young Yusuf was feeling. "And who fired that bullet?" I asked.

"It was an American bullet," he said, from an American sniper. "They are in all the high buildings in Fallujah. The Americans shoot us on the street. They even bombed our school."

At this point, other family members joined in. A cousin with a long beard and only one leg told me he wanted to make an appeal:

All the Islamic organizations in the world [must] stay with the Fallujah citizens. The situation in Fallujah is very bad. The women die and the children, too. You can imagine that we have no time to grieve our dead bodies. Our martyrs are lying on the ground in the streets. We can't grieve them. Never. It's a very bad situation. The Americans claim they are a democracy? Which is the democracy? Where is the democracy? If there is a demonstration they attack it and fire on it. Is that democracy for us? We are coming from other cities to Fallujah to take part in a wedding celebration, but we were surrounded; what is our sin? The children and women they are filled with fear. They cannot sleep at night with the horror and they cannot return to their schools. The only thing that fills my heart with joy is that I see the unity between all Muslims who said welcome to the Fallujah citizens as we left the city. They said welcome to the Fallujah heroes! Welcome with the *mujahadeen*! And they try to cover us with food, with everything, with water."

I offered my microphone to another man from Diala who wanted to speak. He was a wiry man, also dressed in full-length Islamic dress. An uncle of the groom, he had come to Fallujah for the wedding. "There is no electricity or water," he said. "As for the food materials there is nothing. None."

Again, I was skeptical and sure of exaggeration. "I understand there is no electricity," I said. "The Americans have cut it. But what about water? Surely there is water."

"My brother," the man from Diala responded, "because the water pumping has no electricity, he cannot operate it. Because America has cut all the roads, he has no gasoline to operate the backup generator. How can he pump the water for the city? If there is no electric current, how can we use the water pump? So there is no water." A few weeks later, these same facts would appear in statements from the International Red Cross.

"So what will happen?" I asked.

"The Americans can't get inside Fallujah because of the diligent people who defend their city. But we have many injuries in hundreds, maybe in thousands. But God is with us and we will prevail."

I could feel pressure building in my head. It was time to go. The longer we stayed, the more these people merely repeated themselves. Kadem, Andy, and I spoke together for a moment, thanked them for their time, and readied to leave.

"You must stay for lunch," abu Zaid insisted.

"I'm sorry, but we have to go," Kadem said. "We have other appointments."

Abu Zaid insisted again and again Kadem refused. This went on for a while, before a second round of Pepsi was brought. We all relaxed in the front yard of the house for a bit longer, and I suggested that the family pose for a group photo.

Abu Zaid rounded up most of his family for the portrait, though young and middle-aged women were left out because of modesty. In the front row were 15 children under 12 years old. Behind them were two grandmothers with babies in their arms, a cripple, and a dozen middle-aged men.

"You will send this picture to Europe and America?" abu Zaid implored after we took the photo.

"I will do my best," I said. "And I will return here to give you a copy."

"Thank you," he said. "God be with you." Andy, Kadem, and I walked back to the car and we were off.

"Where to?" Kadem asked.

"Back to the Dulaimi," I said. So far everyone had been kind to us since we left the Dulaimi, but given the tremendous increase in anti-American sentiment over the past week and a half, the last thing I wanted to do was press my luck. Andy, newly arrived in Iraq, agreed reluctantly. He had traveled across the world to make a film about Iraq and was discouraged that he was spending most of his time cooped up in the Dulaimi.

But Andy was to get his first "action" in Iraq. As we approached the freeway, we saw an American tank on fire. It was an event that happened nearly every day on the main highway linking Baghdad and Fallujah. American tanks and humvees always moved back and forth on this road going to and from the front. It was not uncommon for mortar fire to hit the vehicle, at which point it would burst into flames.

Still, this was the first time either Andy or I had seen such an event firsthand. Andy asked that the car be pulled over. Then he got out and stood near the on-ramp, pointing his camera at the blaze, a dark red fire with black smoke spiraling toward the sky.

Bullets started flying and Kadem yelled out, "Mr. Andy! It's not safe there! You must come back!"

Andy yelled back that he wanted the footage. After scanning the scene, we spotted a nearby mosque and ran to it. I felt a rush inside me. Bullets were whizzing everywhere. An ambulance sped by, its siren blaring. More tanks sped past us and people shot at them. I hugged the wall to avoid the gunfire. Next to me stood a local sheik. When I told him I was a journalist, he told me his brothers and sons were being held in Abu Ghraib. I took his mobile number and promised to call him to make an appointment to meet with him later.

It was surreal. As I hugged the wall of the mosque, I met the head of a local relief agency. He told me the Americans had thrown out the blood his community had donated. And all of this while missiles whizzed by and the fire in the nearby tank reached precariously close to the main fuel tank.

"We have to go!" Kadem screamed, pointing at the fire that was enveloping the whole vehicle. "When it reaches the fuel supply, the whole tank will explode and shrapnel will fly everywhere. We have to go!"

I rushed back to the car with Andy close behind. Unable to enter the freeway because of the burning tank, the driver turned and directed his car northbound on a side road toward Showle. It would take us an hour and a half to get home this way, but it was better than risking shrapnel from an exploding tank.

In the back seat of the car, I tried to relax. I considered the oddity of the situation. Despite all the bullets around me, I'd felt quite comfortable. In front of the mosque, I'd even had to remind myself that there were bullets flying all around me or I would have simply wandered out onto the freeway on-ramp to watch the tank explode. Maybe I was in shock, or maybe in some kind of crazy state of denial, but I wasn't scared and I didn't feel physically in danger. It was also the first time I'd felt the rush of adrenaline that war reporters talk about.

Still, I worried about my state of mind. I wondered how long I could take the emotional hit of seeing dead and dying people, and explosions, tanks, soldiers, and helicopters, without going totally crazy. I remembered one time I saw Jeremy Scahill speak. An antiwar journalist for Pacifica, he was chugging along at a quick pace, giving a dynamic performance about his experiences reporting on the United States' bombing of Yugoslavia. At one point in the speech, though, he described a scene in a Belgrade hospital where he had seen a young person dying and in order to communicate the horror of the situation he had to put a microphone up to him and ask, "How do you feel?" Jeremy started crying in front of the people who had come to see him speak.

Now I understood Jeremy's emotions. Under the weight of the daily grind of disturbing interviews, I began to cry every day when I got home, before I slept, and almost every time when I had some time to myself. How many people can you interview whose relatives have been killed before you start to crack—or worse, tune it all out?

There was little time to consider such questions, though. The next day brought more news from Fallujah. A friend of ours, British filmmaker Julia Guest, had returned from the city having smuggled herself in with an aid group carrying medical supplies. Eager to get her story out, she headed straight from Fallujah to the Dulaimi, where James had pledged to help her edit the video.

She was visibly shaken. "Unbelievable," she muttered as she set down her gear. "Un-fucking-believable. Your people are butchers. I have to find the technical definition of genocide because your government may be committing one."

As we watched Julia's video, we could understand her outrage. There was footage of an old woman in a hospital bed, an American bullet lodged in her neck, her blood spurting all over the place. "The American snipers have taken up positions on all the high places throughout the city," Julia told us, "and as soon as they see anyone move, they shoot. They aim for the neck. Most of the patients in the clinic were shot in the neck. Women and children. Everyone." The old woman's tortured cries were almost unbearable. Julia said there were other, similar cases. Her voice quaking, she told another story:

When I arrived, I found a woman who I think was in her seventies who had decided to try to help her sons get out of the city. They decided to leave the family group, and so she just had taken the decision to walk out the front door waving a white flag, because they knew they were in a heavily—there was a lot of shooting in their area. And she was shot in the stomach and the foot. So, I found her in the hospital with one of her sons in quite a state and she was evacuated in a small van that volunteered to come out from Baghdad and picked her up and took her back to Baghdad.

I told her the refugees we talked to had accused the U.S. military of shooting at ambulances. She showed us footage of an ambulance covered with bullet holes. The driver had a bandage around his head. An American sniper's bullet had grazed his scalp.

She described the ambulance shown in her picture. "It has blue flashing lights. It was donated by the Kingdom of Spain. It was clearly an ambulance. It's carrying oxygen bottles. The damage to the ambulance was such that two of the wheels are destroyed. They were left without an ambulance after that."

I was amazed at Julia's story. I had always thought that many of the stories I heard were embellished—overstated by an angry population. Accounts from the street, I thought, should be taken with a grain of salt.

I was wrong. In a regular interview on Pacifica's New York station, I explained my new perspective. "The horror of what's happening here is almost impossible to imagine. Even if you are here it's difficult to imagine. It has been my experience in the last two weeks—since the U.S. started its attacks—that the truth is probably much worse than what one can actually confirm and report. It is a disaster here."

The host of the program quoted the American theater commander in Fallujah, who told Britain's *Guardian* newspaper that 95 percent of those killed in the assault on the city were armed militants.

"If they are telling you that there is a small uprising here by a handful of Ba'athists and foreign terrorists," I said over a scratchy international phone line, "then I am telling you that is a lie. That might have been true even a few weeks ago, but now the situation here has changed completely."

Indeed, the next day I had more terrible information to report. A doctor from Fallujah came to the Dulaimi to be interviewed by Julia. Afterward, Andy and I talked to him. Julia asked that I withhold his name for his own safety, but the young doctor, Salam Ishmael al-Obaidi, was a nationalist. He was head of Iraq's young doctors' association and ran a whole group of hospitals. He wanted his name used to lend credibility to the report.

"When you have seen a child, five years old, with no head, what can you say? When you see a child with no brain, just an opened cavity, what can you say? Or when you see a mother just holding her child, her infant, with no head, and the shells all over her body?"

"You have seen all these things?" I asked.

"Yes," the doctor responded. "All this and more." He repeated Julia's charges that Fallujah's ambulance had been targeted by American troops.

He said Americans shot at the ambulance twice while he was in it. He explained that he was trying to bring aid to residents stranded in their homes. The ambulance had been attacked once when it was trying to retrieve dead bodies for burial and a second time when it was attempting to bring food aid to homes cut off by American snipers.

"I see people carrying a white flag and yelling to us, saying 'We are here, just try to save us,' but we could not save them because whenever we opened the ambulance door the Americans would shoot at us. We tried to carry food and water in containers. As soon as you carry food or water, the snipers shoot the containers of food."

I asked the doctor about reports that the dead were being buried in the city's soccer stadium. In recent days such reports had passed the level of rumor. Pictures of the ripped-up field had been shown on al-Jazeera, with new wooden headstones bearing the names of fighting-age men, as well as of women, children, and the elderly. That morning, a journalist from the Associated Press filed a report from the football stadium quoting an aid worker as saying that hundreds of people had been buried there. Dr. Salam told me he had also helped with the burials, which, he said, under the American siege, were risky.

"We buried many in the football stadium," he told us. "It's full now. But the problem is, how are you burying? You cannot stand in the football stadium for a long time, because they will shoot at you. So, we use shovels just to make a hole—a big hole, and we just put the people from one family one over the other, and cover them with sand or—and just go out from there."

It was a sad situation, made sadder by the fact that the Dulaimi was Dr. Salam's last stop before fleeing the country. When he returned to Baghdad from Fallujah, his family told him the U.S. military had come to their house to arrest him. If he showed his face there again, it was likely that the Americans would take him to Abu Ghraib, where he would be held indefinitely with no lawyer and no trial. The next day, Dr. Salam told us, he would be in Jordan. Eventually, he would travel to England where he would speak out full-time against the occupation.

.16.

KIDNAP DRAMAS

Even though I left the apartment less and less, I was able to get a lot done. Somehow, I managed to report a new story nearly every day. I always seemed to find someone to interview: I met family members of the staff of the Dulaimi building who returned from Fallujah with bullet holes in their collarbones (the American snipers were still aiming for the neck). To get another perspective, I met some of Waseem's best friends. A Shi'ite antiques dealer told me stories of the uprising that followed Saddam's killing of Muqtada al-Sadr's father and predicted something similar if Muqtada was killed. A Sunni small-businessman whose father, uncle, and brother had been killed by Saddam told me how he had reluctantly decided to start supporting the resistance after his cousins were taken to Abu Ghraib. "It's the same struggle as under Saddam's regime," he told me. "Now it's been rebuilt by the Americans themselves."

James arranged for me to meet a senior producer from al-Jazeera, Samir Khader, who he knew from his work on the documentary *Control Room*. "In the beginning," Samir said, "most people supported the Americans as liberators. Now, we have reached a point of no return. The majority of Iraqis want to get rid of the Americans. You know there are red lines in this part of the world. When you attack mosques, when you attack women and children. This is a red line."

I asked Samir why he thought so many innocent civilians were dying in Fallujah. "Usually when you have a war it is a war between two armies," he told me. "The problem is that there is only the American army and no Iraqi army to fight. Only civilians and a limited number of insurgents. So what we have seen—what we have broadcast in pictures on al-Jazeera—are F-16s and Blackhawk helicopters killing huge numbers of women and children."

I broadcast my interview with Samir in its entirety on Pacifica to give listeners in the U.S. an opportunity to hear how the events were being broadcast in the Arab media.

During this period, I received a steady stream of phone calls and e-mails praising me for my work. I found this hard to believe. After all, my mobility had been severely hampered by the declining security situation. Nevertheless, I kept hearing the same phrase again and again: *What you are saying in your reports, we can't hear anywhere else.*

How could this be? I was only reporting the obvious, but when I turned on the TV (which I watched more now that I was homebound), the reports I saw rarely showcased the opinions of regular Iraqis and how occupation was shaping their lives. BBC World, the only English-language media I had access to, focused almost completely on the insurgents' new tactic: the kidnapping of foreigners.

The first and most publicized kidnapping was of three young Japanese civilians. All three had come to the country to help the

Iraqi people. They had nothing to do with the occupation. One was a photojournalist. Another was in the country to help clothe and feed street kids. A third had come to research the rise in cancer rates that corresponded with America's use of depleted-uranium-tipped bombs during the 1991 and 2003 Gulf Wars.

The hostage-takers didn't care about their work, only their Japanese nationality. They blindfolded their hostages, put knives to their throats, and demanded Japan pull its 550 troops out of Iraq.

"We tell you that three of your children have fallen prisoner in our hands and we give you two options—withdraw your forces from our country and go home or we will burn them alive and feed them to the fighters," the captors said in a video broadcast on al-Jazeera.

The Japanese government refused to negotiate.

I was deeply depressed about this situation, and whenever I saw images of the captives, tears welled up in my eyes. Not only were the hostage-takers barbaric, but the response of the Japanese government ensured that the cycle of barbarism and revenge would continue.

When the Americans first toppled Saddam Hussein, most Iraqi people were happy, but the U.S. government squandered that trust—they appointed their government and rounded up dissidents and threw them into Abu Ghraib. They failed to restore the electricity, and gave all the jobs to a handful of well-paid foreign contractors. This created rage amongst the people, perhaps feeding into the actions of a small group of men who burned the bodies of a few armed American contractors in Fallujah. The Bush Administration completely overreacted to this and bombed the city flat, a maneuver which, along with the simultaneous crackdown on al-Sadr, turned Iraq into a country full of enemies. That, in turn, created an environment in which these Japanese aid workers could be taken hostage. With the Japanese government refusing to negotiate, I figured, the cycle of revenge would continue and get worse. I prayed for someone to calm things down.

I would not get such help from the media, however. BBC milked the story for all it was worth, showing grainy footage of the kidnappers nearly every hour of the day, along with pleas for mercy from the hostages' families back home.

As the numbers of hostages increased, coverage of the killings of large numbers of Iraqi people by occupation troops withered. It was almost as if these journalists lived in an entirely different Iraq than I did—they stood on the balconies of their suites in the Palestine Hotel speaking about the tremendous brutality of the terrorists, all the while ignoring the thousands of Iraqis being killed by U.S. troops. The implication was: The people who oppose the occupation are barbarous terrorists and we must fight them. I knew that the situation was more complicated.

As if to prove this point, a kind of ethics began to develop amongst the kidnappers. Hostages not directly involved in the occupation were usually released. The three Japanese civilians were let go on April 15, as were a group of eight South Korean missionaries. Six months later, the Associated Press would report that 80 percent of the roughly 170 foreigners kidnapped in Iraq had been peacefully released. Overall, it seemed, hostages directly involved in the occupation fared much worse than their civilian counterparts.

On the same day that the Japanese aid workers were released, an Italian captive named Fabrizio Quattrocchi was shot in the back of the neck, and a videotape of the killing was sent to al-Jazeera. In Italy, there was an outpouring in official circles, with the country's foreign minister, Franco Fartinni, going so far as to call Quattrocchi a "hero."

But the truth was much less glamorous. In many respects, Quattrocchi was similar to the security guards mutilated in Fallujah. He worked for a Nevada-based company called DTS Limited, and his job was to guard Iraq's oil infrastructure.

As I considered these events, another less-publicized kidnapping took place. A group of Western activists bringing food and medical supplies into Fallujah were taken hostage. Their faces never appeared on al-Jazeera, though, and within 24 hours of their capture, they were released.

Initially, I had no idea that they had been taken captive. On the evening of their return to Baghdad, I telephoned one of their party, an Australian, Donna Malbun, and asked for an interview. She gave me a time when they would be available and the address where she and some of the other aid workers were living, a small apartment near a juice stand on Karada, close to the Palestine Hotel.

I found their building and walked up the stairs to their humble apartment. The door was open. "I'm here to take you away," I said in a foolish joke. The residents, two white women in their 20s, gave me a look of horror. "I'm sorry," I said. "My name is Aaron Glantz. I'm a reporter for Pacifica Radio in the United States. We spoke on the telephone."

A sigh of relief ran through the flat. "We're still a little shell-shocked," one of the women explained. She was strong and Australian. "We were kidnapped and we've only been home for a few hours."

"I'm sorry," I apologized again. "I didn't know."

I turned on my microphone and asked them to introduce themselves. The strong Australian woman introduced herself as Donna Malbun. The other woman came from Wales and sported dyed-blond hair with streaks of the original brown. "Can I give you a fake name?" she asked. "My parents don't know I'm here."

I told her any name would do. Her experiences were what was important. She gave me the name "Beth Ann Jones."

"We were part of a group of six activists," the Australian began. "We wanted to use our foreign passports as a shield against U.S. Marine snipers. They've posted themselves around the city and they've been shooting at trucks attempting to bring medical aid to victims of the American attack."

"So what did you do?" I asked. She related the event:

We were accompanying an ambulance from one part of Fallujah to another area that was controlled by the Americans, and we went along with the ambulance, and at one stage we even got out of the ambulance to indicate to the Americans that we were coming through with an ambulance with aid for a clinic that had been cut off. We used a loudspeaker to identify ourselves, we were dressed in bright-blue medical outfits, and we had our passports in our hands with our hands in the air. Then we stepped forward into the street with our hands in the air. We were walking down away from where the soldiers were stationed. And they ended up shooting toward our backs.

I told the aid workers that the U.S. Marines denied shooting at ambulances. I told them that after my story highlighting one such incident in Fallujah had appeared, I had gotten an e-mail from U.S. Marine Lieutenant Eric Knapp. He put the blame for the shootings on Iraqi insurgents, who he said were doing everything they could to prevent aid from reaching the needy. At the same time, he said something contradictory: that insurgents were using ambulances to traffic in arms. "By using ambulances," the lieutenant had written, "they are putting Iraqis in harm's way by denying them a critical component of urgent medical care. Mosques, ambulances and hospitals are protected under Geneva Convention agreements and are not targeted by U.S. Marines. However, once they are used for the purpose of hostile intent toward Coalition Forces, they lose their protected status and may be targeted."

The Australian, Donna Malbun, interrupted, saying the ambulance they tried to enter with was filled with medical supplies, not arms. At least 600 Fallujans had died since the American assault began, she noted, most of them civilians. "There's a big problem getting people to the clinics," she said. "I mean this is the whole point of why we went there, is that people are getting injured and then being unable to travel and get them to the hospital. We saw one guy being brought in who had lost his arm. And he was just taken to any clinic they could get him to, which was our clinic, and because we haven't been able to get to the hospitals to pick up supplies, this guy died, because there wasn't the medical services to deal with what had happened to him."

"But it wasn't only the American army that caused problems for you," I pointed out. "When I came in here, you told me you were kidnapped. That wasn't by the Americans, was it?"

Donna Malbun straightened herself up. "On our way out of Fallujah we were stopped by Iraqi *mujahadeen* fighters. They held us for twenty-four hours."

"What happened?" I asked.

"They wanted to know who we were at the beginning," she responded. "They investigated and they asked questions and looked at our belongings, and once they realized what we were doing, they treated us with great respect. Our delegation was held in a large room and fed well. We were given Pepsi and tea and Fanta almost constantly. They offered us cigarettes."

Beth Ann Jones told me that when the topic of conversation turned to the American assault on Fallujah, the two groups had quickly found common ground:

They would be talking and saying 'My brother's been killed. My father's been killed.' They were telling us details so that we could understand the way that they were feeling, and the obvious resentment

they were feeling towards the occupation, that they were now suffering and a year ago they were promised freedom and liberation from
the Saddam regime, and now they're living in a situation where they
do not have any freedom.

This type of story would become common as the number of kidnappings increased. Over time, a number of my journalist colleagues were briefly kidnapped. They were treated well and released
once it was established that they were not directly related to the occupation. Sometimes, a tribal sheik affiliated with the resistance
would have to intervene to get them released, but overall the kidnappers seemed to understand that their fight was with the occupying armies and not with journalists or aid workers. There have,
of course, been exceptions.

As I readied to leave, the two aid workers told me they harbored
no anger toward their captors. "Fallujah was under siege," Donna
Malbun explained. "Even the women and children who wanted to
leave today, and the men, couldn't leave. And the bombardment
from the air was constant, and the sniper activity was constant to
the point where they were too terrified to leave their houses. These
people were being kept prisoner in their own town and country."

I said good-bye and went back to the Dulaimi and checked the
wires. The U.S. Marines had attacked the city of Fallujah again
with F-15 fighter jets and AC-130 gunships. A military spokesperson had told Agence France-Presse that the maneuvers were
defensive.

Despite the encouraging story from Donna Malbun and her Welsh
colleague, I continued to spend most of my time at the Dulaimi.
Unable to relax, my mental health deteriorated further. I cried at
the slightest provocation.

At night it was worse. For the first time, the tragedy unfolding on the streets of Baghdad and Fallujah began to invade my dreams. In one recurring nightmare, I found myself at a bus depot in downtown Baghdad trying to get a ticket to Istanbul. From Istanbul, I would be able to fly home to California. "I need to get to Istanbul," I would say with great urgency to a myriad of conductors, concessionaires, and drivers, but every time I would be denied.

"There are no buses to Istanbul," a conductor would say as a large 1970s super-liner pulled out with the word ISTANBUL emblazoned on its front.

When I ran to the driver of the bus, he turned to me. "All sold out," he would say with a shrug. This would go on for some time until, eventually, a long-limbed man with a daffy smile and long tongue would approach me with a kitchen knife and cut off my head, in the style of the most macabre Hollywood slasher movie. Blood would spurt from the stump of my neck as my face looked on in horror.

Finally, Waseem would appear and wrestle the knife from my crazy assailant and I would wake.

I also had visions when I was awake. Sitting on my balcony, drinking beer, I looked out past date palms and the Tigris River toward the Green Zone. I saw an American helicopter take flight. Suddenly, I was transported in my mind back to Vietnam in the mid-1970s. I was in front of a building, banging on a closed, dark oak embassy door. A group of choppers lifted off from the roof, the last of the evacuation. Left behind, I erupted in a new fury of banging, knowing there were no Americans left to take me away. As reality dawned on me, I broke down crying, dark men with curved knives coming out from around every corner.

I needed to get out or I would go crazy. Luckily, James was thinking about getting out, too.

James's reasons were different from mine. His sanity remained intact, and he examined the situation with the cruel calculations of a veteran journalist. "It's not a good time to work in Baghdad," he said without emotion. Concerned for Nadeem's safety, Waseem had forbidden his brother from traveling with James, leaving him without the service of a translator.

"Things might fall apart completely on any day," James explained as he arranged his travel. "There is fighting all over the south of Iraq. If anything happens, I need to be able to get out of here quickly and I've got too much stuff here."

James was going north to Kurdistan, where he would take a break in Arbil. The road to Kirkuk was unsafe, but much better than the ones to the west or south. I told James I wanted to go, too.

A few days later, Nadeem and a Kurdish friend, Mohammed, picked us up at the Dulaimi in a beat-up blue van. When they arrived, I packed my belongings and looked around, smiling one last time at the fake ivy and the blue backlighting. I said good-bye to Hamza and the rest of the building's staff.

"You know what they did?" Nadeem said as we sped out of Baghdad. I didn't need to ask who. It was obvious he was talking about the Americans.

I shook my head.

"Last night, the Americans came through our neighborhood with tanks," he said. "The drove round and round and captured people in their houses like they have done many times before. But there was one thing different this time. One of the tanks had a giant speaker on top with an Arab on top of it, reading a statement that was blasted from the speaker."

"What did he say?" I asked.

"He said, 'We know you are a good neighborhood and you do not support al-Sadr. We want you to know that al-Sadr is a very bad man and that we will crush him. If you support al-Sadr we will crush you.'"

There was nothing to say to such a story. Nadeem shook his head and I collapsed onto what remained of the van's seat cushion. I prayed for safety and slept much of the way to Arbil.

Surprisingly, northern Iraq was the same as ever. The streets were calm, the fruit stands open. James and I checked our bags at the Fareed, registered with the *asayeesh,* and walked around the old city stopping for a beer and whisky at a late-night bar. It was nice to be out of Baghdad and back in Kurdistan.

Afterward, James and I went to our favorite Internet cafe, and I read a report that chilled my blood in my veins. Had we left a few hours later, we might have been trapped.

U.S. CLOSES OFF 2 HIGHWAYS INTO BAGHDAD
VOA News
18 Apr 2004, 12:37 UTC

The U.S. military in Iraq has closed off long stretches of two major highways running north and south from Baghdad following insurgent attacks that have affected the flow of supplies to the capital.

Brigadier General Mark Kimmitt says the roads are in need of repair, and must be protected.

A U.S. military statement issued Saturday said the roads are badly damaged and too dangerous for civilian travel. The military also warned that anyone driving on the sections of highway closed for safety and security reasons could be subject to attack.

PART FOUR

BRUTALITY BECOMES THE NORM

.17.

RETURN FROM KURDISTAN

It was nice to be back in Kurdistan, walking the streets, going to the markets and cafes. The vast majority of Kurds still supported America and I felt completely safe, even as I expressed doubt at the tactics of the Kurdish leaders.

"There are a lot of rumors in Baghdad that Kurdish *peshmerga* are fighting alongside American troops against the people of Fallujah," I told Abdullah Fermenda, a Patriotic Union of Kurdistan division commander.

We were sitting in a courtyard outside PUK headquarters in Arbil, drinking dark tea out of small glasses. As we spoke, mustached Kurds with heavy machinery slowly rebuilt the structure, which had been bombed by "terrorists" three months before. Photos of the "martyrs" were posted on the building's walls.

"I don't know if this is true or not," I continued, "but I think

many *peshmerga* are now fighting in the Iraqi army." The United
States had admitted half of the Iraqi army left rather than fight in
Fallujah and Najaf (where the U.S. military had begun laying siege
to al-Sadr), but the Iraqi army nevertheless remained intact fighting
alongside U.S. forces in both battles. This had led to speculation
that the Iraqi army had been bolstered through the use of regular
Kurdish fighters. It was an allegation that took hold despite strong
denials from the U.S. military and the leaders of both Kurdish factions. In Baghdad and the refugee camps outside Fallujah, more
and more Arabs were saying that Kurds weren't interested in being
independent, but were simply working as slaves of the Americans,
and as such were legitimate targets of the resistance.

I explained this to the division commander, but he was unmoved. He sipped his tea and adjusted the AK-47 that was slung
over his shoulder before responding: "We are not going to fight
Arab people," he said. "We are going to stop terrorism. They may
have the opposite idea, but we are not fighting the Arabs in Fallujah and Najaf. We have so many friends there. But sometimes you
see the terrorists are radical Arabs and they want to do terrible
things in Kurdistan and everywhere else."

"But why fight for the Americans?" I pushed. "Why not just
keep your checkpoints at the roads into Kurdistan and say 'We have
our freedom in our Kurdistan and we won't bother you?'"

"We have a debt to America," he responded. "They put down
Saddam Hussein. He was the worst kind of dictator. Now we have
a real chance for freedom and democracy in Iraq. That's something
worth fighting for."

But I was unmoved. I was agitated by the Kurds' aloofness toward
the suffering of their Arab countrymen. It seemed to me that they
were living in a bubble, unable to fully comprehend the consequences of their alliance just a few hours' drive to the south. "Don't
you see?" I insisted. "You are just making more enemies by your ac-

tions. Even if you think you are fighting for democracy and freedom that's not the way a great many Arabs see it. You have to remember that America has its own agenda, its own reasons for being in Iraq. They are only thinking about their own benefit. In Baghdad, they are saying the Kurds have come from the mountains to kill the Arabs. They will strike back at you and you will lose your peace."

The exercise was pointless, I thought, after every interview ended the same way. After a few days of work, I took a vacation day, hiking with Istifan up a mountain near his family's ancestral home in Sheiklawa, an Assyrian Christian community in the hills north of Arbil.

It was spring, and the mountains were green. Children lined the windy road out of town, hawking sweet-smelling wildflowers that marked the arrival of spring. We passed them by and resolved to pick our own.

"There aren't any land mines here?" I asked Istifan as we made our way up a jagged mountain made of volcanic rock.

"No. All the fighting was down there," he said, pointing at the valley below. "Many times there has been fighting in Sheiklawa, but never here in the mountains. You know, in 1974 during the revolution by Mustafa Barzani, Sheiklawa was a very big battle, and in the 1990s when the PUK fought the KDP, Sheiklawa was a very big battle. But no one fought in these mountains and, thanks to God, now we have peace in Kurdistan."

Thanks also to America, I thought, which had eliminated Saddam and succeeded in unifying the KDP and PUK, if only against Iraq's Arab population.

After just five days in Kurdistan, James decided it was time to return to Baghdad. A few days of furious e-mailing had yielded him a new translator, one distantly related to Muqtada al-Sadr and re-spected throughout his movement. From Baghdad, James would go directly to Najaf and continue with his film about al-Sadr.

Every fiber of my body urged me to follow in James's footsteps.

I knew I was missing an extremely important story just a few hours' drive to the south. The American siege on Fallujah contin-ued, while al-Sadr's followers, having lost control of many of the cities they had taken, retreated into the Shia holy city, Najaf. A pro-tracted siege ensued there as well, though American forces—wary of Najaf's status as a Shia Vatican—had thus far spared the city the kind of massive assault they had given Fallujah. If I couldn't report during a time of crisis, what was the point of traveling to Iraq?

On the other hand, I worried about my mental health. I wasn't sure my mind could take another round in the pressure cooker of Bagh-dad. On this front, I had reason to feel better. A friend from South Korea, Eunji Kang, had just arrived at the Dulaimi in Baghdad. A lively woman in her late 20s, she always seemed to be happy some-how, with a loud laugh and a wide smile. Eunji had been to both Pak-istan and Afghanistan since September 11th. Back home in Seoul, she worked for a magazine called *Nation 21,* the only publication in her country that accepted articles by journalists from the Communist North—a country she herself had visited earlier that year.

Most important, unlike James, who always worked alone, Eunji and I could work together, which meant I would have additional companionship to help keep me from cracking. The day after James left for Baghdad, I made up my mind. I woke up early and traveled to the shared taxi depot outside Arbil and was back off to the south.

Arriving back in Baghdad, I called Waseem right away. I suggested that he come to the Dulaimi to talk things over, and he agreed. I introduced him to Eunji and made them both dark tea with sugar. Each took out a cigarette and began to smoke.

"Between the incredible amount of sugar in your tea and the number of cigarettes you smoke each day," I joked to Waseem, "I don't know which will kill you first—diabetes or lung cancer."

"Aaron, let me tell you something about Iraqi people," he said, puffing away. "Not just me, but all Iraqi people. In the first of my life, there was the Saddam regime. And Saddam put me in the army and told me 'You must fight against Iran.' And so maybe the Iranian army would kill me. And after the war, Saddam put me in prison and tortured me. So maybe Saddam himself would kill me. And after that, there were the sanctions and so the food was very bad and the water was very bad and even now the water is very bad and so maybe the food or the water itself will kill me. And if not that . . ." he paused and sighed. "Anyway, there are a lot of bombs going off around here these days. So I will be drinking my tea with sugar and smoking my cigarette."

Eunji let out a small giggle and I shook my head through a weak smile. "It seems like things have calmed down a little," I said. "There is some kind of negotiation now between the Governing Council and the Fallujah people and the Sadr movement."

After they threatened to resign, the U.S. military had allowed respected Sunni members of the Iraqi Governing Council, including the future interim president, Sheik Ghazi al-Yawar, to try to negotiate a truce. In the meantime, America had stopped carpet-bombing Fallujah, although daily fighting continued.

Waseem agreed. "The situation has calmed some," he said. Like many parents, he had sent his children back to school, even as he watched the developments closely.

We started to brainstorm about safe ways to report and eventually decided to visit a refugee camp in West Baghdad that had been set up for people from Fallujah. Visiting the Red Crescent camp was a good idea, he said: "It is very official and also it is very good for the resistance if journalists visit there," he said. "So no one will attack it."

We got into the car and drove west, pulling over and asking for directions from time to time, until finally we reached a vacant lot across the street from a mosque where the Iraqi Red Crescent had begun to set up tents. It was the first tent city for Iraqis caused by the 2003 American invasion (As noted earlier, refugee camps were set up for Palestinians in Iraq, but none was built for Iraqis themselves). Very few Iraqis had been displaced by the initial invasion, and up until this point, Iraqis displaced by the fighting were taken in by their family or neighbors. But the U.S. assault on Fallujah was so large, and displaced so many people, that this familiar generosity had reached its limit.

We arrived while the camp was still under construction. Already, 50 families were living in the tents. "All these families," said Kamer Jabi, the IRC's Director of Youth and Volunteers, pointing around the area, "the Americans destroyed their houses. They destroyed them all. There is no furniture left. No nothing. So they need this help from us."

Jabi told us the Red Crescent had first tried to set up a camp closer to Fallujah, but she said that the area had come under repeated fire from American helicopters. "We established a camp seven kilometers outside of Fallujah," she explained, "but it was destroyed by the Americans. They burned two tents with a helicopter, and even until now we have a lot of tents there but we cannot send our volunteers to bring the tents here because it's very dangerous."

Waseem, Eunji, and I walked around the Red Crescent camp speaking to the new arrivals. One of them was a pudgy young boy, 12-year-old Khalid Anwar Khalidi. He hadn't been to school for almost a month. He said that when his family initially fled Fallujah two weeks before, they all crammed into a relative's home in the poor West Baghdad neighborhood of Washash.

"Before we came here we lived in a relative's house," he said. "There were nine families in that house, so it was very crowded. One family on top of the other. So my parents and my sister and my aunt and her two children moved to this camp. The rest of my relatives still live in that house."

Waseem patted Khalid on the head and smiled at him before walking over to his parents, who were lounging in a corner of their tent. He offered to try to get Khalid admitted to the school near his house, where the neighborhood was marginally safer, and even offered to take him into his home temporarily. Khalid's father smiled and turned down the offer.

It was a good thing, I thought, because Khalid's story repeated itself again and again across the camp. Poor Iraqi families who welcomed their relatives from Fallujah with open arms were unable to support them over what was becoming a long American siege.

"We are refugees in our own country," said one man from inside his tent. "It's so sad. We're just like the Palestinians." He told us his family of 12 had stayed with relatives in Baghdad for two weeks before coming to the Red Crescent camp. He said he had money to rent a house or apartment in Baghdad, but that now that he was a refugee, he didn't have a job—and he said he'd need to use his savings to fix the glass and doors of his house in Fallujah, which had been destroyed by the American army.

"I'm ashamed to be a refugee," he admitted. "I had to cross the street when my brother came to visit the camp. He said it was a shame on our whole family."

"It may be a long time before these refugees have normal lives again," Kamer Jabi said as we shook hands on our way out. "Of course they will eventually be able to go back to their houses," she said. "They have to give them some peace. All the Iraqi people are really tired of the war. For thirty-five years we were under that bastard Saddam Hussein, and now we are under the Americans. We are fed up. We are very tired."

But while the U.S. military had postponed an all-out assault on Fallujah, it hadn't given up on taking the city.

The next day, U.S. Marines launched a fresh assault on Fallujah, sending in air strikes and tanks. Shelling and fierce exchanges of gunfire broke out in midafternoon in areas that had already been pounded overnight by a heavy airborne AC-130 gunship, an aircraft that was first used in Vietnam.

Agence France-Presse reported that the AC-130 gunship unleashed a barrage of fire—including shells from a 105mm howitzer. Gunfire and explosions reverberated for nearly two hours, and an orange glow shone over the area while showers of sparks descended like fireworks.

BRUTALITY BECOMES
THE NORM

One reason that the bombing of Fallujah and the attack on al-Sadr provoked such anger among the people of Baghdad was that these sweeping moves by the U.S. military had corollaries in the lives of nearly every resident of the capital.

In Waseem's neighborhood, Mustansuriye, for example, increased tensions resulted in more American humvee patrols and a greater number of house-to-house searches. Almost every week, the Americans would arrest all the men from a building in his neighborhood and hold them at a nearby U.S. base. The base, in turn, came under more frequent attack, which meant more patrols and more arrests, followed by even more attacks.

"I want to explain this to the American listener," I told Waseem over breakfast at his home. "A lot of people in America think that there need to be more troops in Iraq in order to make the country safer. But it's not really like that. The more troops that are here, the more they make the Iraqi people angry and the more people join the resistance. I want to show how this cycle continues."

"This is very easy," Waseem responded. "In this neighborhood, there are many people who have been arrested. There are two men of religion who have just been arrested. We can try to meet them."

With that, we got into Waseem's purple van and drove toward Palestine Street, the neighborhood's main drag. But even before we got there, Waseem saw a group of men huddled around a busted automobile, their heads under the hood. One of his neighbors was among the work crew. It turned out that he had been among those rounded up by the Americans.

"You can interview him," Waseem said. "He was arrested and now he's been released."

Waseem introduced me, and we all shook hands and walked into the mechanic's house. Pepsi was served. I snapped open the can and turned on my minidisk recorder.

The mechanic, Salihuadul Karem, explained that he had been sitting in his home with his family one day the previous winter when the U.S. Army had swept through the neighborhood on one of their patrols. There were dozens of humvees. "They arrested everyone," he said. "Every man at least." Karem told me he was taken away along with his older brother and his 14-year-old younger brother, who suffers from severe mental retardation. Most of his neighbors were also taken away and incarcerated in the nearby U.S. base, where they were kept for questioning.

"They were looking for someone who had been attacking their base," Karem recalled. "His name was Mazen. So they kept asking us 'Are you Mazen!? Who is Mazen!?'"

Karem said his family was held for two days before authorities located Mazen and they were released. He was comparatively lucky.

He wasn't taken to Abu Ghraib, where he would have been held for months. But he hardly felt secure in his home.

"Two months later they came again, looking for someone else," he said. Again, they took his family to the military base for questioning and released them a few days later. "The Americans don't know the people so they don't know who their enemies are. But every time they do this they make more enemies and now I hate the Americans."

"It's very stupid," I agreed. "The Americans take people to prison and don't give them trials where people can prove whether they are guilty or innocent. They simply put you in prison and interrogate you. Then they decide to release you. Then they drive around your neighborhood with tanks and humvees and say, 'If you join with Muqtada Sadr we will crush you.'"

"You know," Karem said. "I am a Sunni and I am not so poor. Most people like me don't like Muqtada al-Sadr. His followers are gangsters. They're vigilantes. But now I've been thrown in prison twice by the Americans. Really I hate Muqtada. But now with the Americans going after him so strongly and Muqtada speaking out I begin to respect him somehow.

"We will welcome any foreign person from America or Britain or France," he added. "But if the army comes and puts itself in our face we will oppose it every time."

As the interview wound down and I packed up my recording materials, Karem's mentally retarded brother emerged from his room. He held his head at an odd angle and his words were totally incomprehensible. I imagined what it must have been like for him to be marched out of his house by American soldiers in full body armor. I tried to ask him how the events felt, but he was not capable of answering.

———

Back in the van, Waseem asked if I would need more interviews. In these unsafe days, he was always eager to return home as soon as possible.

"Let's try to get one more interview," I said. "Maybe one of the men of religion."

"Okay," Waseem said, sighing as he whipped the van onto Palestine Street. Five minutes later we wound down a peaceful side street lined with date palms and arrived at the Hussein Ali Shi'ite mosque.

"Wait here," Waseem said.

A few minutes later, he returned, a smile on his face.

"We are very lucky," he said. "The old man has just been released and he is excited to talk. Just remember, I told him you are French."

The old man, Sheik Abu Yasin al-Zawi, told me he was 62, but he looked a lot older. His hair was thin and white and he was missing at least two of his front teeth, the spaces between which were on full display as he smiled ear to ear, overjoyed at his release from prison. He invited me to sit on a plastic chair outside the mosque. It was a beautiful day, he said, and he didn't want to be indoors. A parishioner brought tea.

"I called Israel's assassination of [Hamas leader] Sheik Ahmed Yassin 'state terrorism' during Friday prayers," he explained. "I said the Palestinian and Iraqi people are both fighting against occupation. That's why they came to arrest me."

The story seemed in line with normal American procedures. First, they would come with overwhelming force when none was necessary—probably because they didn't know what to expect. They'd simply be acting on a tip from a paid informant in the neighborhood. "What happened?" I asked. "How did they arrest you?"

"They arrived at the mosque at five in the afternoon and surrounded the whole area with hummers and tanks," he said. "And they said, 'You said bad things about the coalition in Friday prayers and your son said bad things, too.' So they took my son, too."

"Did they take you to Abu Ghraib?" I asked. Saddam's most notorious prison was now holding at least 10,000 Iraqis. So many prisoners were held there, in fact, that the U.S. military had set up tents on the grounds of the prison to handle the overflow.

"No, thanks to God," Sheik al-Zawi said. "We were only taken to the American military base near the mosque."

The sheik told me he was kept in a very small cell without any type of bed or blanket. He said the American soldiers didn't allow him to wash for prayer and that they put a hood over his head. He said it was difficult to go to the bathroom because he would be escorted by a soldier who would point a gun at him while he used the toilet. "But I am lucky," he continued. "After twelve days, the Americans released me."

The sheik's quick release seemed to confirm his story. A picture was emerging: The Americans would arrest people who posed no particular threat and treat them poorly while they were in custody. When they realized there was no reason to continue holding them, they released them.

The next day, American television broadcast images from inside Abu Ghraib taken by American soldiers themselves. The images, which were shown on CBS's *60 Minutes II* program, were graphic and disturbing. One showed an Iraqi prisoner with electric wires attached to his genitals; another showed a dog attacking a prisoner; and a third showed prisoners being forced to simulate having sex with each other.

On *60 Minutes II,* the chief U.S. military spokesman in Iraq, Brigadier General Mark Kimmitt, offered an apology. "What would I tell the people of Iraq?" he asked rhetorically. "This is wrong. This is reprehensible." But he hastened to add a caveat. "This is not representative of the hundred and fifty thousand American soldiers that are over here. I would say the same thing to the American people. Don't judge your army based on the actions of a few."

The main source for the story broadcast on *60 Minutes II* had a different version. Soldier Ivan Frederick had written to his uncle, "I questioned some of the things that I saw . . . such as leaving inmates in their cell with no clothes or in females' underpants, handcuffing them to the door of their cell. I questioned this and the answer I got was, 'This is how military intelligence wants it done.'" He wrote that military intelligence had also "instructed us to place a prisoner in an isolation cell with little or no clothes, no toilet or running water, no ventilation or window for as much as three days."

In the United States, the images were met with shock and outrage. In Iraq, they were met with a sense of resignation. Atrocities committed by the Americans, described by so many Iraqis, had finally been confirmed.

As a journalist, I knew immediately what I wanted to do. I wanted to talk to the sheik I met at the West Baghdad mosque at the start of America's assault on Fallujah. He had told me his brother and two of his sons were incarcerated in Abu Ghraib. I knew he would be able to put the graphic photos in the proper context: that regardless of whether the practices depicted in the photos were isolated events, all my interviews suggested that the pattern of throwing people in prison under the slightest suspicion was widespread— and, in any case, just as important.

I ran my idea by Eunji and she thought it was a good one, but Waseem refused to go along to translate. He refused to travel to West Baghdad with us because it was a hotbed of insurgency. It wasn't safe, he said, and he advised us to rethink our plans.

But the job of a reporter is to report, and I saw no reason why the sheik would harm us when he had been so friendly before. So Eunji and I found Kadem, the former Ba'athist minder, and asked him to come with us.

Moments later, we were off, on the highway west toward Fallujah. On the same highway, in an eastbound lane, an American tank was on fire. It was obvious why Waseem had refused to come.

The sheik's street was peaceful, however. Like the other homes in this wealthy suburban neighborhood, his home was expansive. A Jaguar was parked out front. The sheik had dressed up for the interview, wearing traditional tribal robes with gold trim. "Welcome," he said. "Come in."

The sheik showed us into an opulently appointed living room with antique furniture and a crystal chandelier. The most prominent element of the room, however, was a portrait of the sheik's father. He was a general in the old Iraqi army, and in the portrait he was wearing his old Ba'athist uniform, with his thick, Sunni, Ba'athist mustache.

The sheik was courteous. His asked his wife to bring us tea, and when he finished, more tea appeared along with an assortment of fresh fruit. A full lunch was offered, but we declined.

"Can you formally introduce yourself?" I asked. Eunji had brought her camera and was taping the interview.

"My name is Sheik Ahmed Yahir al-Samari," he said. "My brother and two of my sons have been taken to Abu Ghraib. In addition, one of my other sons has been killed by the Americans. I will tell you all of their stories."

He started with his dead son, Nezar al-Samari.

Two of my sons came to Baghdad to go shopping here and then they got on the road to go back to Samara. It was late in the evening and they stopped to fix their car. Then the American soldiers came and saw them. They wanted to frisk them and search their whole car, so they told them to drive to an American base near Samara. They told them to get inside the car and go.

After a while, they told them to get out of the car. Then they ran their car over with a tank. At one in the morning the Americans took them to a dam over Samara. The water is very quick there and very powerful. The Americans told them to jump into the Tigris River. . . . You know it's a place where if you throw a piece of wood it will shatter into pieces. One of my sons survived, but the other one was found dead in the river fourteen days later.

I swallowed hard. I had no way of proving this story was true, but I didn't have any reason to doubt him. The U.S. military would eventually court-martial three soldiers in a similar case, where two brothers were thrown off the same dam-bridge in the middle of the night. A U.S. military spokesperson would tell the online journal *Slate* that—in that case—the two brothers were picked up for a curfew violation and taken to the police station for detention, but the police station was closed, so they were taken to the bridge. The U.S. military told *Slate* that the intention was to drop them off there so they would have to walk back, and that the last thing they saw was the two of them alive, standing facing each other talking, on the end of the dam-bridge.

In any case, Sheik Ahmed Yahir kept talking. He told me his brother, Sheik Katan, the main sheik of his tribe, had been taken to Abu Ghraib after a series of peace negotiations with American military commanders failed, and that he had been kept there for months.

Then he explained how two of his sons—who run an auto-parts store in Baghdad—were arrested by the American army:

I want to give you the picture of the site. They were working in [the mechanics' district] Sheik Omar street in Baghdad. They have a shop where they buy and sell auto parts. The Americans came and surrounded their shop. They arrested my three sons and other people from Samara who came to their shop. They didn't know anything about these people. Only that they are from Samara.

They surround their shop and they arrest them both. They also took two cars. One was a new Mercedes and the other was a Toyota pickup. They also took the money from the shop, both dollars and Iraqi currency. They took all the copy-books, and they tried to break everything that was in the shop. My sons had no weapons, no ammunition, nothing.

Now, Sheik Ahmed Yahir said, he and his wife were doing their best to raise five grandchildren on their own. They hadn't been able to visit either of their sons, but they have been able to piece together a picture of life in Abu Ghraib from a few people who have been released. They didn't repeat any of the grotesque allegations shown in the photographs broadcast on *60 Minutes II*. They said their relatives were being held outdoors in large tents on the grounds of the prison, without electricity or running water.

The Americans had arrested so many people that Saddam's old prison simply wasn't big enough. "Have the Americans made any apology for any of this?" I asked.

"They have given us only one apology," he said. "They have told us they are sorry for destroying our car and they have paid us six thousand dollars in compensation. But they have not apologized to us for the death of one of our sons, or the imprisonment of my two other sons and my brother."

"Is there anything you would like to say?" I asked. "To the people who might be listening to the radio?"

The sheik drew himself up tall and straightened his gold-trimmed robes. "I want people to know this is our country," he said, "and that they are occupiers. So the fact is that we will defend our country. Even the women. Not only the men."

As we got up to say good-bye, the sheik invited us to visit his tribe in Samara, deep in the heart of the Sunni Triangle. "Then you can see for yourself what the Americans do," he said.

I looked up at the portrait of the sheik's father in his Ba'athist army uniform. To be sure, this sheik was one of the "former regime elements" the U.S. military always talked about. Unlike many other Iraqis, his memories of the Saddam era were positive and he saw nothing wrong with trying to restore that status quo, albeit with a different face at the top.

"Does your family have anything to do with the resistance?" I asked, almost as an afterthought.

The answer came from the sheik's wife, Um Omar, who had arrived with another tray of tea and fresh fruit. She offered the type of denial that showed that the family supported armed attacks on Americans. "This is our country and they are occupiers," she said. "So it's a fact we will defend our country—even the women, not only men. I'm angry, because my sons didn't take part in any operation. They were innocent, so I am very, very angry."

Um Omar went on longer, declaring that Saddam was "merciful," and that he "always allowed the families to visit those in prison." I felt uncomfortable around people so obviously out of touch with their countrymen who had suffered so much during Ba'athist rule. But at the same time, there was much truth to what she said. It is absolutely natural to fight an unpopular occupying power, and I didn't think the fate that the Americans had inflicted on the sheik and his family was appropriate for anyone, even a Ba'athist.

Back at the Dulaimi that evening, Eunji and I took our beers out onto the balcony and looked out across the Tigris toward the Green Zone. Tanks went by, and we exchanged stories. Eunji told me that the U.S. occupation of Iraq reminded her of America's occupation of South Korea after World War II.

"What do you mean?" I asked, downing a significant portion of my 16-ounce can.

"As you know," Eunji responded, "for fifty years before World War II, Korea was under Japanese occupation. During that time, there were some Koreans who really tried to get our independence for ourselves. But it was not easy, and sadly we were freed because Japan lost the war and not because of our own efforts to get freedom. . . . Then the U.S. came to Korea as a temporary occupation regime. They controlled Korea for three years. During that occupation, we had a really hard time. The U.S. actually appointed the Korean president, Mr. Lee Seung-man. And just like the present Iraqi Governing Council, Mr. Lee's government was composed of people who were abroad during Japanese occupation. Actually, most of them were in the U.S., studying and working there. So it was just like the U.S. people entered the first Korean government. I wonder if they really wished for Koreans to make their own future, if they knew Korean history, or if they just followed what the U.S. wanted them to do. . . ."

Eunji took a sip from her beer and looked out toward the Green Zone. I sighed, and a time of silence passed between us as she gathered her thoughts, trying to find the best way to explain her country's history in such a succinct way.

"And during that time," she continued, "I mean during the U.S. occupation and early days of Korean independence, there were literally 'witch hunts.' Anyone who was against the United States was killed or imprisoned. They didn't need any other reason but to accuse them of being Communists. You didn't even need any evidence to accuse someone of Communist sympathies. Now in Iraq, it is terrorism. It was Communism in the past of Korea. But it is the same. They were the ones who went against U.S. policy. Then we had a war, the Korean War. The U.S. asked the world to help the U.S. and Korea to be against 'Communism.' It succeeded at that time. The U.S. could earn many countries' help. Just like the U.S. could get many countries' help to fight against the 'terrorism' in Iraq."

"But certainly," I argued, "you are happy that you are not living in North Korea under Kim Jong-Il, that instead of that you are living in South Korea?"

"I only know my system," Eunji answered, "but think about it this way: Even after fifty-nine years of Korean independence, a lot of U.S. troops are stationed in Korea . . . and the Korean government can't be free from the U.S. whenever it makes any decision."

It was a harsh statement. But there was truth to it. Fifty-nine years after Korean independence, there is even a law that says Korean troops cannot be deployed without asking permission from the local U.S. military commander, a situation strikingly similar to the situation of "Iraqi Forces" who fight alongside U.S. troops.

"We couldn't say 'no' to the U.S. when they asked us to send troops to Iraq." Eunji continued. "Why? Because the U.S. helped us a long time ago. . . . How can a small country forget the kindness that the superpower country offered a long time ago? It is the same in economic issues. That's why some Koreans still think we are a country kind of occupied by the U.S.

"Now," she said sadly, "I'm afraid that Iraq may not be able to get rid of the U.S.'s influence even after Iraq has its own election and its own government . . . even the democracy and freedom that U.S. promises to Iraq. Because as you know, Korea is still under a kind of U.S. imperialism . . . a new kind of . . . economic imperialism."

It was late and we were both exhausted, emotionally and physically. "Can you understand what I mean?" she asked.

"I can," I answered. I thought back to a visit I had made six months before to Gwangju, a mid-sized city in the southwest corner of South Korea. On May 18, 1980, protesting students had seized the city, demonstrating against U.S.-backed General Chun

Doo Hwan, who had seized control of the country and declared martial law.

The protestors won the first round. They kicked out the paratroopers and ran the city themselves. Within a week, though, tanks rolled into Gwangju (in an operation code-named "Glorious Vacation"). More than a thousand were injured and even more were arrested. Two thousand students and others were killed.

During the 1980 uprising, student protesters carried signs saying AMERICA OUR SAVIOR, hoping the United States would enter the conflict on their side and help overthrow the military dictatorship.

In Washington, President Jimmy Carter watched the situation closely. Half a world away, Iranian students had played a central role in the toppling of the U.S.-backed Shah and the rise of Ayatollah Khomeini. University students allied with Khomeini had taken over the U.S. Embassy in Tehran and taken 52 Americans hostage.

Worse, from Carter's perspective, Khomeini was trying to export his revolution. In neighboring Iraq, Muqtada al-Sadr's uncle, Grand Ayatollah Mohammed Baqir al-Sadr, had just been killed for trying to make a Khomeini-style Islamic Revolution in Iraq. Across Iraq, Saddam's forces were busy hunting down Sadr's followers, killing them or throwing them in prison. All the while, the Carter Administration stood by silently.

So perhaps it was because of these events that Carter decided to support the Korean military in its crackdown on student demonstrators in Gwangju. As Chun Doo Hwan's paratroopers circled the city and tested its perimeters, a meeting of high-level Carter Administration officials, including Warren Christopher and Richard Holbrooke, gave the nod to the military government to wipe out the rebels.

High-level cables granted to journalist Tim Shorrock in 1996 after Freedom of Information requests show that the officials "counseled moderation, but have not ruled out the use of force, should the Koreans need to employ it to restore order."

All of this circled inside my head in a dizzying haze as I listened to Eunji explain the parallels between Iraq in the present and South Korea after World War II.

"I'm sorry for my poor English," Eunji apologized. "Maybe the logic itself is very poor . . . frankly speaking, I had some alcohol right before . . . maybe it is the alcohol."

"No," I said. "It's not the alcohol; your point is very good and very important." There were definite parallels between Iraq and South Korea, in a way that could give hope for the future. After many years of living under military dictatorships supported by America, the South Korean people *did* succeed in getting democracy. Students demonstrated every year on the anniversary of the massacre at Gwangju and until South Koreans took to the streets for 19 consecutive days in 1987 and forced Ronald Reagan to pull his support for South Korea's military government and join the people of South Korea in supporting free elections. It was not that the U.S. government was opposed to democracy and freedom per se, but that the United States' foreign policy was primarily concerned with U.S. interests and not with those of the other peoples of the world. If Communism is the main enemy, it doesn't matter how many people we hurt fighting it. If Ayatollah Khomeini is the enemy, it doesn't matter how many Iraqis Saddam kills. If terrorism is the enemy, it doesn't matter what our troops do here in Iraq. It is all seen as some kind of collateral damage, a small negative side effect of the great good we are supposedly doing in the world through our main war. But what we don't realize is that each of these countries has real people living in it who suffer horribly when we occupy their country, as in Iraq, or support a military dictatorship, as in South Korea.

After I finished, Eunji sat in silence, staring off into the distance.

Cars passed on the streets below, tanks went by, too, and the speakers of mosques called out for the late-night prayer.

"I'm sorry," I apologized. "It's late. Let's go to bed."

Back in the United States, the issue of torture at Abu Ghraib became a major scandal. Just a few days after CBS broadcast the first photos, Seymour Hersh published an article in *The New Yorker* magazine with a second round of shots. One photo showed a dead inmate at Abu Ghraib wrapped in cellophane and packed in ice. Another photo showed an empty room in Abu Ghraib prison splattered with blood. More disturbingly, *The New Yorker* demonstrated that higher-ups in the U.S. military had known about abuses at the prison. In his article, Hersh cited an internal military report by Major General Antonio Taguba showing that senior Pentagon officials had known about what Taguba called "sadistic, blatant and wanton criminal abuses" for months.

The photos and the facts of Hersh's reporting in *The New Yorker* sparked a fury on Capitol Hill. Hearings were held, and Democratic politicians demanded Donald Rumsfeld's resignation.

In damage-control mode, George W. Bush granted an interview to the State Department–funded Arabic satellite channel al-Hurra (though he declined an invitation to be interviewed by al-Jazeera). "It's important for the people of Iraq to know that in a democracy everything is not perfect," he said. "That mistakes were made. But that in a democracy as well, those mistakes will be investigated and people will be brought to justice."

As I sat in my apartment in Baghdad, the whole spectacle seemed a little strange. The hearings on Capitol Hill were all designed to discover who inside the Pentagon knew what when about the abuses in the photos and who in the administration should be punished.

But no one seemed to be questioning why the prisoners were taken in the first place. Since the end of Saddam's regime, every person locked up in Abu Ghraib had been put there for political reasons (common criminals were sent to other prisons). So all those locked up in Abu Ghraib were there because they were suspected of supporting the armed resistance.

Largly lost amidst the horrors of the graphic torture photos that continued to emerge daily was a leaked report from the International Committee of the Red Cross, which was first published by the *Wall Street Journal.* In their report, the ICRC, the only organization besides the United States military that'd been allowed to inspect the prison, wrote that 90 percent of captives had been caught by mistake. In their report, the ICRC also registered that Coalition forces failed to set up a system families could use to locate their loved ones, creating a situation the report called "missing in custody." It said such a lack of information caused increasing rage among Iraqis against occupation forces.

None of these results surprised me. I thought of the villagers in Abu Siffa I had met months earlier; of Waseem's neighbor, Salihuadul Karem, and his mentally retarded brother. I thought also of the children of Sheik Ahmed Yahir al-Samari. All of their arrests only fed support for the resistance and the growing sense among the public that the U.S. military needed to leave Iraq, and soon.

.19.

DEAD SHEIKS
IN BABYLON

All the while, the situation in the Shi'ite holy city, Najaf, continued to deteriorate. As lawmakers on Capitol Hill grappled with
what to do about Abu Ghraib, U.S. troops backed by helicopter
gunships entered Najaf, clashing with the followers of Muqtada al-
Sadr. The U.S. military claimed that 64 Iraqi fighters were killed in
the first day of fighting, though hospital officials in Najaf told the
Arab satellite network al-Jazeera that most of the 28 injured
brought in from the clashes appeared to be civilians.

It was the first time U.S. troops had tried to enter Najaf. They
had moved into the old Spanish military base on the edge of the
city as 1,400 soldiers from Spain, Honduras, and the Dominican
Republic pulled out of Iraq. It was also the same spot where gun
battles first erupted at the beginning of April after U.S. forces
closed Sadr's newspaper, *al-Hawza,* and arrested one of his chief

advisors. After that, occupation authorities produced an arrest warrant for al-Sadr and announced that they wouldn't rest until he was captured or killed.

"I can't believe the Americans are attacking Najaf," I told James one day, both of us cooped up in the Dulaimi. "It's not impossible that they would flatten the shrine of Imam Ali. If that happens, the rage we will see will be nothing like anything we've seen before. It will be Fallujah a thousand times over."

James disagreed. "The Americans must know this," he said. "They must know better than to completely destroy one of the holiest places to the Shia. They must know it would be all over if they did that."

The initial signs, however, were not good. As the American army readied for its entry into Najaf, Brigadier General Mark Herling told reporters, "We're going to drive this guy Sadr into the dirt."

But inside the holy city, Muqtada al-Sadr was hardly talking about surrender.

In his sermon in Najaf on Friday, the cleric told his followers he would never agree to follow the laws of the American occupation. As before, he demanded a free election in Iraq before giving up the guns of his Mehdi Army. And he quoted one of Shia Islam's most important martyrs, Imam Hussein, to explain his position.

"Our people didn't give our hand to the devil," he said. "We have our dignity, so we can't be traitors."

Since it would be difficult to travel to Najaf, I suggested to Waseem that we interview some of the more mainstream Shi'ite political parties to get their perspective on the standoff. First on my list of priorities was the Da'wa Party, which had been co-founded by Muqtada al-Sadr's uncle Grand Ayatollah Mohammed Baqir al-Sadr with the goal of making Iraq an Islamic state. I especially wanted to talk to the leader of that party, Ibrahim al-Jaafari, a widely respected man who opposed the American assault and had offered to mediate between al-Sadr and the Americans, but when we went to Jafaari's office, his assistant told us he would not be available for an interview.

So we got back into the van and drove toward the general head-quarters of the other mainline Shi'ite political party, the Supreme Council for Islamic Revolution in Iraq, which, like the Da'wa Party, held a seat on the U.S.-appointed Governing Council. After a short wait in their lobby, we were shown upstairs to meet with Dr. Sa'ad Jawad Kindil, the party's deputy director for politics.

"What we are concerned about mainly is the safety of the people and the religious shrines of Najaf and Karbala," he began.

"The problems in Najaf," I challenged him immediately, "whose fault are they? The Americans or al-Sadr?"

"We are trying to mediate between Muqtada al-Sadr and the U.S. military," he replied evenly. "The *hawza* [Shia religious authority] has called on all factions with guns to leave the holy cities, and that includes the U.S. Army. We have asked the Americans to withdraw from Najaf until after the restoration of Iraqi sovereignty June 30th."

He said full Iraqi sovereignty represented the best hope for pro-tecting the people and the sacred shrine of Imam Ali. He took particular exception to the arrest warrant the U.S. Administrator L. Paul Bremer had announced, accusing al-Sadr of murdering a U.S.-backed ayatollah after the American military flew the ayatol-lah back to Iraq from Britain following the fall of Saddam.

"Any outlaw memorandum against al-Sadr must be taken through Iraqi channels and must be dealt with through Iraqi chan-nels and with Iraqi authority," Dr. Kindil continued. "Even if they have a memorandum against al-Sadr, that does not justify Ameri-can military action in the area."

Also key to defusing the dispute, according to the SCIRI's Dr. Kindil, was allowing Iraqis to take a greater role in keeping security in Iraq.

"From the very beginning it was clear American forces would not be able to maintain security," Dr. Kindil asserted. "They don't know the people. The people don't know them and they don't know the country. There is no trust between those two sides as between Iraqi forces and the people."

But Dr. Kindil said SCIRI's plan had gotten a cool response from the U.S. government, which planned to continue not only to command its own force of 135,000 after the political hand-over but also to keep control over the new Iraqi army it had trained after the overthrow of Saddam Hussein.

Speaking on Fox News, U.S. Secretary of State Colin Powell said U.S. control of Iraqi forces is necessary "because you have to have unity of command. You can't have two military forces operating independently of one another. So to some extent, they would yield some of their sovereignty to our military commanders."

What this meant, though, was that the occupation would continue indefinitely, and that the hand-over of sovereignty would be largely a matter of paperwork and not facts on the ground.

As the U.S. attack on Najaf escalated, it became clear that I would need to visit the city and make a report. I had regular e-mails from editors requesting a report from the city. The trick was making the trip in, and out, safely.

Luckily, an opportunity appeared immediately in the form of Salam Talib, a Baghdad computer scientist who had been working with foreign peace activists and left-wing journalists since the fall of Saddam's regime a year before. When James returned from Kurdistan, he had planned to film Sadr's movement with Salam. Unfortunately, Salam couldn't leave Baghdad for weeks, and James thought his presence was necessary to make the film.

James's misfortune was a boon to me and Eunji. In many ways the ideal partner on this project, Salam had close ties with the Sadr movement. His brother was head of the Sadr office in Hilla, near Babylon, and was a longtime organizer against Saddam. When the revolution to topple the regime failed in 1991, Salam had helped many of his relatives escape to Syria or Jordan. In 1998, when Saddam killed Muqtada al-Sadr's father, Grand Ayatollah Mohammed Sadiq al-Sadr, Salam had again helped many escape.

Days went by before Salam judged the road safe. But on the morning of May 2, he stopped by the Dulaimi at 8 A.M. for our trip to Najaf.

I sat in the passenger seat of Salam's car and Eunji sat in the back. "If anyone asks, she is your wife," Salam said to me.

"Okay," Eunji responded, laughing. "What if I want a divorce?"

"You can't get one," Salam responded. "It's for your own safety. Here, wear this." Though Eunji was already clad in a black headscarf, Salam told her it would be smart to cover even more of herslef. So he had brought her a black *chador* that would cover her whole body.

"I can't use my camera under all of this," Eunji complained.

"The people of Najaf are very conservative," Salam responded. "We have to be respectful."

With that, he reached for curtains he had installed along his rear windows and pulled them shut. We were on our way.

As we drove south, we hit a U.S. military traffic jam. The entire highway, both southbound and northbound, had been closed by the Americans because of a bomb scare. In the end, a commander told us that no bomb had been found, but that security dictated the highway be closed at the slightest provocation. After an hour in the same place, we started moving southward.

"What do you think about Sistani?" I asked Salam. The 73-year-old Grand Ayatollah was the most revered religious leader in Iraq, but his accommodating stance with the Americans had angered many of Sadr's followers. So far, Sistani had remained virtually silent on the subject of Najaf.

"Let me ask you something, Aaron," Salam said. "Why did Saddam allow Sistani to live? He killed Mohammed Sadiq al-Sadr and Mohammed Baqir al-Sadr and so many other very important religious men. But he let Sistani live. Why do you think that is?"

"The Americans say it's because Sistani believes in the separation of the clergy and the government and so he didn't get mixed up in politics," I said. Since the Americans had taken over, Sistani's political advocacy could be summarized by one word: elections. Whenever he spoke he seemed to be promoting them, presumably as a way of ending decades of Sunni dominance over Iraq's Shi'ite majority.

"But what kind of man," Salam objected, "sits by for thirty-five years while his people are slaughtered by such a brutal regime? And now we have the Americans."

"Some people call him the quiet *hawza*, the quiet religious authority," I said, "because he only speaks when it's really important. That way, his words carry weight."

"That's why I call him the silent *hawza*," Salam joked. "Everyone on every street is asking 'Where is the democracy? Where is the freedom?' but he remains silent."

We drove by Hilla, where Salam's family lived, and I recognized the remains of Saddam's mass graves from the 1991 uprising on my right.

Two hours later, we were in Najaf.

The approach into Najaf was not what I expected. There was no American checkpoint on the city's outskirts and the checkpoint set up by Sadr's followers was extremely relaxed.

His followers simply waved us through. None of us was searched and the trunk wasn't touched.

On the streets of Najaf, everything seemed peaceful, if overly quiet. The streets were virtually empty. War could reignite any minute, and Shi'ite pilgrims from Iran, India, and Lebanon were staying away in droves.

Salam parked the car as close to the Imam Ali Shrine as we could get, and we walked toward the main office of Muqtada al-Sadr, which was directly across the street from the shrine. Eunji put on her *chador* and we walked up to meet the guards outside Sadr's office.

As they searched our bags, we asked to hear their stories. These young men were the frontline troops of Sadr's Mehdi Army. The night before, 20 of their group had died in clashes with the U.S. military. No American soldiers had been killed. The first one introduced himself as Ali Daoud, from Basra. He said he was 25, but he didn't look a day over 16. He wore a gray, black, and red T-shirt with the words THE BEST FASHION written across the front. "Why did you come to Najaf," I asked.

"I came here as soon as the Americans called al-Sadr a criminal. I have to defend this sacred shrine from the occupiers. My brothers are also in the Mehdi Army," he said. "They are defending Basra. First they were here and I was there, but then we traded off."

"Is it hard coming here," I asked, "being so far from your family?"

"It's not hard to come here," he said. "I just miss al-Sadr when I'm not near him and I want to martyr myself here and go to heaven."

The young men had finished searching our bags, and we had nothing left to ask. We thanked them for their time and walked on past.

The shrine was right in front of us now, a large square building with an elaborately tiled blue-and-green fresco in the entryway. In

front were a number of banners bearing slogans in favor of Muqtada al-Sadr.

Salam asked us to stay and have some tea while he talked to the
sheiks in the Sadr office and arranged an interview.

After just a few moments inside the office, though, Salam
emerged with troubling news. While we'd been driving south
toward Najaf, U.S. forces had raided a meeting of a group that had
been founded with the help of the U.S. government, the Babylon
Human Rights Organization. There, they had killed two senior
sheiks in the Sadr organization and taken at least one prisoner. The
prisoner was Salam's brother, Adnan Onaibi, the head of Sadr's
office in Hilla.

The sheiks from inside Sadr's office came out to make a brief
statement to us. At their center was a tall, black-turbaned man,
with a long salt-and-pepper beard. His name was Sayyed Fadel al-
Mousawie.

"All types of power were represented," he explained. "The political parties and scientists and religious men. They were trying to
figure out what's happening around us. They were discussing everything that was happening in Hilla. They were studying what's happening in our country and what to do about it. They were not
armed and were not fighting."

I would later find the sheik's account to be truthful, but for now
details were sketchy. Sayyed Fadel al-Mousawie said the bodies of
the slain sheiks were on their way to Najaf to be buried as martyrs.
After that, he said, there would be more details. At this time, he
said only that the Americans "showed no respect for anyone in this
attack. They started to beat the people and they attacked their
rights and arrested some and killed some."

"The prisoner, was he taken to Abu Ghraib?" I asked.

"I don't know," the sheik responded. "But we know that what the
Americans are doing in there is nothing compared to what they are

really doing. What's hidden is more than what they show. As we say here, you get what you put in a glass. They disguise themselves as a democractic people, but they hold up democracy and freedom for all the Iraqis."

As the interview continued, Salam nudged me. "We need to finish," he said. A crowd had gathered around us. I thanked the sheik and turned my attention to a businessman who had joined the crowd. He identified himself as Akil Abdul-Munaf Zwein. He said he had been negotiating with American military commanders on behalf of Muqtada al-Sadr.

"The chiefs of all the area tribes are in these negotiations also," he noted. "One condition asked for by Muqtada al-Sadr is to remove the American troops from Najaf because it holds the sacred shrine of Imam Ali, peace be upon him. Second, we demand Muqtada al-Sadr not be arrested or killed by occupation troops and that his fate be determined by a legitimate, elected Iraqi government. In exchange, Muqtada al-Sadr will put down his arms. It is up to them, we don't want to fight."

"Will the Americans agree to this?"

"I think so," he said. "The lead negotiator of the Americans in Najaf has agreed, but it must be approved in Washington also. So we are waiting."

A few days later, the Bush Administration rejected the offer. The two sides would fight for five months before Ayatollah Sistani brokered a peace deal whose terms mirrored Sadr's demands. As soon as the U.S. military dropped its demand that the cleric be captured or killed, Sadr returned to his position as a prominent and somewhat popular political figure.

The interview over, the crowd dispersed. Salam was incredibly calm given the circumstances. He suggested that we remain in Najaf until the bodies of the dead sheiks arrived, and then head to Najaf to see his family. We retired to a nearby store and ate falafel.

An hour later, dozens of followers of Muqtada al-Sadr had arrived from Hilla, singing songs of martyrdom as they carried the coffins of two of their slain comrades into the shrine of the revered Imam Ali. There was no resignation in the voices of the mourners, whose chants spoke of undying loyalty to the Sadr family.

When the ceremony finished, we obtained the names of the two dead sheiks, Methen al-Khzoni and Satchit al-Mahawli.

Then we got back into the car and headed for Hilla.

In Hilla, Salam pulled off the freeway and onto a poorly maintained dirt road lined with palm trees. Children were playing along the road. "These dirt roads are because of Saddam," Salam said. "Saddam didn't let us pave them. He kept all the money for himself. Now the Americans are here and we have the same terrible roads and the same prison."

With that, Salam killed the ignition of his car. We were at the home of his brother Ahsen Onaibi, a logical first step to investigate the raid on the Babylon Human Rights Organization and the detention of Salam's other brother, Adnan. Ahsen was too broken up to speak, so we spoke to his wife Um Ali, a lively woman clad in black *chador*.

"What do you know about what happened?" I asked. "Is Adnan okay?"

"They detained him because he was in the meeting," she said. "They attacked the office and they detained him. I wish I had more information, but I can't because the American soldiers refused. We went to their base but no one would answer our questions."

"Did you try to find out what happened to Adnan?" I asked.

"Yes," she replied, "We tried to go to their base this afternoon, but they stopped us two kilometers from their main base. No one can go in."

Um Ali said Adnan Onaibi had never expected to be organizing against the Americans. "Sayyed Adnan was hoping that Americans would liberate us from Saddam," she said, "and he was happy when the war began because he was tortured so much by the old regime."

She explained that Adnan had been imprisoned in 1999 for giving a fiery speech during Friday prayers. The impetus was Saddam's killing of Muqtada al-Sadr's father, Grand Ayatollah Mohammed Sadiq al-Sadr.

"Why do you think the Americans put him in prison?" I asked.

"He was the head of the Sadr office in Hilla," she answered, "and the Americans are against al-Sadr. But here in Hilla everything has been quiet. There has been no fighting. Everything has been quiet until now. He didn't make any war against the Americans, he just uses words. That's what they told us they were giving us. That's democracy. That means you can express your ideas."

Adnan's brother regained his composure. "We can go to the Human Rights Organization," he said. "We got a phone call and they have a witness. He said that after ten minutes of the meeting, the Americans attacked, that they tied the guards and detained Adnan and then killed two sheiks and then left with their tanks."

Again, it was time to move. Salam, Eunji, and I got into the car and followed Ahsen to the scene of Adnan's arrest.

As the evening call to prayer rang through the air, I looked up at a gigantic sign in English and Arabic. It said BABYLON HUMAN RIGHTS ORGANIZATION. The Americans would have been hard pressed to mistake the building for anything else.

Inside, we found a few members of the community, but none of them had been eyewitnesses to the attack.

It didn't matter, though. The images told the story on their own. Chairs, which had originally been lined up in neat rows for a community meeting, were strewn every which way. One section of wall on the far side of the room was riddled with bullet holes five and a half feet from the ground. Splattered next to them on the wall were fragments of the two sheiks' brains.

Eunji photographed the scene. I wanted to throw up.

"There are only bullet holes on one wall," I noted to Salam. "If there was a fight, there should be shots fired in both directions." Everything about the scene seemed to confirm the basics of the Sadr movement's story: that the Americans had come into the community meeting and killed the two sheiks execution-style while arresting the head of the Sadr office, Adnan Onaibi. They probably thought they could get some information from him through interrogation.

"Shall we talk to the eyewitness?" Salam asked. One of the community members had given him the address of one of the attendees.

We walked back to the car and drove through the twilight to a date farm on the outskirts of town.

I knocked on the farmhouse door.

A man came to the door in his pajamas. His jaw was swollen and he had a gauze bandage around the top of his head; blood was seeping through. He had a huge scab on his lower lip.

Initially, he was disoriented, confused about the purpose of our visit, but Salam explained that his brother was Adnan Onaibi, the one who had been taken away, and that Eunji and I were journalists, and friends.

He introduced himself as Hazem al-Safi, a spokesperson for the Babylon Human Rights Organization and editor of its newsletter. We shook hands, and he called for his children to bring tea. He directed us to sit outside, because dusk was coming and there was no electricity.

"Mr. Adnan was speaking when the Americans came, and he was

very optimistic in his speech," Hazem said. "You know the language that the Americans use is very strange, and the speech that Mr. Adnan gave was very sane. He was asking: 'How can we win our freedom by peaceful means?'"

"We were peaceful," Hazem al-Safi went on. "We just had pens and paper, and Mr. Adnan, he had just his turban, but they came with a whole bunch of arms."

Hazem told us that about 15 American soldiers had entered with machine guns leveled. "They had a translator who ordered everyone down on the ground," Hazem explained. "Then it was just a lot of American soldiers barking in English, so I lifted up my head to ask what was going on, and an American soldier stomped on my head."

That explained the wounds and bandage.

Hazem said that after subduing the crowd, the soldiers ran to the podium and arrested Salam's brother, Sayyed Adnan Onaibi, the head of Muqtada al-Sadr's office in Hilla, placing a black hood over his head. The other man at the podium was also arrested, Hazem said, although he was only present to read the Qu'ran and did not follow al-Sadr.

It would be almost impossible to construct these same events from the American side. Every U.S. official we talked to said they knew nothing about the raid, which was carried out by troops stationed in another part of the country. The Iraqi police in Hilla likewise professed ignorance and told us it was standard practice for the Americans to bring policemen from another town to join them when they had to crack down. Local police officers would be known to the community, so retaliation would be likely.

"What about the two sheiks?" I asked Hazem. "What happened with them?"

"They shot them in the head," he responded. "They just walked across the room and shot them in the head. They shot them right where they were standing and you can see from the blood that they shot them from just one or two meters away." Like other witnesses, Hazem didn't see the killing itself because his head had been forced down on the ground.

"What do you think will happen now?" I asked, eager to finish up. Darkness was falling. I didn't want to be on the road late at night.

"America lost this fight," Hazem concluded. "The people in this meeting were from the whole spectrum of the city and they all saw what happened. So the Americans are losing very good people who were in this meeting.

"I'm embarrassed very much," he went on, "because I was representing the peaceful ideas. You know, I was a friend of [U.S. Deputy Secretary of Defense] Paul Wolfowitz. He came to our center last year to talk about the importance of human rights."

"You were friends with Paul Wolfowitz?" I asked somewhat incredulously.

"Yes," he responded.

"Do you have any proof of this?" I asked. "Some letter or photo to prove your relationship? This will be very interesting to people listening to the radio in America."

Hazem said he had many photos. He asked his children to go back into the house with candles, because the electricity was still out. A few minutes later they returned with a stack of photographs of Hazem al-Safi and Paul Wolfowitz shaking hands.

"I was a friend of Paul Wolfowitz," Hazem al-Safi repeated, "but they lose when they detain someone like Adnan because they make new enemies for themselves."

I was amazed at this turn of events, and despite the pictures provided by Hazem, I thought there must be some inaccuracy somewhere. But when I researched the issue later, I found an account in *American Forces Press Service* of Wolfowitz's October 23, 2003 visit.

According to the article, the deputy secretary told the assembled crowd that "democracy means many things to people," but that successful democracy requires the involvement of its citizens. He said: "The key to preventing another dictator is to participate in the political process and to work to ensure that all people's rights are protected." The report said Wolfowitz had told the group that each of them had the power to make a difference and urged them to strive to make positive changes in their country.

But in the six months since his visit, events had transpired that Wolfowitz may not have anticipated. People in Iraq were becoming more involved in the political process, but primarily to band together to oppose the U.S. occupation.

We said good-bye to Hazem and got back into Salam's car to head back to Baghdad. But before we started, Salam asked if we could make one last stop, to the big military base in Babylon near Hilla, which was maintained by Poland. His family members had not been allowed to approach the base, he said. Maybe Eunji or I could find out where his brother was being held. "Maybe," Salam said morbidly, "he is dead. It would be important to know."

But there were no answers at the Polish base. After wading through a stilted communication with a number of soldiers who spoke neither English nor Arabic, Eunji and I were pointed toward a telephone in the base's entry checkpoint that connected us to an English-speaking press officer inside. When we asked about the raid on the human-rights association and the detention of Adnan Onaibi, the press officer said he knew nothing about the affair.

"We have no American soldiers in this base," he said, "and we do not do any raids like the ones you speak of. All of those activities are done by the Americans. They must have come from another town. Have you tried the CPA headquarters in Baghdad?"

"No luck," I said to Salam as we got back to the car. It had been a long day and we headed back to Baghdad in silence.

The next day, Eunji went to the CPA office to find out about Salam's brother. They told her it was against policy to tell anyone anything about where any detainee was taken until at least 10 days after the arrest. It would be a month before Salam would learn that his brother had been shot in custody and that he was being held in Abu Ghraib. Two months after that, the Americans would finally charge him with the murder of a member of the Coalition forces, but they would refuse to name the date and place of the alleged murder.

.20.

VICTORY RISES ABOVE
A MASS GRAVE

Meantime, in Fallujah, the rhetoric of the American side cooled down. After the death of more than 100 American soldiers, U.S. military officials stopped talking about "punishing" terrorists and foreign fighters in Fallujah. Speaking on CNN on April 29, Secretary of State Colin Powell said he hoped "the fight in Fallujah would no longer be a fight in Fallujah." He threw his support behind local negotiators "who will be able to talk to the people inside the town and say 'Let's end this; let's bring this to a conclusion.'"

"We want to help the people of Fallujah," he said. "We want peace in Fallujah, not war in Fallujah. We can find a peaceful solution and that will be over, and we can get on with the process of getting ready for the transition to a sovereign government."

In his weekly radio address two days later, President Bush said the American effort was designed to "ensure an atmosphere of se-curity as Iraqis move toward self-government."

General Jasim Muhammad Saleh, a former commander of Sad-dam Hussein's feared Republican Guard, entered Fallujah in his old Ba'athist Army uniform to command a new Iraqi-only force called the Fallujah Protective Brigade. Refugees, waiting outside the barbed wire where the Marine Corps had cordoned off the city, cheered his arrival. Americans began to withdraw to checkpoints outside the city. The barbed wire was bundled up and thrown away.

The end of the siege was in sight. On Saturday, May 1, the Prophet Mohammed's birthday, I decided it was safe to go to Fal-lujah myself. So Eunji and I got into a car and drove west out of Baghdad.

On this day, Eunji and I decided to work with Kadem, the for-mer employee of the Ba'ath Party's information ministry. He was the wrong person to work with most of the time, but exactly the right person to travel to Fallujah with, because Fallujah was one of the few places in Iraq where Saddam's regime was popular.

As usual, the road to Fallujah was the center of conflict. A U.S. military truck on the opposite side of the highway burned out of control and dark black smoke billowed into the air, but when we arrived at the outskirts of the city the mood was one of exhaustion rather than anger.

The day after General Saleh entered Fallujah, most American troops had left the city and set up new checkpoints off the main road. By the time we arrived at nine in the morning, long queues of cars had already formed—many of the cars filled with entire fami-lies eager to return home after a month as refugees. Others carried a single male resident of Fallujah, returning to see if the situation was safe enough for the rest of his family to return.

To avoid waiting in line, we decided to leave our car outside the city and walk through the checkpoint. U.S. Marines checked our documents and searched our bags, but they allowed us to pass through ahead of the refugees, whose vehicles took much longer to inspect. Once across to the other side, we hailed a taxi and asked the driver if he would be willing to drive us around for a few hours. He took our offer.

The first place we went was a shopping center that had been bombed by the U.S. Marine Corps. The roof of the block-long complex had collapsed in on itself, rendering the three-story building a pile of rubble. A group of locals quickly crowded around when we got out of the car. A bald middle-aged man stepped forward from the group and introduced himself as Mohammed Abas al-Ashrawi, a small businessman.

"This commercial complex was destroyed," he told me, "but it doesn't mean we lost. We won because the Americans left Fallujah. They want to destroy the entire Iraqi civilization, but we broke the noose of America and we are the winner." Everyone around nodded in agreement.

We asked Mohammed if he would be willing to take us to the Golan District, where the heaviest fighting took place. He agreed and we all piled into our taxi and slowly made our way through deserted streets to a small alley where two *mujahadeen* were relaxing—young Iraqis, their faces covered by red and white *kaffiyehs*. "There's still U.S. Marine sniper fire in the area," they warned us. "Stay close to the buildings and be careful."

Most of the houses around us had been destroyed. Whole streets had been reduced to rubble; stray bits of normal life peeked through to the surface in full color amidst the gray cement debris— a stray pillowcase, a bit of sofa, and a teddy bear littered one lot that used to support a house.

The *mujahadeen* wanted to take us to a nearby mosque that had been bombed by the Americans. "There were no fighters inside the mosque," one rebel insisted when we arrived there, "only people who had come to pray."

"They killed our Muslim brothers and raided Allah's house," the other one added. "They shot the minarets and the sanctuary in the time of prayer and they destroyed the Qu'ran."

Our first stop at the mosque was the room of the man who reads the call to prayer, which would normally be broadcast from the minaret's speakers five times a day. The windows of the room had been shattered, and the room itself had been burned. Looking up, we saw that the minaret had been shot—probably by a helicopter gunship. The pulpit where the imam delivered his Friday sermon had also been destroyed.

"This is the blood of our Muslim brothers," the first *mujahadeen* said, pointing at a dried red trickle on the mosque's carpet. "Is that democracy? Is this a democracy? The houses of Allah and the sacred places—they don't respect it. You can see by your eyes we are defending our religion and our country."

I scanned the mosque, looking for shell casings. I doubted that the rebel claims were correct—that they had never stockpiled any arms in this mosque. But I was nonetheless surprised that the U.S. Marine Corps thought it appropriate to bomb the sacred building, because—regardless of who was inside—most Iraqis would be irate when they saw that the Americans had destroyed a house of God.

We crossed town to another mosque. This one was larger and more important, the head of the Sunni Association of Islamic Scientists, which had negotiated the release of many of the foreigners taken hostage by resistance fighters that month.

Two giant craters caused by American air-strikes had filled with raw sewage. Despite the destruction all around them, most of the men gathered here felt they'd won a hard-fought victory. Ayyad Tapid Abbas was amongst the crowd: "For twenty-five days they used everything they had—tanks, planes, helicopters—everything and many other kinds of weapons. They couldn't enter this heroic city."

My translator Kadem realized that Eunji had walked away to take photos and went to make sure she was safe. I was left alone in front of the mosque talking to Fallujans I'd just met.

"God is with us and we are right," Abbas continued. "If any American appears on the street we will shoot him."

The sheik of the mosque, Abdul Kadr al-Isawie, walked up to me and introduced himself. He said the images released showing American soldiers torturing Iraqi prisoners at Saddam's old prison, Abu Ghraib, showed that suffering and cruelty are the norm under U.S. occupation. "This torture will not pass without punishment," he tells me. "This is against our dignity. That's what the residents of Fallujah say."

Sheik Abdul Kadr al-Isawie was hardly cowed by the fury unleashed by the killing of four American contractors—whose dead bodies were dragged through town and then hung from a bridge. He said a similar fate will meet the members of the U.S.-appointed Iraqi Governing Council if they fail to respond to the allegations of brutality against incarcerated Iraqis.

"I swear to God that we will pull out the members of the Governing Council and we will hang them on the old Fallujah bridge," he said. "Those are the men who brought America and this destruction and they will hang on the doors of all the houses in Fallujah."

Sheik al-Isawie denied that such actions constitute terrorism: "Is there any terrorist in Iraq?" he asked. "There is no terrorism and that's a fact. We only defend our houses and our city."

Clearly, the assault on Fallujah had done nothing to stop the armed insurgency. I thanked the sheik for his time and went looking for my translator and our guide, small-businessman Mohammed

Abas al-Ashrawi. He told us he had to go, but before leaving he asked us if we wanted to come to his house for lunch.

We declined. We still had a long list of places to go in Fallujah before we left. He insisted, but we told him we wanted to visit the soccer stadium that had been turned into a graveyard.

On our way to the municipal soccer stadium, we spotted a group of locals outside a single family home. Many of them were wearing surgical masks, so we pulled over.

We found the head of the medical team and asked him what was going on. He explained that volunteers from his clinic had come to take the rotting corpse of a middle-aged woman to the soccer stadium so it could have a proper burial. For three weeks, he said, the woman's body has been rotting in the front yard of this house as the owner waited for the bombing to stop.

When I asked for his name, the head of the medical team turned his name-tag around and asked to speak anonymously. His clinic's ambulance was shot by U.S. Marine snipers twice during the siege. One of the clinic's volunteers was killed.

"The Americans are dogs," he said. "They try to kill anybody who works in humanitarian aid. They attack any humanitarian-aid worker, doctor, or ambulance to kill him."

The volunteers in surgical masks lifted the woman's rotting corpse from its shallow grave in the front yard of a single-family home. The owner of the house explained how the woman came to be lying dead in his front yard. He said an American warplane bombed her car as she fled the city with her husband, who was now buried in the garden of the house next-door. The charred remains of the car still sat a few meters away from his front door.

"We couldn't give her a proper burial," he says, "because every time we would go outside, American snipers would shoot at us.

They even shot at us when we retreived her body from the car after the Americans bombed it."

In the meantime, the aid worker said that many corpses continued to rot under buildings, which collapsed on top of them amid a hail of American bombs.

The volunteers poured formaldehyde onto the woman's body to cut the stench, then placed it on a gurney and took it away in a small pickup truck. I was struck by the sad, intense eyes of one boy—not more than 12—who was helping with the operation. His hair was cropped short. His shirt was white, his pants were white, his surgical mask was white—and none of them seemed to carry a speck of dirt. He didn't blink as he stood in the back of the open bed of the truck next to the woman's body, which was now covered in a white sheet.

The truck sped away. The boy was still standing, his hands on the side of the truck. In ten minutes, he would help to bury a middle-aged woman he had never met, in the municipal football stadium alongside 600 other "martyrs" killed in one month by the U.S. military.

The soccer stadium turned out to be a lot smaller than I imagined it. Watching al-Jazeera and talking to medical doctors who had been in the city during the siege, I had imagined something much larger—but Fallujah is a relatively small city and so its municipal soccer stadium is also rather small. The bodies are buried very close to one another, and each mound has a small concrete slab as a headstone, the name of the person hand-scrawled with red paint. Sometimes there are more than one name.

"There was not enough space in the city's graveyards," explained 30-year-old Fadel Abbas Khlaff, who helped bury the dead in Fallujah's football stadium for five days before picking up a gun to fight the U.S. military. "Sometimes we would bury two people in the same grave to save space."

The area was dusty. All the turf from the soccer field was dug up to reveal regular dirt, which blew around in a dry wind.

With the bombing over, area residents had begun to file through the graveyard looking for their loved ones. One young man placed a palm leaf on his relative's grave and poured water onto the dirt that covered the site until it stopped kicking up dust. Another man, 50-year-old Ahmed Saud Muhasin al-Isawi, found two cousins, aged 18 and 13, buried in the stadium. It was his first day back in Fallujah after three weeks as a refugee.

"They stayed in their houses and didn't go outside," he said, "but they're still dead." He said the rest of his family tried to leave but were prevented from doing so by persistent American sniper fire.

Ahmed Saud told me one of his nieces also died in the U.S. military assault, but he hadn't yet been able to find her body—nor had he been able to locate any of her eight children, who went missing after her death.

"Every day the Americans show us that Saddam Hussein made many mass graves," he said. "Resistance to occupation is normal. How could they do this? Even the little children and the families are dead." As Ahmed Saud continued, a crowd began to gather around him. Aware of his new audience, he began a speech he knew the other mourners would agree with. "The Americans came to Iraq and said: 'We will make Iraq a symbol of freedom and democracy.'" He pointed at the new headstones all around him. "Is that a symbol of democracy and freedom? If the answer is yes, we can say good-bye to life."

It was only two in the afternoon, but Eunji and I decided it was time to leave Fallujah. We'd had enough for one day. We couldn't imagine what it would be like to live in this city.

When we got back to our apartment building, I sat down almost immediately and started typing, eager to bang out a news report as fast as possible as a way of processing the death that I had seen. When I finished at ten o'clock at night, I went to Eunji's apartment—two floors down in the same building—to check on her progress. She was viewing each of the haunting pictures she'd taken, again and again, trying to cope with the pain of the events she had witnessed. I tried to pull her face away from her computer. "If you're not going to work, you should relax," I told her, and asked if she wanted to check if there were any good Hollywood movies on the satellite. She declined.

Instead, she joined me for a beer on the balcony and we tried to drink away the events of the day.

PART FIVE

TOWARD A BETTER FUTURE

.21.

KINDERGARTEN COP

After visiting Fallujah, I lost all desire to report. I spent most of the day drinking and watching bad American movies on Channel 2. I saw *Dirty Rotten Scoundrels* with Michael Caine and Steve Martin and a lot of old James Bond movies with Sean Connery or Timothy Dalton. Most memorably, though, I remember watching *Kindergarten Cop,* an Arnold Schwarzenegger comedy.

In the film, Schwarzenegger plays a police officer who has to go undercover as a kindergarten teacher in order to catch a killer. Initially, he flails away, unable to keep a motley crew of 30 five-year-olds in line so they can learn. But then Arnold gets the hang of things. He turns the elementary school into a boot camp, with the children marching in lock-step military formation and shouting out the answers to math problems.

Eunji simply laughed at the absurdity of the scene, but for me the humor landed a little too close to home. I railed against the television. "This shows exactly why the situation here in Iraq is so bad!" I screamed. "Look at this. This is the Americans' idea of humor, turning kids into little soldiers. All they know how to do is war. They don't know how to turn on the electricity or clean the water. They just know how to make little soldiers who come over here and kill."

After a year of occupation, the water was still dirty and there were still only a few hours of electricity each day in Baghdad. Parents were afraid to send their children to school. Conservative estimates put unemployment at 70 percent. Only the killings and torture of the old regime seemed to remain.

I was obviously frayed at the edges, coming apart inside and out. In my mind, I saw the rotting corpse of the middle-aged woman again and again. When I was awake she hovered directly in front of my eyes with a kind of translucent quality. When I was asleep, she appeared whole in the ground. I drank more and worried I was developing post-traumatic stress disorder, a psychological disease that often strikes soldiers and others close to severe violence.

There was nothing more to report, I thought. The whole country had just become a vicious cycle of violence and revenge. From this point on, I felt, every story would be the same. I had nothing left to say. It was time to leave.

"I'm going," I said to James, "first to Kurdistan and then Istanbul and then back to America."

I called Waseem and told him I was leaving. The next morning I loaded all of my stuff into a car of one of the staffers at the Dulaimi and went with Eunji over to Waseem's house. (Eunji would also be heading north to Kurdistan, in order to investigate a story on South Korea's decision to send 3,000 troops to Arbil.) Waseem had told me he would help us pick the taxi that would take us back to Kurdistan. He would help us negotiate the price, and more important, ensure that the driver was honest and would not turn us over to the resistance.

"*Habibi,*" I said as I left Waseem at the taxi stand. "I will see you again in better times."

"*Habibi,*" Waseem responded, and we hugged. Intellectually, I had every intention of coming back after a month of rest back in the States, but somewhere deep inside I knew it would be a long time before we would see each other again.

In Istanbul, on my way home a few days later, I walked the streets of the city's Aksary neighborhood. An old part of town, it was one of my favorites because of the proliferation of public baths. I walked into my favorite one, a slight building down an alley near one of my favorite kebab restaurants.

Inside, I took off my clothes and wrapped a towel around my waist. Sweating in the steam room, I considered a question one of my editors had asked me the night before: what Iraqi people thought about the killing of 26-year-old Nicholas Berg.

My first reaction had been "Who?" I told her I had been traveling for two days and so I hadn't been as on top of the news as I was before. She told me he was a contractor, who owned a company called Prometheus Methods Tower Service, and that he had been found beheaded on May 8, 2004. But the incident still didn't jog my memory.

When she told me a videotape had just been released showing Berg being decapitated by five men wearing ski masks and headscarves, I still had no reaction.

"The thing is," I said, "when you are in Iraq every day you see so much death with your own eyes. I have seen the brain parts of a senior sheik who was shot by American soldiers in a human-rights office and the body of a dead woman rotting in the garden of a neighbor's house. I have met so many people whose brother or sister or father or mother has been killed by the American army so when I hear about something like what has happened to Nicholas Berg it doesn't shock me the way it may shock most Americans. It just seems like a small incident. A small incident in the sea of destruction and death that is Iraq."

"Well, what do you think most Iraqis are saying about Berg's execution?" she asked.

"I can't tell you about Berg exactly," I said, "because I am in Turkey and not in Iraq, but I can say that usually when something terrible happens to an American—like the hanging of the charred corpses on the old Fallujah bridge in March—that the reaction of most Iraqis I know has been fear. They have no time for any other emotion like compassion. All they have time for is fear—fear for what the United States will do in retaliation for the killing of one or two or three Americans. All you have to do is look at Fallujah, where the United States killed hundreds of people in retaliation for the killings of a few security guards from a company from North Carolina, or the way the Americans take everyone from a neighborhood or a house to Abu Ghraib when one person in an entire neighborhood attacks them. If people in America are talking a lot about Nicholas Berg, I think it's a mistake. He is only one man, and however terrible the facts of what happened to him, the overall horror of life under American occupation in Iraq is ten times worse."

As I considered the conversation in the Turkish bath, I tried to think of other words I could have said to the editor that she would better understand. An argument was building in my head for the need to withdraw all American troops from Iraq immediately, but I still needed time to consider it.

When I arrived back in the United States, though, I found a populace that was hardly ready for such an appeal. There was increasing questioning about the toll the occupation was taking on America—with close to 1,000 U.S. soldiers killed and dozens of contractors taken prisoner. There was increasing rage at the still-missing stockpiles of weapons of mass destruction and at the tens of billions of dollars of handouts to giant corporations like Bechtel and Halliburton. But there was no one of stature who talked about how terrible life was for the Iraqi people under U.S. occupation, and there seemed to be a consensus across the political spectrum that the American military needed to stay in Iraq to keep the country from completely exploding.

Some people spoke about the possibility of civil war in Iraq, with Sunni Arabs, Shi'ites, and Kurds in a kind of Wrestlemania free-for-all. Others said they were concerned about the emergence of a Shi'ite Islamic state along the lines of Iran under the ayatollahs. Still others worried that Iraq would become a safe haven for al-Qaeda–type terrorists if America left. Returning home from the war zone, I found these scenarios to be valid concerns, but I failed to see how a continued U.S. troop presence would prevent any of them.

"The U.S. military doesn't do anything positive in Iraq," I would argue, "so there is no reason to keep them there. In fact, by its very presence, America exacerbates each of the disasters you seek to avoid. After all, it is America that is taking Kurdish *peshmergas* from the north and asking them to fight Arabs in Fallujah, and it is America's constant humvee patrols, its arrests, and mass incarcerations in Abu Ghraib that make armed resistance an attractive option to regular Iraqis. As for the possibility of a fundamentalist Shi'ite state, you have to understand that at some point America will be forced to leave, and at that point the will of the people will prevail in some form or another. In the meantime, the occupation will make Iraq more dangerous, and the people, who will be looking for protection, will find it in the most bellicose of their religious leaders.

"A little bit of humility is in order," I would conclude. "What kind of arrogance is it that says that only America can solve the problems of Iraq?"

But it seemed no one was listening. When I turned on the TV and watched the speeches of Democratic presidential hopeful John Kerry, I saw him accuse George W. Bush of fighting "the wrong war, at the wrong place, at the wrong time." But his prescription of what to do in Iraq would have been just as damaging to the people. On the campaign trail, he talked repeatedly about the importance of "finishing the job," implying that a longer occupation would result in a more positive outcome in Iraq. This is because, like Bush, Kerry saw the conflict in Iraq as a purely American problem. He almost never mentioned Iraqi civilian casualties. He rarely, if ever, made mention of the mass incarceration without charge of thousands of Iraqis in Abu Ghraib prison, which was still run by America two years after the fall of Saddam.

Instead, he criticized Bush for not being tough enough. "What I want to do is change the dynamics on the ground," he said during the first presidential debate. "And you have to do that by beginning to not back off of the Fallujahs and other places, and send the wrong message to the terrorists."

Less than a week before the November election, an article appeared in the *Lancet,* the United Kingdom's most prestigious medical journal, titled "Mortality Before and After the 2003 Invasion of Iraq: A Cluster Sample Survey." The survey represented the work of a team of doctors from Johns Hopkins University in Baltimore who had sent a team of researchers door to door throughout Iraq, visiting 30 neighborhoods in nearly every province of the country to ask who had died and how.

Their result: 100,000 Iraqis—many of them women and children—had died prematurely since the start of the U.S.-led invasion, 58 times more than in an equal period during the last years of Saddam's regime. According to the researchers, in the years before the invasion, most people had died as a result of heart attack, stroke, and chronic illness. (Most of Saddam's worst atrocities—including the gassing and forced relocation of the Kurds—occurred in the 1980s, when the U.S. government backed his regime, or after the 1991 Gulf War, when George H. W. Bush urged the Iraqi people to rise up and then withheld support for their revolution.) After the invasion, about the same number of people had died from these "usual" causes, but there had been a massive increase in the numbers of violent deaths.

Indeed, since the invasion, Johns Hopkins' Dr. Gilbert Burham told me, occupation troops had become the number-one inflicter of death. "Women and children were the most common group of the dead," he added, "and houses that said the deaths were due to Coalition forces mentioned that these were primarily due to aircraft."

What happened to this crucial piece of information released days before the presidential election, deemed by many "the most important in a generation"? Neither candidate spoke about it; and the issue of Iraqi civilian casualties stayed out of our national dialogue.

On the issue of Iraq, this was nothing new, of course. After all, the debate around Iraq has always centered on the result for America and "our safety" or "strategic interests." For all the current talk of globalism, Americans are an essentially tribal people. We care far more about 1,000 dead U.S. soldiers than about 100,000 dead Iraqis.

It is the same on the Right and the Left. This is why, I think, before, during, and after the invasion many antiwar activists focused on the lack of weapons of mass destruction or a strong link to al-Qaeda rather than daily life for Iraqi people, and why many on the Left were unwilling to address the brutality of Saddam's regime when George W. Bush first made the case for war.

Michael Moore's film *Fahrenheit 9/11,* like most journalism by the antiwar Left, presented Saddam Hussein's Iraq as a peaceful place. The only image of prewar Iraq in the entire film was of a small child flying a kite on a clear day. In the film, no mention was made of mass graves or mass incarceration by the Ba'ath regime.

At the same time we protest against war, we must also put forward solutions, however partial, that could help the targeted people escape the tyranny of their brutal regime. Consider these words from Iranian human-rights activist and 2003 Nobel Peace Prize winner, Shirin Ebadi. In September 2004, she told *The Progressive* magazine's Amitabh Pal:

> North Americans do not understand that you do not throw down human rights like bombs on the Iraqis. I want to take my American friends back to the end of World War II, when the Universal Declaration of Human Rights was formulated. A group of thinkers met to come up with ways and means to prevent yet another war. Mrs. Eleanor Roosevelt played a crucial role in assembling this group of people. And that is why the name of the United States is synonymous with the cause of human rights around the world.
>
> Now what has happened to the glorious American civilization that has brought us to the present phase when we see those despicable pictures of mistreated Iraqi prisoners? What do you think Mrs. Eleanor Roosevelt would have said if she were alive in this day and age?

Perhaps Eleanor Roosevelt would suggest that we try to create a new internationalism; that we focus our efforts on building up institutions that can bring dictators to justice using legal rather than violent methods, like the International Criminal Court in The Hague.

In the meantime, we should focus at least as much on human beings as we do on weapons of mass destruction. We should do everything we can to avoid giving people a choice between war and dictatorship.

ELECTIONS AND BEYOND

At eight-thirty in the morning on Iraq's election day, January 30, 2005, dozens of buses and battered Toyota pickups were already arriving in the small Kurdish farming village of Pir Dawud, southwest of Arbil, the regional capital of Iraqi Kurdistan. The truck beds were full of Kurds headed to the polls. The buses were full, too, furnished with giant Kurdish flags on their outsides.

Nine months after leaving the country, I had returned to Iraqi Kurdistan to check up on the situation. I didn't dare go back to Baghdad. A number of my colleagues, including Eunji, had been kidnapped, and while they all had been safely released, I was unwilling to take the chance that my face would appear on al-Jazeera as the victim of the latest act by the resistance's radical fringe. I expected to find the elections to be a kind of a joke. Based on previous experience, I figured the Americans would find a way to ensure that former CIA asset Ayad Allawi would continue to sit in the prime minister's chair in Baghdad.

The Iraqi people, though, had other ideas.

Thirty minutes later, at nine A.M., the polling station at Pir Dawud was mobbed. Thousands of Kurds of all ages milled around, waiting for their chance to queue up. Others pushed forward to try to get to the front, prompting local *peshmerga* fighters to push them back, firing bullets into the air.

"Now we are free from the Arabs," seventy-year-old farmer Rhasid Pirbal told me. He was dressed in traditional baggy *sharwal* pants and a black-and-white checkered *kaffiyeh*. Like everyone else, he was prepared to vote for the Kurdish slate. "They looted our houses. We have been killed and have lost our honor. Finally, we feel we are human and we are Kurds."

It wasn't just the Kurds who mobilized for the election. In the south, Shi'ite parties led by the Supreme Council for Islamic Revolution in Iraq and inspired by Grand Ayatollah Ali Sistani turned out in tremendous numbers. They garnered more than four million votes, a near-absolute majority of those cast. In Baghdad, the slate's leader, Abdul Aziz al-Hakim, announced his slate would govern in coalition with the Kurds. The Shi'ites would take the prime minister's post. Kurdish leader Jalal Talabani would assume the largely ceremonial role of president.

In Washington, the election was being hailed as a victory for George W. Bush's policies. Violence was minimal, and despite a boycott by Sunni Arabs (twenty percent of the population) and massive voter irregularities in the northern cities of Kirkuk and Mosul, it was clear that the Iraqi government—for the first time in generations—would represent at least a large portion of the people.

Indeed, the Iraqi people went to the polls as a kind of peaceful resistance. "No one welcomes the foreign troops in Iraq. We believe in the ability of Iraqis to run their own issues, including the security issue," the Shi'ite list's spokesman Abdul Aziz al-Hakim told Reuters on the eve of the election. "Of course this issue could be brought up by the new government."

Ibrahim Jaffari, the head of the Da'wa Party and another leader of the victorious Shi'ite slate, had spoken out repeatedly against the U.S. military. "I oppose the use of arms by any citizen in the new Iraq," he told United Press International in August 2004. "I also object to any violent retaliation that would further escalate the situation as it happened in Fallujah and Najaf before. . . . I also object to the killing of such a great number of people in holy Najaf and the use of force in any other region."

Unlike the U.S. government, Jaffari and others on the Shi'ite slate, including the firebrand cleric Muqtada al-Sadr, believed in the political process: "New Iraq should be politically motivated and capable of accepting the other, by using all means except the military option. It should also avoid being drawn into violence and counterviolence. At the end, we are responsible for building a state which is not based on violence but on political stability."

Listening to Jaffari and Hakim's statements around election time, I realized how little their platform had changed since the early days of the occupation. Then as now, they thanked America for toppling Saddam, but rejected the tactics of the U.S. military and the extended length of the occupation. I remembered back to the villagers in southern Iraq whose family members were killed during the invasion. Posters of the Shi'ite slate leader's now-dead brother were plastered everywhere, and in the same sentence in which everyone thanked America, they also voiced concern over when the U.S. would leave.

It is curious then—as now—why it took America so long to finally hold these elections. As early as February 2004, Muqtada al-Sadr had successfully organized polling in Najaf and a number of poorer Shi'ite areas throughout the nation. That same month, thousands of Iraqis took to the streets, demanding elections be held immediately, but such entreaties were rejected in Washington. Had the Iraqi public been permitted to express itself sooner—while the U.S. was still regarded as a liberating force—the armed resistance might have been averted and thousands of lives saved.

In early 2005, it remained unclear what kind of hold the U.S. would have over the newly elected government. The ability of Iraq to recover, to attain freedom, and to restore the stability of its daily life hinged on the Bush Administration's willingness to accept that the will of the Iraqi people might be different from its own.

—Aaron Glantz
February 2005

HISTORIC AND POLITICAL FIGURES

THE SHIA LEADERS

Ayatollah Sayyed Mohammed Baqir al-Hakim (1939–2003) was one of the foremost Shia Muslim leaders in Iraq until a car bomb killed him along with nearly 100 worshippers while he left a mosque in Najaf where he had led prayers. The son of Ayatollah Sayed Muhsin al-Hakim, the worldwide leader of Shia Muslims from 1955 until 1970, he cofounded the Islamist political movement in Iraq with Muqtada al-Sadr's uncle, Sayyed Mohammed Baqir al-Sadr. After Saddam killed al-Sadr and repressed attempts at Islamic revolution in Iraq, al-Hakim fled to Iran and founded the Supreme Council for Islamic Revolution in Iraq, a Tehran-backed group dedicated to the overthrow of Saddam Hussein. His brother and political right hand, Abdul Aziz al-Hakim, was appointed by the Bush Administration to the Iraqi Governing Council and led a unified slate of religious Shi'ite parties to victory in the country's January 2005 elections.

Ibrahim al-Jaafari (1947–) was the nominee for prime minister of the United Iraqi Alliance, the coalition of religious Shi'ite parties that won the U.S.–sponsored Iraqi elections in January 2005. A medical doctor who became an activist in the Da'wa Party of Grand Ayatollah Mohammed Baqir al-Sadr when Ayatollah Khomeini came to power in Iran, he fled to Iran in 1980 and organized attacks against Saddam's regime designed to bring an Islamic state to power in Iraq. In 1989, he moved to London. When Saddam was overthrown, he returned to Iraq, and the George W. Bush Administration gave him a seat in the Governing Council.

Grand Ayatollah Sayyed Mohammed Sadiq al-Sadr (1943–1999) was a prominent, widely respected leader of Iraq's Shi'ite majority, especially among its poorer classes. He was originally elevated to a high position among the Shia by the Ba'ath Party following the 1991 Gulf War in an attempt to find a puppet amongst the Shi'ites. But al-Sadr did not play along. Instead, he used his position to call for reforms and religious freedom in public. He was killed by Saddam's regime on February 19, 1999, along with two of his sons. His death sparked riots throughout Shia Iraq, which were brutally repressed by the regime. His surviving son, Muqtada al-Sadr, is now head of his father's organization.

Grand Ayatollah Mohammed Baqir al-Sadr (1934–1980) was the uncle of Muqtada al-Sadr and an author of two major Shia theological texts, *Our Economy* and *Our Philosophy.* He was also a founder of the Islamist political movement in Iraq and a supporter of Ayatollah Khomeini. Saddam Hussein imprisoned him for his political activity and and eventually had him executed.

Sayyed Muqtada al-Sadr (1974?–) is the son of Grand Ayatollah Mohammed Sadiq al-Sadr and heir to his father's organization. In the aftermath of the fall of Saddam Hussein, he built an organization dedicated to public service in the Shia slums of eastern Baghdad, which were renamed Sadr City after his slain father. He is very popular among poor Shia, but less popular among the middle class. He called for the end of U.S. occupation immediately after the end of Saddam's regime and turned to armed rebellion at the end of March 2004 when the U.S. closed his movement's newspaper and arrested one of his chief advisors.

Grand Ayatollah Sayyed Ali al-Sistani (1930–) is the primary Shia *marja,* or religious reference, in Iraq. Sistani believes in the separation of the clergy from politics, and this has helped to keep him away from the attention of the Ba'ath Party, notorious for its ill-treatment of Shias. Shortly after the American occupation began, he issued *fatwas* calling on Shia clergy not to get involved in politics. Still, he has criticized American plans for an Iraqi government as not being democratic enough and regularly called for direct elections to replace the U.S.-imposed government.

THE KURDISH LEADERS

Mullah Mustafa Barzani (1903–1979) was the father of modern Kurdish nationalism and the Kurdistan Democratic Party (KDP). After World War II, he fought a series of wars against the central government in Baghdad. To do this, he built a force of *peshmerga* (lit.:

"after-death men"), guerrilla fighters who continue to make up Kurdish militias today. At different times, he received arms from the United States, the Soviet Union, and the shah of Iran, all of whom used the Kurdish people in geopolitical struggles against one another.

Jalal Talabani (1933–) is head of the Patriotic Union of Kurdistan (PUK), which controls the eastern section of northern Iraq. Talabani has a long history of involvement in Kurdish politics. A military leader of the KDP during its 1961 revolt against Baghdad, Talabani was part of a group that split from the KDP in 1964. At the time, he criticized Mullah Mustafa Barzani for being too tribal and dictatorial and for not espousing socialist and democratic values. He also felt that Mullah Mustafa should enter into peace talks with Ba'athists in Baghdad, so he went behind his back and negotiated with the Ba'ath government. Talabani's PUK sided with Ayatollah Khomeini during the Iran-Iraq war and then fought a war with the KDP in the mid-1990s for control of northern Iraq. After reaching a settlement to share northern Iraq with the KDP, Talabani's PUK *peshmergas* joined the U.S. military on the front lines of the 2003 invasion.

Masoud Barzani (1946–) is the son of Mullah Mustafa Barzani and the president of the Kurdistan Democratic Party, which controls the western half of northern Iraq. In the mid-1980s, the KDP sided with Iran's Ayatollah Khomeini in the Iran-Iraq war and then in the 1990s fought a war with Jalal Talabani's PUK for control of northern Iraq. In that war, he called on Saddam Hussein for help in kicking the PUK out of Arbil. Afterward, he met Ali Hassan al-Majid (aka Chemical Ali) at his headquarters in Salahudin. After reaching a settlement to share northern Iraq with the PUK, Barzani's KDP *peshmerga* joined the U.S. military on the front lines of the 2003 invasion.

Abdullah Ocalan (1949–) is head of the Turkish-Kurdish organization PKK (Kurdish: *Partiya Karkerên Kurdistan*), or Kurdistan Workers Party. For 20 years, the PKK fought a war of national liberation for the Kurds of Turkey against the Turkish government in Ankara, which banned Kurdish speech, Kurdish newspapers, and any discussion of a Kurdish nation. More than 30,000 Kurdish civilians died (mostly killed by the Turkish army) until Turkey captured Ocalan in Nairobi in 1999. Locked away in his own island prison in the Marmara Sea, Ocalan called a unilateral ceasefire, and most PKK forces retreated into northern Iraq. The Turkish army maintains two bases in northern Iraq and has asked for America's help in attacking PKK forces. In 2004, the PKK (now named KONGRA-GEL) called off its ceasefire and began carrying out attacks in major Turkish cities.

THE SUNNI LEADERS

The Association of Muslim Scholars is the primary organization of Sunni religious clergy in Iraq. Immediately after the start of the occupation, the organization favored negotiation with the Americans. But as the occupation dragged on and became more brutal, AMS began to openly support the armed resistance. AMS called for a boycott of U.S.-sponsored elections. The organization has also played an important role in negotiating freedom for many of the foreigners kidnapped in Iraq.

Mohsen Abdel Hamid (1937–)is secretary general of the Iraqi Islamic Party, the largest political party of Sunnis in Iraq. An Islamic scholar from the northern city of Kirkuk, Abdel Hamid has written more than 30 books on interpretation of the Qu'ran. Appointed to the Governing Council by the Bush Administration,

Abdel Hamid threatened to resign during the April 2004 bombardment of Fallujah. In November 2004, he quit the interim Iraqi government over the second U.S. attack on Fallujah and has called for a Sunni boycott of U.S.-sponsored elections.

THE CURRENT "IRAQI GOVERNMENT"

Ayad Allawi (1945–) former Ba'athist turned CIA and MI-6 agent (he onced bragged that he had been on the payroll of 14 foreign intelligence agencies) who ran a U.S.-government-funded organization that promoted a military coup in Iraq before the U.S. invasion in 2004. He was made prime minister of Iraq by the U.S.-appointed Iraqi Governing Council. After taking over as prime minister, Allawi imposed a state of emergency and approved a second major assault on Fallujah.

Ghazi al-Yawar (1958?–) is a major tribal sheik who was professionally educated as an engineer in Saudi Arabia. Appointed to the Governing Council, he threatened to resign after the first U.S. assault on Fallujah and was allowed to help negotiate a settlement. The Governing Council appointed him president in June 2004. From this position, he regularly criticized some of the more heavy-handed tactics of the occupation.

THE AMERICANS

Ronald Reagan (1911–2004), 40th president of the United States, supported Saddam Hussein during his long war with Iran in the 1980s. He criticized Iran's desire to topple what he called "the legitimate government of Iraq." In 1983, he removed Iraq from the

U.S. government's list of "nations that support international terrorism" and sent Donald Rumsfeld as a personal envoy to Iraq, where Rumsfeld met with Saddam Hussein and Iraqi Foreign Minister Tariq Aziz. According to a State Department memo made available by the non-profit National Security Archives in Washington, Rumsfeld told Aziz that "the United States and Iraq share many common interests," adding that the Reagan Administration had a "willingness to do more" to "help Iraq." Military and economic assistance followed.

George H. W. Bush (1924–), 41st president of the United States, invaded Iraq after Saddam Hussein invaded Kuwait. After pushing Saddam out of Kuwait, he called on Iraqis to rise up and promised support for their revolution. When Iraqis rose up and seized most of the country, his administration sat by silently as Saddam massacred tens, possibly hundreds of thousands of people. After that, his administration pushed a tough sanctions program on the country through the United Nations, claiming that Saddam needed to be disarmed of chemical, biological, and nuclear weapons.

George W. Bush (1946–), 43rd president of the United States, invaded Iraq and toppled the regime of Saddam Hussein. He claimed that Iraq had weapons of mass destruction, but no such weapons have ever been found. In May 2003, gave a speech on the U.S.S. *Abraham Lincoln* aircraft carrier declaring, "Iraq is one victory in the war on terrorism that began September 11, 2001 and still goes on." Since then, he has occupied Iraq with more than 135,000 U.S. military personnel.

L. Paul Bremer (1941–) was the second U.S. administrator in Iraq, serving from May 11, 2003 until June 28, 2004. A longtime diplomat, Bremer began his career as assistant to Henry Kissinger from

1972 to 1976. In 1981, he became executive secretary and special assistant to Ronald Reagan's first secretary of state, Alexander Haig. Bremer retired from the Foreign Service in 1989 and became managing director at Henry Kissinger's company, Kissinger and Associates. When he arrived as the civilian administrator of Iraq, Bremer dissolved the old Iraqi army and police force and appointed the Iraqi Governing Council. Bremer retained veto power over their decisions.

INDEX

ABOUT THE AUTHOR

Aaron Glantz is a reporter for Pacifica Radio and other media outlets. He has visited Iraq three times during U.S. occupation: for a
month immediately after the fall of Saddam Hussein; from February to May of 2004; and during the elections in January and February of 2005. In addition to Pacifica, Aaron Glantz's radio work
from Iraq has been heard on Radio France Internationale and the
Christian Broadcasting Network. His work from Iraq has also been
syndicated to newspapers around the world by Inter Press News
Service. A native of San Francisco, he lives in Los Angeles with his
fiancée, Ngoc Nguyen, and her family.